Truth's
Daughter

a memoir

Barbara Santarelli

Black Rose Writing | Texas

The author grants the final approval for this literary material.

First printing

This is a work of fiction. Names, characters, businesses, places, events, and incidents are either the products of the author's imagination or used in a fictitious manner. Any resemblance to actual persons, living or dead, or actual events is purely coincidental.

ISBN: 978-1-68433-713-2
PUBLISHED BY BLACK ROSE WRITING
www.blackrosewriting.com

Printed in the United States of America
Suggested Retail Price (SRP) $20.95

Truth's Daughter is printed in Sabon

*As a planet-friendly publisher, Black Rose Writing does its best to eliminate unnecessary waste to reduce paper usage and energy costs, while never compromising the reading experience. As a result, the final word count vs. page count may not meet common expectations.

"Honesty is often hard. The truth is often painful. But the freedom it can bring is worth the trying"

-*Fred Rogers*

Contents

Truth's Daughter

Part *1*

1 Anecdotal Truths

This is what I know about Charles Payne, my father. His handwriting was like calligraphy, all loops and flying ribbons that distracted from the intention of the words. He preferred complex and impressive words to simple language.

I have proof of this fact. There were several letters sent to us in his initial seven-year absence from our lives. The letters were read aloud to my brother, Stephen, two years my senior, and to me. Mom read, her voice laced with disdain and in exaggerated, theatrical enunciation of his words. He'd written:

"1963 has seen me subject to a number of serious m-e-t-a-m-o-r-p-h-i-s-m-s, each with attendant furious manifestations of my own reactions thereto."

"Jesus Christ! He is crazy," my mother shouted as she shook and abused the paper decorated in word ribbons. "Can you believe this crap?" She then attacked and wildly flapped the envelope it was mailed in, also beautifully calligraphed and sent via Air Mail from Fontainebleau Boulevard, Miami Beach, Florida, her flailing, looping arms ironically mimicking his handwriting.

I thought it special that the paper had traveled from my imagined pink and green paradise of Miami to our drab and cold rented railroad flat in the Bronx. I imagined flamingos carrying it to a mailbox. Never mind that, she shook it furiously at its opened side edge, trying to dislodge the check she hoped for. I watched silently, waiting for a cue. At eight or ten years old, I was never sure. Should I laugh, comfort, shout, or just remain silent? I always chose silence. In silence, I could recall and try to reconcile the only image I had of him in my mind. That image, imprinted when I was three years old, was of a sandy-haired man sitting in a chair, nothing more. My mother seemed to approve of silence in all things "Charles" related. The silence was tacit and persistent. It lasted most of my life. I remained unsure of how to react or how to feel about him well beyond childhood. He was a part of myself that was missing without an awareness of ever having being missed.

Here is another thing I knew with certainty. He graduated from the NYU School of Engineering in 1941. He became a successful civil engineer.

My proof is a heavy, ornately embellished, ten-karat gold college key with tiny letters and the image of a spidery suspension bridge in relief dangling from a charm bracelet. I no longer wear the bracelet because it is dated. His college key is flanked by a heart-shaped Sweet Sixteen charm and my own nursing school graduation key. The charms reminded me of late Autumn acorns waiting to fall from grace to the ground, clinging to stems against the reality that their time has passed. They are fragile connections to what was: now, about to be squirrel stash or meltdown gold for cash.

He designed great buildings in Miami Beach in the building boom years of the 1950s. I was, by then, enjoying my first decade in the Bronx in a miserable apartment that had mice, cockroaches, and a landlady that hated us for reasons unclear to me then. I understood we were a different kind of family.

When I was fifteen in 1962, I visited The Castaways, one of his most famous buildings. It was, at the time, an iconic specimen in a collection of beachfront resort motels on Collins Avenue. I loved the name. Of course, it was designed to be redolent of remote Polynesian jungles. It was designed with peaked roofs defined as Oriental modern. I thought, perhaps it was named in honor of his castaway children in New York.

I never mentioned my father or his connection to the motel on that long car drive south with my best friend, Rennie, or to her parents. I was just fifteen, and I had no cause to brag. After all, in the two years we had been best friends the subject of my missing father or his whereabouts was not on the radar. As much as I adored Leo, Rennie's athletic, acerbic, and overprotective dad, the absence of my own father was simply a given. He just did not exist in our lives.

Some afternoons on that trip, I enjoyed sitting in a low, nubby, cloth-covered orange Tulip chair in the lobby of the Castaways to study the vast space that existed under the sweeping lines of the peaked roof. I imagined him drawing those lines on graph paper, the edges persistently curling up at the sides and being gently nudged away with bent elbows covered up under the rolled-up sleeves of his "manly" shirt. I imagined him chewing on the stem of a meerschaum pipe as he worked.

He did smoke that pipe. He left the honey-colored artifact with its engraved tooth marks on its stem sitting in a very heavy star-shaped Swedish crystal ashtray when he disappeared. I was just three, but somehow, the tableau of the pipe reclining in the hollow of one of the star's points remained in place on a dark oak bookcase like a loyal dog waiting patiently to be the subject of an owner's affection. It stayed there for sure until I was thirteen and we left the hated apartment.

Here is another thing I know. Here is, again, hard evidence about him. I value hard evidence in my search to understand who this man, now gone, was. There are perhaps a half dozen photos of the man in question. Most are in the post-war early forties. They are of the dating or "pre-children" marriage years of my parents. They are dressed in the excessive bulk and strange sensuality of men in high-waisted slacks and women with nipped-waist dresses and peep toe shoes. But the photo I offer as evidence in the mystery of my paternal heritage is of my father's mother, Nora Payne.

In this photo, circa 1920, she is dressed in a black tank bathing suit. She is on a beach (Brighton Beach, Brooklyn, I'm told) and she is holding a large beach ball aloft over her left shoulder. It is, of course, a black and white or sepia toned photo and somewhat faded. It is, in its absence of color, a gift to imagine color. Her hair is a short, severe *dark—almost black—bob of the day. In my adult mind of now, she is an art deco bathing beauty of artist George Barbier. She is not an elongated, elegant Erte of the day. This is a woman of short, strong, and muscled stature. She is solid and has a most disproportionate and top-heavy build. Her breasts are huge. In another photo of Nora with young Charles, she is wearing a stylish flapper dress, and her son is in knickers, clinging to her side. He looks up at her. Clearly, his view of her face is blocked entirely by those bosoms.*

A favorite tale my mother told was of Nora's talent. According to my mother, Nora could hoist her pendulous breasts up and catapult the heft of them into the air, above her shoulders where they would succumb to gravity and land on the reverse side of her body. My mother, quite proud of her own triple-A sized pre-pubescent breasts, usually added a disgusted grunt to the story. It would remind the listener of a dull thud or "whack" that could be heard on landing. She hated Nora. I lived in fear from ages eleven to fourteen that I might inherit the gene for behemoth breasts. I did not.

Everything else I know about my paternal grandparents is anecdotal. There is no physical evidence of their lives I possess. I have no first-hand memories of them. I must consider only the anecdotes in my search for facts as clues. If nothing else, these anecdotes will always entertain me. They are like the beach ball in the photo of Nora. The observer imagines the colored sections of the ball in bright orange or blue wedges offset by white. The truth is, there is a great possibility those were, indeed, the true colors. And so, I am going forward believing the stories with a caveat. I need to consider what other options there were in the narrative that colored my understanding of who Charles Payne and his parents were.

In fact, the Castaways narrative is anecdotal. Surely, it was my mother who told me he built and designed the iconic motel. Perhaps in a letter promising her child support he assured her of his ability to fulfill this promise by bragging about this potential or realized contract. It evolved into this recurrent diatribe. "Did you know your father is famous now? Making a fortune designing fancy hotels in Miami for rich people." As she offered us a choice of Chef Boyardee cheese ravioli or a Swanson fried chicken TV dinner (a favorite) she'd continue, "Bet his new family will be able to have a swimming pool now, why not?"

I responded in the safety of silence.

The impact of that anecdote is more notable because the Castaways project receded in importance. I was plagued with recurrent bad dreams about my father's imagined new family. There were always other daughters. They had long blond hair in braids. When I watched them, they ignored me. I was invisible. I outgrew the dreams at some point but clung, like moss to a shaded rock, to the comfort of the Castaways project.

On my visit to the Castaways at age fifteen, I noted but dismissed the absence of my father's name on a cornerstone or lobby plaque. Twenty years later, I researched and found that architects Wilmer and McKirahan had designed the fantastical place. No matter, I still credited him with the sweeping ersatz pagoda roof lines. After all, as a civil engineer he was at least responsible for the issues of drainage and building stability. The very integrity of its foundation was due to him. The lofty architects had a dream and design, but without his genius, rain and wind would certainly have caused the stress points responsible for the roof to crumble in disgrace. So that is how I wanted to define some small quality of a man I did not know. If I was expected to resent his behavior and the inescapable fact that he was responsible for my mother's misery, and by extension, my own, I also needed to find redemption for him. Perhaps that is simply the conundrum of acknowledging the biologic reality of having two parents. It helped me to consider genius as I configured his identity. After all, we were related.

And so, I understood at an early age it was possible to conceptualize an identity that was neither present nor absent, loving or not, selfish or not, famous or not, a liar or not. I could create a narrative based mostly on anecdotes, and the malodorous fumes of angry rejection or the flight of wispy dandelion seeds blown with hopeful breath. I chose both, and so, the truth about my father has always eluded me.

If I embrace an anecdote it is because it pleases me to consider. I loved every story my mother ever told about Nora. They were intended to forge hatred or shame. But how to hate a woman with a talent for breast acrobatics? Yes, she harbored the woman my father was sleeping with while married and the father of two. But she traveled to Havana constantly, smoked cigars there, and danced with rebels and dissidents.

Of course, I'm told, she cheated on her husband, fifteen years her senior and a staunch WASP whose distant relatives may or may not really have arrived on the

Mayflower. While he worked long hours as a conductor on the New Haven Railroad, she busied herself with her spoiled only son or with nightclub life. But how can you not be amused and intrigued by a woman who was said to have kept a crucifix, a Jewish star, a Muslim Star and Crescent, and Buddhist Shinto in her purse as props for whoever she might have wanted to impress? Oh, those anecdotes so fed my lust for belonging to something uniquely my own. Meant to poison me, the stories served instead as an escape from the reality of an ugly apartment and social isolation.

I grew up on a foundation of fanciful stories and discordant voices. Along the way, there were real events which shaped opinions. But if I consider those events, the actual time I spent with my father from age three to sixteen, and then never again, I know it was insufficient in finding truth. By my calculation, there were between twenty-five and thirty hours in total (eight of which were spent asleep) spent in the company of my father.

Does it matter? Is reconciliation important? Are there term limits on our ability or need to find a truth that no longer matters? After all, both Charles and Charlotte, my mother, are long dead. I'm sure no one cares but me. I am seventy years old and should no longer care either. But there is this longstanding question I really hate to take to my own grave. Who was Charles Payne? Who was my father? Is his identity, and by extension my own, dependent on a truth best left undiscovered?

2 A Letter

September 10, 1980

Dear Stephen and Barbara,

I have just talked to your mother, and it was my unfortunate duty to advise her of the death of your father, Charles Payne, on March 16, 1979. He died as the result of stab wounds when Charles was attacked by a crazed Negro in the Miami Shores area. It occurred without provocation or incident. It was simply a crazy man yelling something to the effect that he was doing the will of God. Charles survived for a short period and died in the hospital.

Since March of '79, I have been trying to locate you and your mother, but even skip tracing agencies provided me with no information until I called directly to the telephone company and fortunately located your mother.

Your father died leaving no will; however, he left surviving him his wife Nancy and two children, Rebecca

Payne, now age 18, and Charles Payne, now age 11. Most of his assets were held jointly with his wife. The only probable assets are those items shown on the inventory filed in the estate, a copy of which is attached. There can be no claims as the expenses of last illness were astronomical. The burial expenses and legal fees far exceeded any assets...

Signed: (lawyer's name)

The letter goes on to request our signatures as necessary in closing the unresolved estate issues. It was from a law firm in Miami Beach, Florida. My first reaction was to laugh. It was 1980, and while far from being post racial, the use of the term *crazed Negro* was jolting and a questionable label. Imagine, not hearing from this man between my junior year in high school and next at the age of thirty-two, celebrating my second son's first birthday and getting this news? Would surreal be a good choice of words? So, I focused on the most ridiculous part of the news.

"Mom, did the letter really say he was stabbed to death by a *crazed Negro?*" A child of the sixties, I was offended. After all, by 1980 even the US Census Bureau had changed the racial identity question to read African American / Negro. And then there was what would become a lifelong lasting vignette played over and over in my thoughts. A Black man with wild Afro hair (this before dreadlocks arrived on the fashion scene) stabbing a terrified sixty-year-old "innocent?" man repeatedly and shouting it was God's will? I considered the fact that the guy may have had something there. I imagined the stab wounds in his neck and chest. I'm not sure why, but I thought the concomitant blood loss would make for a dramatic scene.

Do I add this to the *What I Know* column? It is not anecdotal. I have saved that letter forever. My mother read the letter and waited in uncharacteristic silence for our reactions. "Yes, Barbara," she said, "a crazed Negro with no particular issue."

"Oh my God, Mom, that was no 'crazy Negro.' Who just stabs a guy walking down the street in a good neighborhood for no reason? Bet he was either a hit man, or my father screwed him over, too." I wondered what happened to the Black guy? I felt no loss or sadness. Not horror or curiosity. *So, this is how it ends*, I reasoned. *I can release myself from uncomfortable silence and lasting questions.* It later became a chosen part of my own athenaeum of colorful facts about my life. The amusing litany of facts I might decide to include if anyone asked about my family history.

"Well yes," I might say. "I grew up in a single-parent family in an Italian-American neighborhood. I was the only Jew. I loved stuffing cannolis in my best friend's family bakery. I won the Brotherhood Award in fifth grade for an amazing poster depicting children of many colors on a staircase. It read, 'Brotherhood: Stairway To A Better World.' I have saved the medal I received along with the lawyer's letter about my father's death. My paternal grandparents were descendants of Americans who arrived on the Mayflower. My paternal grandmother could fling her breasts over her shoulders and smoked cigars in pre-Castro Cuba. My father was stabbed to death by a crazed Negro in 1980. Oh, but before then he designed the iconic Castaways Motel in Miami Beach. My father had an affair with a cocktail waitress he met while designing buildings in Poughkeepsie, New York. He then had an affair with a stepdaughter who attempted suicide by jumping out of a fifth-floor window (a fact). Then he eventually had a whole new family in Miami and had two more biologic children. I think the daughter may have long blond braids."

But mostly, I kept this narrative to myself. I'm not sure if it is too unbelievable or too painful. I do know it is as entertaining as hell. Is it sick to say I love it? I love it as I love the story of my maternal grandparents. Those uncomplicated Russian Jews who fled pogroms and came to New York at the turn of the century to work in unsafe factories as a seamstress and a coat maker. I love it all. Maybe I am more like Nora after all. I love Yiddish as much as I love Italian pastries and as much as I love the thought of a grandmother who may have slept with Fidel Castro and smoked cigars and had remarkable breasts and a father who may or may not have been a genius or a loser. I love the possibilities of weaving it in to a cohesive story with an end. But that is where I fail. Does it end in truth? And so, I return to facts I have and those I need to find to complete myself. The narrative amuses but does not satisfy me. It does not all ring true. It has never helped me feel confident in my own identity. I am a collection of half-truths and fanciful stories. I am the human version of a hybrid car. Fueled by blood and biology and extraneous unseen energy that moves me forward. It is efficient but missing the purity of a simpler version I can believe in.

Here is a fact I know. I have a listing of my father's final assets at probate.

$133.64 in a savings account
1974 Mercury Comet Value $1,000
1976 Mercury Comet Value $1,600

I know he liked Mercury Comets and was either dirt poor or great at hiding the vast wealth my brother and I were deprived of as children. My brother's reaction was so different than mine. "That motherfucker, let's get a lawyer and see where he hid the money. Good that he's dead, I hope he suffered."

I was happy not to be so angry. I was happy not to care. I never felt anger. I never felt hatred. I did not care if he was dead or alive. After all, he was never more than anecdotes and thirty hours of time spent together.

Time moved on without him occupying space on the planet or in my thoughts most, if not all, of the time. Until it didn't. I was happy to forget those five times, thirty hours within six years that brought me no closer to claiming a father or knowing the man. Still, thirty hours in a lifetime could not be dismissed entirely. Those thirty hours were primary evidence. If I recalled the details of those hours would I now find some hidden truth? Would I discover who he was? Would it help me claim a credible and complete identity for myself? Would I better understand the unknown and unclaimed part of myself still missing? The finality of his death tripped a need to consider the five meals I'd shared with the sandy-haired stranger. For decades, those memories lodged in the deep recesses and shadow cast by the bright light and sunshine of everyday life.

3 A Phone Call

The heavy black rotary dial phone was not an important part of life in our house. I can't remember ever making or receiving a call in my childhood, but I must have. My mother occasionally called a friend or my grandparents, who lived in Long Branch, New Jersey. Otherwise the heavy instrument sat unceremoniously on a dark wood table aptly named "the telephone table." It had a diminutive squared-off attached chair that married the pair to the promise of a lifetime dedicated to human discomfort and aesthetic suicide. In fact, humans weighing more than one hundred and forty pounds were not welcome to sit at all. The weight of the phone and marriage to the wall and table were the equivalent of a ball and chain. A shelf set low enough in the table's interior accommodated the Bronx and Manhattan telephone books. The table lived in the middle room of our railroad flat. The middle room was my mother's. It seemed appropriate that it was sandwiched between the shared bedroom of her children and a narrow living room with a door to nowhere. The door had once led to a porch on the second level of the ugly lime-green clapboard house of no architectural pedigree. The landlady who hated the sexy young divorcee and her two children had, one fall afternoon, ordered her brother and sniveling husband to climb up on a ladder to the second floor and with sledge hammer and repressed lust for my mother driving their energy, destroy the structure. No problem, her husband soon discovered that he could climb to a ledge that flanked the kitchen window and peep in quite easily. He was sometimes rewarded with a warm smile and quick glimpse of long freckled legs in snug shorts as she warmed those cans of cheese ravioli.

Lou, the landlady's husband, worked in a lace dying factory in a commercial area of the Bronx. It was a perfect job for a man that often filched hot red or bright pink lace panties and bras. These were left mostly as "anonymous" offerings to my mother on the narrow overhang where a clothesline was affixed to the exterior window frame and a steel pulley that drove the line to a large tree in an empty lot, this luxury assuring his visitation to the demilitarized zone of the structure. It was highly unlikely that his fat, balding, miserable wife, Sebastiana, ever wore garments more suited to Playboy centerfolds.

My mother's room was sparely furnished. Other than the telephone table, there was her single bed, covered in a white chenille bedspread that in subtle relief showcased a geometric maze inviting my fingers to find a beginning and end. A simple maple dresser with three drawers topped with a mismatched mirror completed her room. I rarely spent time in her room. The only time I gravitated to it was on days she sat in the telephone table chair which offered great light from the only window facing south and skillfully plucked her eyebrows, her oval face painted on one side in a splash of gold. Her head tilted and lifted to catch the sun, she held a magnifying mirror in her left hand and flat edged tweezer in her right. I watched as she arched a brow in an arrogant expression and hunted stray black hairs. I enjoyed the changing light and shadows that played on her face. Her narrow-bridged ski nose and huge brown eyes in shadow or full light were always compelling. No one I knew had a more beautiful mother. I understood I looked more like my father. I held little hope of ever growing into a similar beauty. Mostly, I was content knowing she was mine. In fact, if having only one parent in my life was my lot, I was proud of having this one. She had, clearly, been a constant source of learning, fun, and high expectations for her children. Her colorful and irreverent vocabulary was balanced by an expansive and impressive knowledge of literature and cultural facts. She read Walt Whitman poems aloud from her favorite collection, *Leaves of Grass*. We listened to Rachmaninoff piano concertos and powerful Vivaldi pieces. Our favorite concerto was the *1812 Overture*. Stephen and I waited with delight for the canons to sound. Then, we would grasp our chests dramatically, spin in feigned surprise and with agonal breath as we twirled and fell to the floor— dead.

She was an intellectual snob despite being caged in a railroad flat with little income, a high school diploma, two children, a door to nowhere as the centerpiece of her living

I had a head start on digesting the information, time to consider options and my mixed-up emotions. Oddly, I wondered how tall he was and what his voice sounded like. I had no memory of his height, girth, gait, or the sound or timbre of his voice. I was as afraid as I was curious. Thinking my mother might accompany us, I considered saying yes, but, conditioned to the safety of silence, I waited. I had adopted a feline quality when considering how to react. Crouching, in full alert, ready to pounce or retreat to the hiding place that was the dark inner space of my thoughts.

Twelve-year-old Stephen set the wheels in motion for an outcome I should have foreseen. "NO WAY. Are you kidding me? Why is even here? Not me!" He screwed up his face in righteous indignation at the suggestion of his going. My mother and brother turned to me in unison. My turn. "Are you going, Mom?" I asked.

She looked directly at me and answered. "No, I am not. I don't think he actually invited me."

Great, I thought, now there was no neutrality. It was a choice of loyalty to them or betrayal if I chose the enemy. She upped the ante. "Neither of you *has* to go. He's here on business, so I imagine he can find other things to do." A subtle reminder, I thought, that even now we were not his priority. I understood that without the reminder. "Why don't you both think about it overnight? He is calling tomorrow morning to make plans. I think he just wants to pick you up and take you to lunch. That will be nice. He likes good restaurants."

Ha! Yes, the deal was sweetened. We almost never, ever ate out. Every couple of months, we went to a Horn and Hardart cafeteria style restaurant in Yonkers. It was in an outdoor shopping mall we loved to visit, one of the first in the country. We bypassed the stores and queued up happily with our plastic trays on a line that promised a steamy adventure through food "Adventureland." This was the Disneyworld of dinner. The choices were merely food foreplay, each of us knowing already what we would order and where this would end. Mom loved their creamy chicken pot pie with flakey crust. Stephen loved calf's liver and onions with mashed potatoes and creamed corn. My choice was carbohydrate heaven: mashed potatoes, mac and cheese, and crinkle-cut sweet potatoes. We all had Boston cream pie with whipped cream for dessert. I imagine now I was in training to build an ample supply of fat cells that would accompany and plague me throughout life. I was sold. I would offer myself up as the sacrificial lamb, or perhaps in a new status as family traitor. I wondered as much about his height as his taste in food. Did I look like him? Did he like mac and cheese too? "Okay, Mom," I said with exaggerated and false reluctance, "I'll go."

**

Amundson Avenue was unpaved in 1957. Two years later, a ubiquitous strip of brick row houses joined the five old clapboard homes on the dead-end street. Smooth black pavement replaced the sand-colored gravel, a surface better suited to chalked hopscotch grids and bicycles. The slow crunch and give of those pebbles that day heralded his arrival. Sound preparing me for the unknown. I waited with my mother on the front steps of the lime-green house.

We were wordless, ensconced in lime-green shingles, blue hydrangeas and anxiety. Stephen remained inside, having opted to ignore the visit. I wore my navy-blue corduroy school jumper with a white petal-collared blouse. It was July, but this was my best outfit, last worn for my fourth-grade school photo in November. Last fall's navy and white saddle shoes felt snug in July and in contrast to my canvas summer sneakers. The clothing matched a loose internal discomfort.

The rented Ford Galaxy crunched forward on a targeted path. It was a two-toned late model in sharp cadet blue and white. The chrome trim reflected strong summer sun. I thought how somber our dull black 1948 Studebaker looked, and felt another stab of guilt for comparing the cars. After all, the black "rocket" as we called it was our ticket to visiting grandparents in Long Branch, New Jersey, and weekend *Let's Get Lost* adventures. I knew the car was purchased soon after my birth by parents happy to have a new car and baby girl. The rocket was my little sister and good friend. It deserved some loyalty. It was a good source of adventure and entertainment.

Let's Get Lost trips were our favorite. "Okay, Barbara, your turn—right, left or straight ahead?" she'd ask. The questions alternated between us, and she followed any command. The intention was to explore new neighborhoods, get lost, and maybe discover a treasure. Sometimes, I feared we wouldn't find our way back home. "Mom, do you know how to get back home? This is really far away."

"Yep, I think we are lost for sure," she'd answer. "But did you see that pretty little pond at the end of the street we just passed? That might be a good place to catch some sunnies. Stop worrying about getting lost. For God's sake, if you can speak English, how lost can you be?" We grew up hearing that refrain over and over. A sense of adventure and independence were early lessons I am grateful for. But fun was also an important element in our lives.

Now and then the lost car became a boat. She would suddenly be piloting a boat across an unseen river. "Okay kids, watch out, I see a raging river we must cross to get back home." We loved imaginary bodies of water. "Hold on, I have to navigate the waters." Then, she'd change how she held the steering wheel. Curled fists just resting on the outside edge, it looked like she was holding the knobs and spokes of a ship's wheel. She'd jerk the wheel in tight movements that rocked us back and forth. "Safe," she'd announce, and we were out of the water and headed home. We always arrived safely home. But now, an adventure she wasn't piloting lay ahead. I waited for her direction and held my breath.

4 Grilled Cheese

My mother stood up first. I followed as we walked to the now parked car. My father, in slow motion, swiveled in his seat and opened a bright blue door. New car smell greeted me before he even stepped out. I preferred the more familiar odor of our Studebaker's motor oil and gasoline. Before my mother or he even spoke, we stole furtive glances, each taking short sips of appraisal.

She spoke first. "Hello, Charles, good to see you."

He reached out for a friendly hug. "Hi, Chickie (his nickname for her). You look great. Happy to see you."

The ground rules of civility were established, temporarily freeing me from the misery of feeling like a traitor. They both turned to look at me. I smiled hesitantly, preferring to steal a better look than to speak. There was a familiarity in his face I understood was not the recalled memory of a photo. I saw the broad forehead, slightly bulbous nose, and full lips that might greet me in a mirror. There was no escaping our genetic link. It gave me no more or less comfort or confidence. "Hello," all I could offer to the stranger. And so, charged with taking parental control for the moment, he was forced to offer his plan for the next few hours. These would be the first three of the thirty hours I would spend with him for the duration of our lifetimes.

"I think Barbara and I will just grab some lunch at the Bee Hive for starters," he told my mother. The strangeness of my name on his lips was unnerving. It was good to know we would be at a restaurant my mother and I knew in nearby Mount Vernon, the closest commercial area. There was never a thought that he would want to kidnap me, but getting into a car with a stranger felt better knowing my mother could at least know where I was. I got in the passenger side as they hugged goodbye.

"It's good to get to see you again," he offered. I smiled. This was not going to be easy. First of all, he was a man. At ten years of age, I had no template for or comfort level with speaking to men other than to my grandfather or uncle Walter. Visits to Grandpa occurred every few months and consisted of being "shushed" so he could watch Walter Cronkite or listen to politics on the radio. These were sacred rituals everyone respected. Quality time with grandpa was associated with a drive in his '57 Chevy to the boardwalk in Long Branch. He smoked Philly cigars, gave us a handful of pennies for the penny arcade, and joined his buddies to talk more politics on a bench, waiting for us to exhaust our pennies on iron claws that grasped ineffectively at celluloid toys or on the fortune teller who spit out a pre-printed card we took very seriously. Somehow, I understood his love and would always love the smell of a stinky cigar. Uncle Walter was a once weekly presence in my life. Visits to their garden apartment in Alley Pond Park in Queens alternated with Sunday visits to us in the Bronx. Uncle Walter did not engage in much conversation with the children (Mark, his only son, or Stephen and me). His role was to punctuate his wife's (Aunt Dorothy's) opinions and stories with clever affirmative quips or to tell corny jokes. He also acted as mediator when Dorothy and my mother engaged in arguments over extremely competitive Scrabble games. Almost every game included a fight over proper spelling or accepted use of obscure words. I loved Uncle Walter's ability to diffuse a fight with humor or distraction. "Hey Dot," he'd laugh, "I saw you turn over that letter. Now there are three blanks out there, ha-ha." He was kind and gentle, but not a man who asked how my day was or hugged me comfortably. The only primary men in my life were pleasant visitors I loved, albeit from a safe distance. These men existed outside the membrane of the nucleus I called home. There were no neighborhood fathers I engaged with. Their weekends and evenings at home were times I was absent or fleetingly present. There was never a male teacher in my elementary school. Men were, in essence, foreign creatures existing in a parallel world. And now, I sat in the front seat of a rental car alone with a man I hadn't seen in seven years but who, mysteriously, looked like me.

"Do you like the Bee Hive?" he asked, finally breaking the silence. I'd only been there once. Blessed with baby teeth that seemed destined to share a long future with my permanent teeth, the dentist suggested pulling them out three or four at a time. I was rewarded for good behavior and bravery after the first visit with lunch at the Bee Hive. It was on Fourth Avenue and just a block from the dentist. I fondly recalled a perfect grilled cheese sandwich and vanilla fudge ice cream sundae for dessert. The ice cream was served in a silver-stemmed metal cup with fluted edge. It was a dessert fit for a princess. And now, warmed by the memory of icy crystals coating a silver dish, my inhibition eased. "Oh yes, I love the Bee Hive. I went there after I had all my baby teeth pulled out."

I never thought at the time if he considered how much of the trivia and events of my life he had missed. He smiled at the story and took my hand in his. I stiffened but allowed my imprisoned and cold hand to remain captive and resting on the long low center console between our seats. All thoughts of ice-cream were now replaced with discomfort and panic. No man had ever held my hand in a car. Other than crossing a street with grandpa to get to his car, no man had ever held my hand. I didn't want to offend a long-lost father, but I felt an urgency to disengage my hand that I could not ignore. A bobby pin which held back the last vestiges of growing-in bangs saved me. Pretending to secure the errant strand, I removed it with both hands and made an exaggerated effort at replacing it. Then, I breathed out as if winded, clasped my hands together and laid them in my own lap. I hoped he didn't feel rejected. He might feel better, I thought, if I spoke to him. "So, after we eat, do you want to go to see my school? I could also show you the roller rink. It's right across Scott's Bridge and close to the Bee Hive?"

"Well," he smiled as he spoke, "I don't think I've roller-skated in a very, very long time. But, Barbara, I would love to see your school." Hearing him say my name again was as strange as hearing a cow or dog speak my name. We ordered our food and set about the business of eating.

My father took the cloth napkin, snapped it open with a flourish, and placed it on his lap. It looked like a magic trick was about to happen. Would a rabbit appear on the table next? I never realized napkins should leave the table, a logical and closer place to wipe your mouth. He cut his food with a fork and knife but kept the fork in his left hand after he cut, bringing the food directly to his mouth. The fork looked upside down to me. There was no clumsy transfer of the fork to a dominant right hand. I was happy to be eating a grilled cheese sandwich requiring no utensils. My napkin had been discreetly lowered to my lap. I enjoyed the ice cream with a long-handled spoon. We had navigated through the first meal together that I painfully recalled decades later. It was an awkward beginning to the next four meals and twenty-eight hours which comprised the entirety of shared time with my father. I can't remember what he ate. The car was parked on the same side of the street as the Bee Hive. No need to hold my hand.

A ride past PS 68 was next. We looked at the summer-shuttered building. I thought of school things he didn't know. Should I tell him about the fourth grade teacher who humiliated me because I just couldn't learn to tell time? She called on me every day to visit the huge oak wall clock in the corridor and return to announce the time to my classmates. After two or three incorrect answers and sufficient snickering from my classmates, I was permitted to sit as a smarter child would be called on to complete the task correctly. Maybe I should tell him about the poster contest I won for Brotherhood Week? I was so proud of the bronze medal and red, white, and blue ribbon it hung from. Would he like to know I was the best Hula-Hoop twirler in the school? Should I tell him about Mrs. King, the lunch lady who always gave me the peanut butter sandwich that had the end piece of crusty bread flipped and hidden in a layer of peanut butter paste? I suspected it wasn't random and she hated me. Instead, I said nothing. The living things I remembered were not compatible with the soundless, slow summer warmth PS 68 now sat in. He must have understood this. We stood instead, side by side for a few moments, staring at the school. It might have looked like reverence, but it was the quiet echo of those seven silent years.

* * *

The question of who he was receded into the background over the next two years and twenty-eight hours of contact. Those next three visits were easier and had large gaps of time in between. Those gaps were peppered with the same meager checks and apologetic letters arriving in air-mail envelopes decorated in his dancing script. Still, in my naiveté, he was mine to rediscover in a shared future. I was a twelve-year-old girl confident in the likelihood of good outcomes. His absence and silence in the ensuing four years eroded that hope with the corrosive burn of reality. I was sixteen, angry, and defiant when we shared a last meal. That final and unfortunate visit ended with my hurling any collected currency of trust into an irrevocable abyss. The other visits receded into that dead space. I slipped into adulthood cradled in the abyss. I made no attempt to retrieve alternative truths until it was too late.

5 The Abyss

The egocentric frenzy of setting and meeting goals, driven in equal parts by hormones and societal expectations, negated any tendency to reflective thought. Milestones were shrouded in a thin layer of vaporous speculation about him that I casually shrugged off. Should my father know I had graduated high school, nursing school, gotten engaged, married, had a child? When I did summon the courage to ask my mother about informing him of an event or milestone, I was given a stock answer. "Of course, you can let him know. It's totally your decision. Personally, I don't think he deserves the respect or honor of knowing, but it's up to you." I was perpetually trapped in the same prison I'd first confronted before my tenth birthday. A useless conundrum of guilt or betrayal had latched on for life. All her love, sacrifice, suffering, and nurturing could suddenly be for naught if I chose to include him. I was the same girl standing next to a father who silently stared at an empty school building. There was too much history and too many living, breathing, unshared days to consider including him. Sharing had become an insurmountable task that loomed too large. I came to accept its overbearing presence and the shadow it cast. I stood in that long dark shadow for five decades, respecting the sweeping elegance of the Hemlocks arms as they shielded and hid me and kept me close and tethered to their safety.

It was the move to my current home that allowed some dappled sunlight to dance in the darkened space I'd grown comfortable in. This was the sixth home of my adult life and the first I'd moved to since my mother's death a few years before. I was sixty-two years old. Every move included the usual transfer of overly taped sturdy cardboard boxes. Three of those cartons had earned the honor of continued storage in an attic, basement, or extra closet. The contents of the boxes were marked in my neat printing in bold, black letters. The large boxes stated they held old photos, photo albums, video tapes, yearbooks, diplomas, kids' camp letters. One was labeled "Cissy." The Cissy doll had accompanied me, without question, on every journey. She had survived the donate or save question other artifacts had not. I had almost forgotten about that box until a change of seasons and storage of winter hats and scarves found me in the attic. *Cissy*, I thought, *why are you here?* There were now granddaughters who might like her. But they didn't seem to care for dolls, and Cissy was too special to imagine her tossed into a toy chest or, God forbid, subjected to a bubble bath. Cissy was now in her fifties. We were both old girls now. How could that be? Perhaps she was a valuable collectible now. *Ha!* I thought. *Finally a gift from my father that could be turned into cash.* I remembered the details of his missing last will and testament. But, like the charm bracelet that could become melt down money, this was evidence I needed to keep. Evidence of what? The question of Cissy had never been asked.

Now, I thought back on the meaning of Cissy and how she might tell me who my father was. Why had I never considered the meaning of Cissy? I hadn't saved Penny, my first beloved doll. That Madame Alexander baby doll with painted face and molded hair was a first birthday gift from my parents. They named her Penny because she "cost a pretty penny." I loved Penny as a child. I made shoe box cradles and dish towel blankets for her. I worried she might be too hot, too cold, wet, sleepy, or uncomfortable. Thank you, Mom, for teaching me compassion for dolls, teddy bears, and all living and inanimate representation of living things so effectively. As an adult, I am guilty of retrieving dirty and ripped stuffed animals from the trash to apologize for their fate. I carefully consider my right to end the life of intrusive insects and suffer disproportionately when I see a stray or sick animal. But somewhere over the span of those busy young adult decades, Penny was a donated item. I am sure I must have apologized before giving her away. How and why had Cissy escaped the same fate? She was evidence, I knew, in the question of my father. His identity, and more importantly, my meaning in his life were linked to Cissy.

Three months after the summer visit with my father, I turned ten. Stephen turned twelve the day after my birthday. Days before, a large parcel addressed to me arrived at the house. The only other time I'd received a package was the delivery of a secretly ordered fake fly entombed in a plastic ice cube, pink rubber Whoopee cushion, and magic periscope glasses advertised in the back pages an Archie comic book. I'm not sure how I managed the financial end of that even now. Cissy was a grown-up Madame Alexander doll. She had to have cost more than a pretty penny. She was a doll that embodied a life of luxury. Encased in a large red metal steamer trunk with silver fittings and rail and steamship stickers, befitting a debutante or movie star, she entered my less fortunate life. Her wardrobe included a real mink hat, coat, and muff; a spring coat and hat ensemble; a tennis outfit; nightgown; evening gown and matching sets of shoes; and drawers full of hosiery and toiletries. I know my favorite items were the tiny rolls of toilet paper and tissues. She was a beautiful brunette with green eyes and gold earrings. I loved her, dressed and undressed her, and combed her hair. I still preferred baby dolls and was almost too old for any doll to amuse me as they had. But Cissy was in a class by herself. I can't remember if Stephen was ever sent a birthday gift. At some point, both Penny and Cissy were given equal status and relegated to lives of storage in dark spaces as the little girl who was me grew and changed. Cissy stayed on. Perhaps it was her obvious value as a luxury item or as a potential collectible. I hate to consider the abstract question that both *play life* and *real life* assigns more value to those who own mink coats and travel than to their less fortunate sisters. There were, right now however, other questions that keeping Cissy had evoked. What had Cissy been meant to tell me, then, and now?

Had this luxurious doll been intended to compensate for the years with no gifts and no contact? Why had seven years passed without hearing his voice or his having sent a card or letter sent to his children? What had happened in his life during those years that created the vacuum? Had he been moved by my willingness to see him that July? Had he been struck by meeting the nine-year-old chubby girl who looked like him and wore too-tight winter clothes in July? Was he trying to offer up an alternative of luxury I might consider as enticement to a continued relationship? It was only after I had decided to offer up Cissy for sale on eBay as I approached my seventh decade that another question was considered. Had my father once tried to love me? Was Cissy an expression of love?

Cissy sold for nine hundred dollars to a doll collector in Maine. The little girl Barbara was secretly relieved she would have the warm mink coat as she moved to a colder New England climate. I was happy she would get to see the light of day and bask in the glory of her intrinsic value. I was happy I'd held on long enough to realize her appreciation in value as a luxurious collectible. That money was earmarked for a weekend trip to a favorite bed-and-breakfast on Block Island. Thank you, Cissy. Thank you, Dad.

I wrapped her beautiful vinyl face and extremities in new white tissue paper. I dressed her for the final voyage in her light blue gabardine flared spring swing coat, smoothed her hair, and pinned the matching hat in place. I made sure all the drawers inside the trunk were tightly secured and bid farewell to toilet paper rolls in half-inch scale. I secured the silver latches to close the trunk. I lowered the so familiar trunk into a sturdy mailing box and filled it with too many Styrofoam squiggles. The box was taped, labeled, insured, and sent away. She was no longer mine. Finally, I considered a last simple question. Was Cissy his way of simply telling me he loved me? Did I really want to walk through that mine field of dangerous speculation? That unknowable outcome was as elusive as knowing who he was. How, at almost seventy years old, did the sight of that grown-up doll make me still feel like a child? Cissy was no longer mine. She had never helped assure me, anyway. The piece of me that kept her all these decades had relinquished any hope.

6 Gifts

There were another twenty-six hours we spent together to consider. In the absence of concrete things like gold charms and a now departed rich girl's doll, what did I know? There was a wristwatch with a mauve colored, enamel face shaped like a flower I received a month after Cissy, a Christmas gift. My brother denies ever getting a gift from our father, but I remember a Polaroid camera that year that captivated him and produced shiny, wet images he flapped to and fro to dry them. I loved the acrid chemical smell that wafted around the newborn images. My memory of the luxury is that my father sent it. Some sadly faded photos survived their battle of daylight and handling. They are in a "survivors" box of photos. The watch was stolen by a visiting classmate soon after I received it. I knew that Antoinette, a motherless friend, loved the watch and had snatched it from my dresser. I saw her wear it to school one day. She never admitted it. Compassion always dominated our life lessons.

"Barbara, she probably stole the watch," my mother agreed. "That poor girl, it's just her and her father in that house. Her mother died when she was just four. He doesn't even speak English," was her calm response to my outrage. "Just think, if we call him up, how angry he will be at her. You might get the watch back, but he might shame her and punish her for taking it. Also, she might lie to him and that would be terrible. In either case, you know she can never wear the watch or enjoy it. Let's hope she returns it."

"But Mom," I shouted in outrage, "that's not right. It's my watch. Why should she get away with stealing?"

"You wouldn't want to trade places with that girl, believe me. Do you think she will ever enjoy it now? Do you think she might be sad because you are mad, and now she can't visit our house anymore? I bet she feels completely miserable about ever taking your watch," her final word. My anger only slightly assuaged and replaced by sadness.

I couldn't imagine life without a mother. It had to be worse than life without a father. I thought of her father, a man who rarely spoke, wore gray looking undershirts, and seemed to take his only pleasure from a lush garden that yielded perfect tomatoes. Her small house was always filled with the scent of freshly made tomato sauce. Hers was not just a single parent home, it was also a single sensory home. The watch was never returned or seen again on her wrist. Thank you again, Mom, for a valuable lesson in compassion. Now, through the lens of maturity, I wonder if my mother was also happy not to have the gift on my wrist as an irritating reminder of Charles. The irony of not knowing how to tell time until two years after the watch was stolen does not escape me. Stolen watches and telling time were parallels to having a father yet never having one. Missed opportunities, bad timing, or something other?

How strange it must have been for my mother to adjust to his new-found interest in fatherhood over the next two years. She'd spent seven years comfortably in her role as our only viable parent. His parental claim was staked in erratic, casually constructed visits that now included my mother and Stephen. The first three visits, each about three hours, were shared meals in exotic restaurants. I was unaware of the grown-up underpinnings, which changed the dynamic to include them. In retrospect, I like to imagine he was so smitten with me and having a reclaimed daughter that he began to send child support checks more regularly. My brother's change of heart was driven, no doubt, by his need to please my mother at any expense. He never failed to reward her with his good looks, excellent grades, and ability to charm anyone he met. The irony is that she often reminded him of how he had inherited his father's brilliant mind and easy charm. His rejection of the man he resembled may have been fueled by distorted guilt about those tainted genetic gifts. He needed to make up for his father's misdeeds. If she had relented and would share some time with him, so too, would Stephen. Unlike me, he remained a staunch critic, aloof participant, and, I believe, a permanently lost son. His role was casual observer, mine was willing participant, and our mother took on alternating roles cast as either martyred savior or femme fatale. Her sensual beauty was a commodity which empowered and diminished her in equal parts. It was a new and short chapter of life with two parents. Life with just one parent was less confusing. There is something to be said for its simplicity.

By eleven, I was aware of the role sexuality played in her life and in my nascent understanding of how men fit into the larger picture of our lives. It had gone beyond the creepy landlord's black lace panties left on a ledge. My mother had begun to date other men when I was ten. Along with lessons in compassion, classical music, literature, and adventure, there were now passive lessons about men. I hated their interference in our treasured triumvirate. Like my father, they were never people who shared the hour to hour, day to day, reality of my life. I assumed, legitimately, they had no interest in children. Poverty aside, we were provided with love, attention, and gifts few children claim from a single adult seeing them through to maturity. We simply enjoyed life together. She taught us how to swim, ride bicycles, fish, identify birds and flowers. We were signed up for scouting. She was never short on irreverent humor and cryptic analysis of people and politics. She made us intellectually curious and perhaps too cynical. She provided a feeble attempt at religious conviction though she lacked her own commitment. We celebrated Chanukah and Christmas. We lit sabbath candles on Friday night in defiance of being the only Jews in the neighborhood. It was with contrived and anemic anger that she scolded me for going to confession at the Catholic church on Saturdays with my friends. I loved the smell of dying votive candles and the beautiful stained-glass windows at Our Lady of the

Blessed Nativity. I liked the statues of saints and hated the cruelty of Christ's crucifixion. It was all mysterious theater and a larger-than-life offering. She countered this appeal with humorous considerations. "So, don't forget that Jesus was actually a Jew. Unfortunately, he was living at the wrong time in the wrong place. Nowadays he'd be a great Democrat like Adlai Stevenson." A lesson in ancient and contemporary politics.

* * *

Now, there was the occasional man she talked about who could distract her from the single mission of growing and nurturing children without a father. I resented their intrusion. It was different from the possibility of that other man, the father I wanted to know. The man who gave me his bulbous nose and large hazel eyes. The man who gave Stephen his brilliant mind and winning ways with people. Unlike the other men, he seemed interested in *her* children. And now, we were taking tentative steps together over the course of several hours and strange new foods to experiment in family life as we never knew it. It was a crazy experiment of disparate objectives and, like Jesus, being together at the wrong time at the wrong places. My life was one of considering wrong places at the wrong time. And here is an irony greater than losing a beautiful watch before I could even learn how to tell time. I had a father who seemed to have been in the wrong place at the wrong time. It was too late for my brother to care. It was too late for my mother to want him back. Her distrust was deeply ingrained. I don't know the events in his own life which led him to seek us out. At that time and place I am certain I wanted to know more about him. I would have four more opportunities to search for answers. But, twenty-six hours then and now, in retrospect, have never yielded the answers a daughter deserved. Still, in my final decades it seems important to look back more carefully at those hours in case I had missed a clue. I forced myself to bring back the memories. They had not been as easy to retrieve as a beautiful doll in a large red steamer trunk. But they were there.

7 Vichyssoise

"I really want to stay home. Can't you two just go without me?" Stephen had no desire to have a fancy lunch with his visiting father. This time, my mother had accepted his invitation to meet at his motel room in Riverdale (where the wealthy lived in the Bronx) and drive together to a Japanese restaurant in Suffern, New York. This was upstate and an hour's drive. A reluctant Stephen, dressed in his good khaki pants and clean, white short-sleeved dress shirt, tagged sullenly along. My mother wore a mid-calf, very flared skirt. Huge black and white flowers swirled and undulated in slow motion with each step, merging the sensuality of human and botanical potential. A wide black belt at her tiny waist acted as the conductor of the dance. All energy and purpose was driven from that center. It was late May. I wore a white organdy dress with flared skirt and a collar designed to look like flower petals. This dress was an original design created by my mother's friend Mary. An accomplished seamstress, it was her gift to me for our school's May Day celebration. I'd worn it two weeks earlier, proudly weaving a pastel ribbon through a human braid of ten-year-olds binding an unadorned twenty-foot pole into a glorious pale rainbow-plaited stem. We were all wearing our best to meet Charles. What, I wonder now, dictated the need to present a collective of good packaging to the man who had left us without concern for our most basic needs?

Was this my first foray into a lifetime of believing others could not value the inside unless the outside was attractive? Was Stephen's righteous indignation and resistance a healthier response? I have come to believe righteous indignation is too often coupled with anger. At least in his case, it has always seemed that way. The need to please and be accepted is laced with hope. It stems from a desire to be loved and love in return. Our twin legacies of anger and hope are as tightly bound, plaited and woven through our lives as the ribbons around that bare Maypole. Dressed in costumes that belied our reality, we piled silently into the black Studebaker and headed west to Riverdale to meet Charles.

My mother knocked timidly at the door of his motel room. I'd never been in a hotel or motel. I was impressed with the concept of owning your own room for as long as you like in a place you didn't live. It was three years before we moved out of the miserable lime-green house to an apartment house ourselves. At that time, everyone in our lives lived in private homes. I was aware of the anonymity of this place. It was strange and secretive and foreign. The three of us stood anxiously in the foreign place waiting for a response to her knocks. It felt hollow and empty. "Be right there," a very nasal but decidedly male voice finally answered. I recognized it from my last encounter. It was permanently imprinted, something I may have subconsciously recalled from infancy. Soft—barefoot?—steps could be heard, and I'm sure none of us were breathing. The dark-blue door flew open.

And there was my father, barefoot indeed. He wore only white Jockey shorts and a wide grin. "Oh my God, Charles, for Christ's sake, where are your clothes?" My mother had bypassed the need for social niceties. No breaking the ice here. We were plunged into the ice-cold lake that was Charles and Charlotte. Stephen and I were bolted to the blue carpet. It was like playing a favorite old schoolyard game of Red Light-Green Light and freezing on command. Recalling the scene now, it seems like a frozen frame of white objects—my white organdy dress, Stephen's freshly ironed white shirt, and my father's white underwear—and a portrait emerges. Perhaps I would give this work of art a formal title: *Juxtaposition In White*, for surely the innocence of our clothing and awareness of his exposure were in stark contrast to the other white subject and object in the tableau.

Our mother strode quickly across the room to come face to face with the almost naked man. I realized they were the same height as they stood staring at each other. I studiously averted looking at his underwear. There was, however, no question in my ten-year-old mind that this male body differed from my brother's. If any doubt remained. My mother clarified any first impressions I may have repressed. "Honestly, Charles, no one wants to look at your bulging balls," she hissed under her breath, her words audible to me. I gathered the courage then to steal a glance at his thickly muscled legs. Just a few inches above those tree trunk thighs, the offending bulge sat unapologetically wrapped in white cotton. By the time I could avert my eyes, he'd turned and casually went into the bathroom behind him. "No problem, Chickie, I'll be right back."

In his absence she regained control. "What was he thinking? Honestly, I think he was trying to impress me—Chickie? Oh that's just great. Endearments and nicknames. Your father is really special. I do believe he wants me back." She plunked herself down on his queen-size hotel bed. "The nerve of him!" She looked into the large wood-framed mirror facing the bed and tucked a lock of thick chestnut hair back in place with an indignant flip of her head. Moments later, he emerged from the bathroom wearing a thick white terry robe. Here we had another opportunity to consider the absurdity of the scene. Looking back, I am uncertain that at ten and twelve years of age we registered each frozen frame as a stored memory for future consideration. Now, I question the order of impact on our minds. Mom was now "Chickie." Mom and this man had a strange musk of tense sexuality we were too young to comprehend completely but were aware of. Mom hated this man? Loved this man? Which? Who were they before? And then there was the imbalance of our formal clothing. A now white-bathrobed man standing across from our seated mother and the two statue-like children waiting for the adults to take control. The frozen frame of three white-clad figures were standing in place waiting, expectantly, for the black-belted center of power to move us forward in some new direction.

We were about to be choreographed in a four-hour long performance of unfamiliar actors swirling about in white organdy and billowing, undulating black and white skirts blowing in the wind. The scenery changed as did the costume of the male lead, now in pleated and cuffed charcoal dress slacks and a fine white linen, open collared sport shirt. This was an intermission of sorts. There was a stop along the New York State Thruway where the first dandelions of spring popped out to begin their own battle for survival in their unfortunate birthplace of toxic carbon monoxide along the busy road. Flowers and children alike challenged with their circumstance. It was a good place to take some photos of Charles with an arm draped lovingly over the shoulders of his offspring. Both Stephen and I appear to be either nestling against his chest or trying desperately to extricate ourselves from his clutches. It is a matter of subjective interpretation. The photo is just one more piece of real evidence I have saved. It answers no question at all. The next hours of dining and playing our roles continued to be surreal. They left no concrete traces to consider years later. The memories of a Japanese restaurant set above a high mountain, a koi pond, and vichyssoise were as foreign to me as the memory of the bulging white cotton of tight Jockey shorts. And yet, I can forget none of it. What child can forget the first visit to the circus or her performance in a school play? Perhaps it is the fear-tinged flying trapeze acts or the too-tamed tigers we most remember. Most probably it is the millions of flashlights in the darkened tent that are the memory. Maybe it is the play where you got to be the Tin Man or the Good Witch or maybe just the wind of a tornado spinning and spinning and changing the world as you knew it. It is always remembered. You will frame it in your mind's eye and remember it as you will. And I could remember the details of the second shared meal with my father over the next few hours as easily. The salient question of who he was remained, unfortunately, just an image with blurred edges and speculative thought. There are chalky, ghostly smudges where I long for crisp black and white. Yes, the white remains an important part.

"Mrs. Payne will have the vichyssoise," he tells the young skinny Asian waitress in black skirt and white tailored shirt. I didn't like the sound of what he ordered for her. It sounded like something that may have little "fishies" swimming in it. I also didn't understand why he had to speak for her. This made no sense at all. Before he could do it again and order some fish thing for me, I gathered the courage to ask what it was. This was serious business to me. Food was a no-nonsense area, and I wanted to decide what I would ingest. It has always been that way. I have taken control and lack of control of food my entire life. A subject for later discussion perhaps. On that day, I did not care what the choreographer had intended.

"Excuse me, Dad, I don't know what 'fishysoise' is," I said. "I'm not sure I want that."

"Oh, it's delicious Barbara. It's actually a cold soup made with leeks and potatoes and some cream." He looked at me with self-assured benevolence.

Is he kidding? I thought. *Cold soup to begin with. Whoever heard of eating soup cold?* My chicken noodle soup from Campbell's or Mom's rare homemade offering was a hot item. *Anyway, what is a leek?* I wondered. It sounded bad also. We had leaks in our bathroom pipe that caused rusty stains on the wall. Was it some distilled extract from pipes that got to be salty and could be put in soup? The potato part was okay, but I also liked them hot and mashed up with butter and salt. "Do they have chicken soup?" I asked.

"I don't think so. But you will like this if you try it, I promise." He proceeded to order the cold soup for all of us. Stephen had the resigned posture of a person waiting to have a tooth extracted in a dental chair. He was silent and ready to bolt if he could. My mother was uncharacteristically quiet but difficult to read. It seemed as if she might be enjoying her special role as submissive wife and amused mother in this scene. I was not sure if having a normal family with a dad was actually a good thing. I was sure I hated the vichyssoise.

After lunch, we walked the grounds belonging to the Faux Japanese restaurant. There were a series of shallow rectangular koi ponds as the central feature. I remember spikey grasses surrounding the pools and several scattered creamy lotus blossoms floating in the water. The fragile flowers appeared to be tethered by green roots to a bottom. The umbilical-like connection reminded me of small dogs straining against tight leashes. An exotic evergreen stacked in horizontal layers marked the end of the path. Stephen and I took the opportunity to escape the now *two* unfamiliar adults and skip across granite stepping stones evenly spaced and set in white marble chips. We surreptitiously watched our parents in animated conversation we couldn't hear. "I still don't like him, and anyway this place is stupid. All he talks about is himself."

This insightful remark by my brother was in response to lessons over lunch on the finer things in life which included both vichyssoise and the sliding doors, thatched sweeping roofs, and use of wood in Japanese architecture. I can only speculate now on the timing of this meal and its possible influence on another Faux Japanese creation in Miami I would visit years later.

It does seem as if our parents had at least one thing in common. They both subscribed to a theory that children were vessels best served by filling them with facts. Mom's version was immersion in good music, art, literature, the natural world, and her opinions on everything from Albert Einstein to adultery. We were excellent "vessels" and absorbed and retained both opinions and facts, secure in her devotion and sovereignty. But Charles had earned neither our trust nor receptivity to his opinions. He seemed disinterested in knowing what we actually liked to eat or in any other interests we had. I was back in the schoolyard with him in summer. There was too much he didn't know. He was out of season and out of synchrony with our lives. Perhaps what I learned on that day was that he may have been a narcissist. This fact is speculative and from the vantage point of maturity. At ten, I was impressed with his fancy manners and take-charge attitude. He was a man able to at least temporarily inhibit my mother's ability to make her own decisions and magically neutralize what I knew was her venomous opinion of this irresponsible, philandering man. I understood he was a charming and charismatic figure. He was a snake charmer. Unlike Stephen, I was more impressed than dubious. If he was a snake charmer, so be it. As the two white-clad children flitted like butterflies from stone to stone and flower to flower, they were disparately attracted and repelled to the object of their attention. The male and female offspring so bound by their origins and experiences would leave this particular span of time with divergent impressions. My own hope and willingness to explore possibilities was in sharp contrast to Stephen's abject distaste and distrust of his father. I imagined there would be other opportunities for change. After all, this day marked less than eight collective hours spent with my father. I was still ten years old and believed that time was not so much an indeterminate luxury as it was my entitlement.

It was dark when we returned to retrieve our car and leave him at his hotel. There were quick hugs and promises to be in touch. Stephen and I sat in the back seat and waited for our mother to speak. She sat stiffly and silently in front of us. We didn't need to find her eyes in the rear-view mirror to assess the coming storm. Fine-tuned to her body language, we understood the first words spoken would rupture the silence and any positive inclinations lurking in my thoughts. "I still can't believe he flirted with me all afternoon. Guess he is between girlfriends now or he wouldn't have visited anyway." We double downed on our silence, happy to be sitting in shrouded darkness, now, her audience. "So, it's been seven years. That should be about enough time for his charm to wear off and be looking for greener pastures." She started the car and it lurched forward. "Don't hold your breath for the next visit kids. And don't hold your breath for the next check to come either. We are returning to normal."

She was mostly correct. The next check was late. There were no phone calls for several months and life returned to "normal." The visit was forgotten. We didn't see him again until June of the following year. Stephen returned to good grades in school and Wednesday night Boy Scout meetings. He built intricate wood and plastic model airplanes. He visited friends and played baseball. He had five stitches in his forehead from a baseball bat flung by a friend that made a home run. He got stuck in the crotch of a huge tree in the empty lot next door. He was attempting to climb it when his foot lodged in the space. Mom called the fire department to extricate him. They had to cut a huge limb off as neighbors watched. He hid indoors for three days following the incident, so great was his shame. A month later, he threw a huge rock tied to a rope over a higher limb on the same tree. It missed the limb and returned to earth with increased velocity, slamming him in his head. He nursed a huge egg with ice and a bit more grace. Perhaps the tree wanted revenge for losing its previously yoked twin. Stephen seemed to be accident prone. He was otherwise a perfect boy. Of course, the father who should have shared, witnessed, cared, or been aware of the day-to-day events was absent and unaware. And in his absence, Stephen's resentment and anger solidified. Now, baked into the perfect boy was a perfect anger that would be as permanent as the little keloid above his left eyebrow where a baseball bat once hurt him.

My own return to normal was not as dramatic. The visit and images of bulging white Jockey shorts and koi ponds receded quickly. I was two years into what would be a lifelong battle with "the heartbreak of psoriasis."

Mom told me I'd inherited this plague-like condition from my father's mother. It seems the gene for psoriasis was more dominant than for Nora's huge breasts. I know for sure that the genetic association with the woman my mother professed great hatred for burdened me as much as the itchy, ugly thickened scale-like plaques on my legs, elbows, and scalp. There were tar ointments and derivatives of tar that stained the sheets black and smelled like the newly paved road down the block. There was an oily concoction of salicylic acid and sulfur worn under a plastic shower cap most nights. Once removed, the task was for my mother to use a fine-toothed comb to remove the collection of greasy flakes and loosened scalp. She never complained, nor did I. Certainly, I felt bad enough to have inherited Nora's genes. My mother was committed to helping me. We tried any new medical or folkloric suggestion. A trial medication at NYU ended in fatigue, jaundice, and liver damage. Urine-soaked gauze yielded only repulsion, frequent baths, and no improvement. Ultraviolet light therapy gave me sunburn and skin cancer in my fifties. Eventually, my mother discovered an amazing cosmetic paste available in three skin tones (none which matched my olive skin) that enabled me to minimize the appearance. A finishing powder minimized the slick surface and set the disguise in place through several baths. Lydia O'Leary Cover Mark was my new best friend. I don't know how Mom had discovered it. Years later, I learned it was invented by a cosmetician to help disguise strawberry hemangiomas and dark nevi that disfigured people even less fortunate than me. I am sure my father was unaware of having passed on this "gift." He was certainly unaware of the time, associated expense, and anguish spent in the quest for normal skin. I became immune to frequently being asked, "What's wrong with your skin?" I'd robotically offer, "It's a skin condition and it's *not* catching," registering their repulsion and relief.

Only once did the insensitivity cross the line into cruelty. By fourth grade I was firmly established as a sweet but subpar student. I had not mastered telling time and read out loud in a hesitant manner. Overshadowed by a brilliant brother who had skipped a grade or two and was in "S.P." Special Progress classes, I saw no reason to compete. The anonymity of underperforming was going along well until my path found me in the classroom of Mrs. Wilson. A handsome woman whom I would now describe as being either gender neutral or more in touch with her masculine side, she wore fitted gray suits with mid-calf straight skirts and tailored shirts. Her hair was steel gray as well. The only nod to femininity were her shoes. They were what the Irish would call brogues and had chunky heels that marked them as feminine shoe gear. She was tall. She only smiled at two select students who sat in front of her desk and seemed to have perpetually raised waving arms. Is this a form of priapism? They had the correct answers to any question. She had daily rituals which included a quarter turn to the obedient red geraniums on the window sill for perfect sun exposure. A half hour each morning was spent with a lint brush taken to her lapels. She seemed to snarl involuntarily during this activity. She studiously avoided engaging me directly and sat me in the back row. Only when she called on me to tell time would she look at me, knowing the outcome would be failure. In preparation for the annual Maypole festival, our class was making tissue-paper flowers in pastel colors to adorn the pole once it was braided with ribbon. We were instructed to get a supply of tissues from her closet when our row was called. I was the third student in the last row. I approached the closet hoping there would be enough yellow tissue left for my flower.

The painful thwack to my right hand and wrist removed all thoughts of yellow flowers—all thoughts of anything. Mrs. Wilson loomed over me wearing her familiar snarly expression. She looked directly into my questioning eyes. "Not you!" she spit out. "Do not touch those tissues with your hands. You cannot touch things with that skin." She had slammed the heavy golden oak closet door closed on my hand. I don't remember returning to my seat or reacting. The room had become silent and still, frozen in time. I am able to recall the still tableau of that moment even now. And thus began my first foray into disobedience. I was not indignant, I was ashamed. In my shame, I chose to not share the incident with my mother or to react in any way that could lead me to relive or recall it.

Recollection included returning to the scene of the incident. Without formal planning, I knew I was not returning to Mrs. Wilson's class. Feigning a bellyache would not afford me more than a day or two respite. My plan was to avoid returning to school. I became a runaway kid. I was almost successful at elusive invisibility. Did I know even then that existing under the radar, subpar and basically unremarkable in a world of smarter, prettier, two-parented kids, was fodder for survival? It's easy to get lost in a crowd or a classroom if you are ordinary. I easily got lost each morning in the huddle of babbling children waiting for the school doors to open, enabling them to filter into a morning assembly area and ultimately to classrooms. The moment the doors flung open, I sidled off to the schoolyard side, down a staircase, and out to freedom. For three days, I entertained myself in weak April sunshine with walks to Seton Falls Park where only a few disinterested dog walkers and strolling young mothers preoccupied with their charges ignored me. Sometimes a favorite stationery store about a half mile away was the destination. I liked the gondolas with costume jewelry best. No adult questioned my presence on a school day. I was either lucky or invisible for sure. The luck lasted just three days. On a Thursday morning, my mother received a call from the school office asking if I was feeling better and returning to school. "You must have the wrong number," she casually told the secretary. "Barbara is in school today and has been there all week."

I was discovered by my mother, sauntering back to school as she took to the Studebaker to search the neighborhood. Silence prevailed as I was driven directly to the principal's office where the stooped and kindly old man and my mother sat facing me, both expecting a reasonable explanation. "I just don't want to go back to school anymore," I offered without elaborating.

Mild-mannered and soft-spoken Mr. Tully, who looked like a white candle that had melted into his chair on a too-hot day, stared at me impassively. He rarely visited classrooms or walked the halls of PS 68. He probably hadn't observed the long-ago tenured fourth-grade witch, Cruella, since before I was born. "Well,

Barbara, it's April now. What has changed your mind at this late date?" he asked.

They both looked at me and waited for an answer. "I don't like Mrs. Wilson, she's mean," I near whispered.

"Is she mean to you or everyone?" my mother asked. The safety of being able to respond directly to her enabled me to recount the incident. Their eyes went directly to my right hand looking for evidence. Only a fading dusky colored discoloration remained. It was unimpressive but evidence enough for my mother, now rising from her seat in reflexive righteous indignation to react. "She is *not* returning to that class. Actually, I always thought that old hag was a sourpuss. No surprise to me she could do this. Would you like me go in there now to tell her, or will you be doing that Mr. Tully?"

Poor old Mr. Tully, caught between a rock and a hard place, shifted a bit, sluggish and listing from side to side in his soft waxy nest. "Well, I definitely will be speaking to Mrs. Wilson to get her version of what happened. I will need to start there. For now, why don't I walk Barbara back to the class so she can get back to learning today."

Mom glared at him and stood above him, gathering her full height of sixty-eight lean, engorged with anger inches above the amorphous man. "For now, I will be taking her home and considering the need for legal action. You will need to consider another class placement for the remaining nine weeks of this school year." She took my hand and led me out.

She was on a tear. I prepared for a raging verbal firestorm. Her words were bullets and she had a robust arsenal. She loved words. Words in a Scrabble game, words in poetry, lyrics in a song, words in best sellers and classics, and now, words as weapons where a lawyer might be more appropriate, where a father and husband might diffuse her wrath and support her need to protect her child and right this wrong. "She is an anti-Semite for sure, an iron-clad bitch. I should have just gone in there and swung the closet door open and closed it on Eva Braun's right hand. Why did it take you three days to tell me about this, anyway? Walking around the neighborhood for three days is not smart. Doesn't matter now. On Monday, we are going to school to meet your new teacher, then I will request a meeting with Mrs. Wilson. Ahh, Mrs. Wilson, you are about to meet a formidable adversary. You might enjoy reverence from children, but you are not in Narnia and this child has a mother who will protect her from the wicked white witch. I'm sure the police or school board will be interested in this incident."

The diatribe was mostly meant to diffuse her anger, not, in fact, a dress rehearsal for an actual encounter. It served to quell her rage but also to distract me from the anxiety I had about starting in a new class. What should I fear more, being a new kid in the class at the end of the year or having a crazed mother embarrassing me in public? I finished fourth grade as an under-the-radar, underperforming quiet girl in the back row of Mrs. Burke's class. The trauma of this experience, which had occurred shortly before the dinner of vichyssoise and lotus blossoms, was unknown to my father. It had never occurred to me then to want him there or to speak about it afterward. It had nothing to do with him.

How would my father know about my brother's brilliance or stitches and bumps and bruises if the letters came so rarely from Florida? If the phone never rang on either end? Had he noticed the red patches on my elbows and knees over a couple of shared meals? He had missed over seventy-five hundred meals together in the past seven years. He had missed my winning the Brotherhood Week poster contest, and he had missed Mrs. Wilson's cruelty and my response to it. He had missed knowing his children. In his absence, my mother had done a valiant job. There was a necessary absence of reflection necessary to efficiently navigate the daily rituals that occupy the hours in a day. Reflection is an adult's purview, anyway. In the vacuum of physical distance, reflection was irrelevant. The void deepened. That is how we became lost to each other. He may have reflected, but there was no evidence of that. This is how we remained strangers in spite of good intentions, benign neglect, or genetic links that seem to work better in the natural world of swans and apes. It may have simply been his apathy. We remained strangers.

Still, there were those few hours existing outside of the daily universe. There were the unexpected calls that caught us off guard. They existed only in the space of the less than the two years between the ages of my being almost ten and almost twelve years old. For unknown reasons, that is when he had taken a hiatus from his existing routines to consider the existence of his children again. Was he suddenly reflective or just lonely and between other women in his life? The answer was soon revealed. Those two years existed in between next lives and next families for him. He found himself now, at age forty-eight, in free fall from a devastating and scandalous relationship with no viable means of redemption. It was probably a good time to consider a ten-year-old daughter and twelve-year-old son. Perhaps their beautiful mother was still beautiful. Perhaps he should consider the past as an option for the future. My mother was brilliant and intuitive. Her impressions of the man in Jockey shorts were not misguided. She was fond of the quote: *Hell hath no fury like a woman scorned*. I knew there would never be a reunited family. Both my brother and my mother seemed to hate this man. I'm not sure why we continued to accept the rare invitation to see him when it came. From my vantage point at ten and twelve, it seemed she was either conflicted about her feelings or desperate for financial relief. I know for certain she held on to her children protectively and selfishly. I felt it then and believed it always.

"Your father called. I told him you were graduating from sixth grade. He wants to take us out to celebrate next week. The Bastard doesn't deserve the honor, of course, but I thought you might like to go to a fancy restaurant." A quandary for me. Did I want to betray her and be with the Bastard, or did I want to see him again and also enjoy a fancy dinner? This recurrent question t shadowed me for every major milestone in my life going forward. It was a basic question and choice between loyalty and curiosity. And always, a matter of hope hid timidly between the two. A choice between the antagonist or the protagonist in the novel that was my childhood. I could be my mother's daughter or my father's daughter, but not both. Completion in either case was impossible. The stage was set and the actors in place. My mother, the director and arbiter of the script's integrity and objectives, set the wheels in motion. The stranger would remain a stranger forever. But first there remained another meal and opportunity to gather pieces of the puzzle. Four more hours were added to my collective of information. I was almost eleven years old. Still, perhaps a cygnet eager to follow a distant but handsome swan she understood she belonged to. Still hopeful.

8 Lobster

Wearing a lavender cotton shirtwaist dress with a lightweight crinoline that created the illusion of a waist above the airy folds, I felt pretty and special on that day, privileged to be able to select the restaurant. "I would like to go to the Red Coach today." The wagon wheel chandeliers and deep red coloring of the interior were familiar to us from the outside. The more expensive restaurant sat high on a hill towering above its neighbors in the shopping center where our Horn and Hardart cafeteria served meals to hurried shoppers. The Red Coach was a destination restaurant, like the Japanese restaurant in Suffern. These were upscale restaurants that reminded people of their good fortune. Price and time spent dining are unimportant factors to the privileged. Eating in well-known expensive restaurants may validate your sophistication and status in life. My father subscribed to this doctrine. At ten years and eight months of age, I was impressed with the lighting and colors. I understood that it was too expensive for us.

We met after the graduation ceremony at the restaurant. I never questioned his absence in the auditorium. Why would I? My school life was unknown to him, as hollow and silent as the day we stood looking at the empty building in summer. He was waiting in the lobby, surrounded by large plants and soft light. This time he wore a cream-colored linen sport jacket. It had tiny flecks of blue that matched his shirt perfectly. I noticed he had blue eyes. My brother's blue-gray eyes were definitely similar. He was handsome. He was comfortable and in charge in fancy places. I understood that my father was used to finer things. Did he know I was anxious? Stephen and I looked at each other and waited. "Hello, I'm so happy to see all of you. How was graduation?" He asked all in a single breath, without waiting for an answer. He casually kissed my mother on her check and headed to the reception desk. "Good afternoon. The Payne family is all here. We have a reservation." He said "the Payne family" as if we really were a family, and a distinguished family as well. A tall man in a more formal black jacket looked at my brother. "We would be happy to offer the young gentleman a jacket for the dining room," he said in a condescending tone. Stephen stood in place and scanned the interior of the room. All the men wore jackets. He was not quite thirteen and did not own a sport jacket or suit. In just a few months my mother would be confronted with that expense when he had his Bar Mitzvah. For now, she was struggling with paying for a small reception and his resistance to learning the long Hebrew Torah portion he had to perfect and recite. Her agenda today included not just my graduation but asking Charles to help pay for the party. "Of course, sir. I am sure you have a suitable size for the young man," my father offered with a knowing smile. Steve was outfitted in a dark blue jacket with sleeves he quickly rolled up. His silence and sour expression were noted mostly by me and lasted throughout the meal.

We were seated in heavy dark oak captain's chairs with spindled arm rests. They felt like a strong embrace. Steve gripped the curved end caps with white knuckles. There were Hobnail glasses and pewter colored silverware resting on red cloth napkins. I feared vichyssoise would appear on the menu. I waited for my father to whip and snap the napkin into obedience before placing it on his lap. I watched my brother flinch a bit at the ritual. We placed our napkins to follow his lead in a subdued version of the task. Now seated and covered in red loincloths, we were presented with oversized menus that looked like small leather-bound textbooks.

"Barbara, have you ever had lobster?" he asked.

Was he serious? I had of course not had lobster or filet mignon or caviar or truffles. My preferences ran toward crunchy peanut butter and grilled cheese. Was he trying to impress me or expose me to finer things? "No, I don't think so," I answered timidly.

"Okay then, perfect, we will order you a lobster for lunch."

I have no memory of the other food that day. Overwhelmed by the site of a huge dead red insect sitting on a plate in front of me, I was overcome with fear and disgust. The animal had large claws, two long and two short hairy antennas threatening to move and dead eyes daring me to move first. Smaller legs lined the hard plates of its body. The tail fanned out in some grotesque impersonation of a pleated skirt. *Why would anyone want to ingest such a repulsive thing?* I thought. How would I begin? I took note of a nutcracker as the waiter tied a bib around my neck.

"So, my dear, we begin with the claws, my favorite." My father smiled benevolently at me. He picked up the nutcracker and put it in my hand. He clasped his hands over my fingers to guide them. The pressure of his hands enclosing mine was as unfamiliar and as disconcerting as the task at hand. I hoped the animal was good and dead. He squeezed the tool, and I heard and felt the ruptured surface simultaneously. I remembered stepping on a water bug in our bathroom then. The nausea associated with the crushed exoskeleton of a repulsive life form was identical.

"Great start. So now, let's have you finish cracking open the shell. You are in for a treat. Just take that pretty little fork on your plate and pull out the sweet white meat."

Stephen and my mother watched closely. I think my brother may have smirked. I picked up the nutcracker and grasped the edges of the crescent shaped claw, now revealing a trickle of clear fluid running from the thin crack. It slid a bit in my grasp, but I took a deep breath and squeezed hard. The pressure caused the wet claw to pivot in the jaws of the instrument. Now, the continued pressure propelled it toward freedom. Airborne, the claw followed a short trajectory to the left and landed on Stephen's lap. He swatted it to the floor in one swift jerk of his bulky cuffed sleeve. A moment of stunned silence was followed by my father's offer to eviscerate the insect for me. The claw remained under the table for the entire meal. I slumped forward and slid the ballet flat on my right foot forward to push it as far away as possible. I took small bites of the shreds and chunks of lobster flesh, which I diluted with pieces of a sweet roll and a sip of water before swallowing. Grateful for the distraction of adult conversation, I moved pieces of it under the cover of a large baked potato skin. *Here, Mr. Lobster*, I thought, *a new shell for you.*

"So Chickie, it's been a bit of a rough course," he began. He relaxed back into the arms and cushion of his own captain's seat. It seemed he was about to tell us all a long and interesting story. "You know, of course, I'm in New York because the best doctors are here." My mother's eyes came alive and she was suddenly attentive. I imagine she thought he might be very sick. Of course he looked healthy and ate most of his meal and part of my lobster. "So, I don't know if I ever told you about Alice's oldest daughter." We all knew that Alice was the "other" woman. The singing cocktail waitress he had met in a bar in Poughkeepsie while on a job. Steve and I knew some tawdry facts about her. She was older than him by a decade. She had three daughters and an ex-husband. She was given safe harbor in Nora's apartment in the Bronx where she was able to have clandestine visits with Charles until he could manage to leave his marriage and family. These were just things we grew up knowing. Facts like our grandparent's lineage from Russia or our cousin's middle name and our father's infidelity, just family facts. "Well, anyway, her oldest daughter, Betsy, is needing more rehabilitation and help learning how to walk again. She's had an awful time." He furrowed his eyebrows and looked down sadly.

"Was she in an accident, or is she sick?"—a logical question from my mother.

"Well, it's really complicated actually. It was a suicide attempt almost a year ago. Poor thing, so confused. She jumped out of a fifth-floor window in her apartment house. Fortunately, the fall was broken by a huge hibiscus bush, or she would have died. Even so, she was in a coma for a week and sustained a fracture of her spine. She has gotten back partial use of her legs but spends most of her time in a wheelchair. That's very difficult for a girl in her twenties. I haven't been able to work as much as I should. I guess you noticed that the money is just not coming in. I take her to doctors and therapy most days. It's been challenging." Again, he lolled his head in a hang dog way.

My mother was quiet a minute or two and then asked, "Why isn't Alice taking her to the doctor's visits? I really don't understand why you have to neglect your job to do it all the time."

Silence, a long and pregnant silence, ensued. "Alice and I are no longer on speaking terms." He fiddled with his red napkin, wiped his already clean mouth, and continued. "It's more complicated and hard to explain. Especially hard to explain to you." Stephen and I pretended to be disinterested. We toyed with melted ice cream and looked away. We knew the word suicide, probably from TV. I was more interested in knowing about the daughters who had plagued my dreams. Was Betsy the one I envisioned with long blond braids? Was she the prettiest one, or were they all pretty? I had mostly outgrown the recurrent dreams of pretty girls but definitely remembered having them.

He continued. "Well, Betsy was a troubled girl. She was always a little wild and hard to control. Anyway, she was better with me and we had a special closeness. It was just a special closeness to me and nothing more. We did spend a lot of time alone together because she was out of school and then only part-time in college. She was home a lot, and so was I. Do you remember how much time I spent at home drawing up plans? That's just the nature of my work." The air had become charged. I didn't realize why. I knew my mother sat up straighter and something was different, something unpleasant. It was the same as the still and dark summer sky that heralds a bad storm. He continued. "Betsy thought I was in love with her. She misread my affection, of course. When Alice became aware of her feelings she confronted me. She accused us of having an affair. Of course I loved her, of course but..."

"Oh my God, Charles, you are not to be believed! Do you expect me to believe you were alone all the time with a beautiful twenty-two-year-old girl who seduced you, and you resisted? Wow, what a story! So you cheated on Alice in your own home, and now you have a paralyzed stepdaughter that is your responsibility. I'd say good doctors in New York are the least of your problems."

He waited a respectable few seconds and continued. "My plan is to get her the best care I can afford and hopefully some psychiatry. She's young and can have a full recovery. She has moved back home with her mother but hopes to get her own place someday."

I pictured her long blond braids draped over the back of a wheelchair. I felt sorry for her living in a wheelchair.

I didn't think my father lived in the same house with her now. His beautifully addressed letters written on onion skin paper had a new return address on the envelope. That special celebration of elementary school graduation lasted less than three hours but occupied enormous and lasting space in my young mind. My mother articulated the questions that were still taking form in my own innocent and still hopeful mind.

The trip home was fueled as much by her anger as by gasoline, the car always a perfect place for limited timed venting of her anger. We sat in the back seat and waited. "So now we know why he was in New York. Only the best for Betsy," she spit out. "Aren't we lucky he could be here to celebrate his own daughter's happy day?" she glanced back to make eye contact with me. I looked down. A daughter with diminished expectations, I never expected him to be at the graduation. I was confused and afraid but not disappointed. Content with a celebratory lunch, I was newly confronted with a different reality and unanswered questions. Was he there to tell us he had no more money because of Betsy? If he was now as poor as us, how could he afford fancy restaurants and the best doctors? Was he in New York for me or for Betsy? The last question was the most troubling. I suppose we were lucky that we weren't met at the Red Coach with the shocking sight of a beautiful and paralyzed stranger in a wheelchair. I imagine she might have been better schooled in the art of cracking lobster claws. The conflicting facts marked the first sludgy trickle of the poured concrete foundation of unanswered questions and lost hope. Lingering hope was now replaced by thickening doubt. The irony of that shaky and unstable foundation being the design of a talented civil engineer has not escaped me. Almost eleven, I was less impressed with his sexual misconduct and vision of an airborne girl landing in a hibiscus bush than I was with the lobster claw that sat under the dinner table. After all, I still didn't know if she really was beautiful and which one of us brought him to the table that day. I was left with a lifetime aversion to whole dead creatures served up as food. Trout almandine, halved chicken, shrimp with fanned tails, and whole lobster still repulse me. Perhaps my repulsion is associated with repressed thoughts of crushed spines and twisted vertebrae.

* * *

The question of money for a Bar Mitzvah party was more easily answered. Mom understood that the option was figuratively and literally "off the table" that day. The shock of the scandalous story muted even her ability to find snarky words. Maybe it was just as well. There is something inherently wrong with discussing kosher food in the presence of a big red *traif* (forbidden kosher food) lobster. She would have to find other resources for a new suit and modest party. There was only one potential resource available.

Aunt Dorothy and Uncle Walter lived with their only child, my cousin Mark, in a familiar yet alternative universe. Mark and I were six weeks and several worlds apart. He was indulged, good in school, arrogant, and uncommunicative. They lived in a two-bedroom garden apartment in Alley Pond Park, Queens. Even the name Alley Pond Park denoted affluence to me. A neighborhood with a title seemed special. We lived in a uniquely ugly house that existed in an unnamed neighborhood. I saw the two-story solid brick cubes with white shutters and rows of low attached garages behind them as nothing less than an enclave of privilege. Their second-floor unit boasted lush, sculpted, cream-colored wool wall-to-wall carpeting. They had a sectional sofa and Duncan Phyfe end tables with green leather surfaced tops. Uncle Walter had a burled walnut Baker desk where a carved wooden antelope and Steuben glass bowl rested. A small black shaded desk lamp provided subtle light and attention to this area dedicated to business and accomplishment. Uncle Walter was an advertising agent for Ogilvy and Mather. Those two names were always spoken with reverence. If we were Christians we may have genuflected as we spoke them. Uncle Walter was kind, intelligent, and irreverently funny. Taller than his sister, he had rich and expressive hazel eyes, graying hair, a cleft chin like my mother's, and an overbearing and ambitious wife. Aunt Dorothy was short and well-dressed but dumpy. She had wealthy friends who played mah-jongg and gave her hand-me-down clothes for her less fortunate niece and nephew and their single mom who visited every week from the Bronx. Aunt Dorothy was routinely and bitterly defeated at Scrabble by her unfortunate sister-in-law. Occasionally, the hand-me-downs were too good for her to part with. On one visit to our house she wore a tan colored chesterfield coat. Mom said it was made of camel hair. I couldn't understand how the hair from a camel could be fashioned into a coat. "Oh Dorothy, I love that coat. It is so classic. It's so different from your usual choices." My mother's left-handed compliment was poorly received. True, Dorothy liked trendy clothes in bright colors and bold patterns, but who wouldn't love a classic? Even if the classic was several inches too long on her five-foot-three-inch frame. Did my mother sense this coat did not reach its intended recipient?

"Well, actually," Dorothy said in a matter-of-fact tone, "Bea Schiffman sent this coat for you. She's a size larger. But when I saw it, I just had to try it on, and—voilà!—it fits." There was always an undercurrent of friction between them. Walter did his best to offset their sparring with silly jokes and unrelated distractions. He liked to write cryptic "throwaway" letters to famous people or his bosses at Ogilvy. They were hilarious and laced with off-colored words and sexual innuendo. There was usually a reference to Kelsey's Nuts, a well-known brand of peanuts. We came to understand this meant Mather's balls. I imagine now that some of the catharsis in those letters was displaced anger toward Dorothy. There was a great ritual of reading them aloud and then crumpling them into a tight ball. He would pitch it overhanded into the leather clad waste can under his fancy desk. I loved it. Visits ended with a stack of free *Life* magazines from his job and some change for the tolls at the Whitestone Bridge.

Aunt Dorothy impressed me with her ability to dominate her husband and son. She was unquestionably in charge. She was self-assured and opinionated. My mother once told her she thought she was too opinionated. "Well Charlotte, that's because I'm a grown-up and having opinions is what grown-ups do," ending further discussion. She was a retired nurse who thrived on telling gory tales of her glorified days as the head nurse on a surgical unit at Monmouth Memorial Hospital in New Jersey before getting married. I loved the dramatic stories of amputations and gangrenous loops of large intestine. She was fearless. She was smart, and she made nursing as exciting as the stories I read in my favorite Sue Barton books. Early on, I knew nursing would be my chosen career. Was it better to be loved or respected? Without consciously considering that question, I understood that being respected offered important rewards. One of those rewards was a tall handsome husband you might be able to boss around, even if he was just afraid of you. He was funny and kind and wealthy. He may have been the template for choices I'd make in my own future.

9 Kosher

Against this backdrop, my mother was confronted with asking her financially secure brother for help beyond loose change for the Whitestone Bridge. Bypassing Dorothy would be a challenge for both of them. "I think I can get an inexpensive suit, unless Mark has something that might work," Mom suggested. Mark was overweight and spent most summers in a fat camp in Maine. He returned home each August magically transformed for a short-lived time until fall saw him fattened up like a turkey. He had nice clothes in varying sizes. He was a bit shorter than Stephen but false hems were a possibility. As far as a party, plans were whittled down to sponsoring a "Kiddush" (after services bagels and salads). and a dessert party in a conference room at a local hotel. Still, an offering to the synagogue was expected. He had attended Hebrew School on a complete financial scholarship. The least she could do was pay for ritual wine and bagels. The modest hotel party for family and several friends was within striking range if Walter could help out. Had he more carefully dug into his son's closet one Sunday morning to explore possibilities, he might have spirited away a suit. He might have quietly gotten away with helping.

The phone rang the following Sunday evening. "Hi Charlotte, it's Dorothy. So, Walter went rummaging through Mark's clothes for a suit or jacket to lend Stephen. Looks like they are all the wrong size. Maybe the Goodwill store has something. Kids grow like weeds and I bet they have just his size. Let me know how you make out." Of course, my mother understood the likely scenario as clearly as she understood her veiled message and failure to offer help. The suit was not her problem. Charlotte's situation was not her problem. She was disdainful of her poverty. Her disdain may have been tinged with jealousy and legitimate questions. How does an unusually beautiful and intelligent woman end up needing help? Good questions posed in 100% pure camel-haired arrogance. Several weeks later, Uncle Walter handed my mother an envelope with three hundred dollars. There was an unspoken agreement that Dorothy would never know of the exchange.

My father was not invited to his son's Bar Mitzvah. He knew the date and agreed with my mother that he would not be missed by his ex-wife's parents or other family. Surely Stephen was relieved by his absence. I claim amnesia about my feelings at the time. Only five months had passed since our famous meal at the Red Coach. Unlike my mother, who was raised by Jewish parents and celebrated major Jewish holidays and cultural pleasures, my father was raised by a Protestant father and self-hating Jewish mother. He had not had a Bar Mitzvah. His religion was pretty women and the luxurious trappings of wealth. He did seem to understand that a luxurious gift was in order for the special day. He was always good at luxuries.

Stephen may have hated his father, but he loved the Wollensak tape recorder that arrived for his thirteenth birthday. The heavy, gunmetal gray cube was the size of an overnight suitcase. Two large reels sat over color-coded controls with functions for fast-forward, playback, or record. There were volume and sound quality functions. In 1958, this technology was not a common household luxury. Home entertainment was provided by portable radios, black and white televisions enclosed in heavy cabinets, or record players accommodating both 33 and 78 RPM records or smaller 45's with an adapter resembling the cardboard inner tube of a toilet paper roll. Stephen spent hours recording conversations (secretly at times) and later added bird calls, whistled tunes he perfected, and his rendition of a Julius La Rosa song he loved. He so loved the song "Everywhere I Wonder" that even hearing it played back in his own flat and changing, out of tune voice did not compel him to use the erase function of the Wollensak.

I don't know if either of us ever thanked him on the phone or wrote a note acknowledging how much either this gift or my Cissy doll or mother-of-pearl and mauve enameled flower-faced wristwatch meant to us. We received these gifts with well-hidden gratitude for fear of hurting our mother's feelings. We knew instinctively that she regarded these gifts as burnt offerings. His generosity was driven by either guilt or an inability to understand the greater need for rent, new shoes, and a well-stocked refrigerator. She made sure we considered his insensitivity at every opportunity. "That tape recorder must have cost a hundred dollars. It sounds great but could have paid for your Bar Mitzvah suit." This time she was wrong. No suit could have given him as much pleasure. I know for sure it was a fixture on his dresser until he started college. It didn't enjoy the same longevity as Cissy did in my life, but it was beloved.

What did those luxurious gifts represent? What did he hope to convey in giving them? I cannot deny the expense, but I will also not negate the thoughtful effort it took to select perfect gifts for children he didn't really know. Was it just guilt? If so, why not just visit or call more often? What rational person would conclude it was a feeble attempt to impress us with his good taste in gifts? He was well aware of our financial struggle. It was more likely a misguided attempt to show his love. We were, ironically, unable to believe and to associate our love of these gifts with an ability to believe he ever loved us. Can love be metered out in short fits and bursts with long intervals and still be counted as legal tender in the emotional bankbooks we hold so dearly in our heart's inventory? I am allowing this belief to be considered in the larger question of who my father was and if he loved us.

10 Pressed Duck

Just a month later, my father called again. This was the shortest time span that had ever elapsed between calls. We listened attentively that Sunday evening over the sound of Ed Sullivan introducing Mario Lanza on the television. We didn't care about Mario Lanza. We homed in on our mother's lowered voice. She didn't normally lower her voice on the phone. Stephen snuck up to the TV in a low soldier's crouch and lowered the volume. "I don't know," she said. And she said, "I don't know" at least four more times. "I'm not sure I'm comfortable with flying for them. Also, it would be a long time for them to be with you if it's overnight. When do I have to let you know?" A long pause while she listened to him talk about details.

Stephen and I looked at each other and voicelessly mimed open-mouthed shock. Flying? Hotels? Overnight? I assumed it was an offer to fly us to Miami and stay at his house. It made no sense. I replayed the last visit in my head. If Alice was no longer in the picture and Betsy was still paralyzed, where and who does he live with now? Maybe he really is alone and wants us to live with him? Could he force us to go there? Why wasn't Mom going with us? I was not getting on an airplane without my mother. I wasn't sure I'd even want to get on an airplane with her. We heard her say goodbye and assumed a more normal slumped posture on the couch, feigning rapt attention to the next guest on Ed Sullivan. She watched quietly through a comedy sketch with Alan King, not once laughing at his one-liners. Finally, she spoke. "That was your father (we knew that). He has to be in Washington, D.C., in two weeks for some business meeting. He will be there for a few days and thought you might enjoy seeing Washington."

It was my turn to ask questions. I knew instinctively Stephen hated him and would never say yes to being with him at all if he could help it. Being with him overnight was out of the question. But I wasn't sure how I felt about any of it. I thought it was good that moving to Miami was not a possibility, at least for now. "Do you want to go, Mom?" I asked.

"No, he wants to treat you and your brother to a special time. I think he likes the idea of having you to himself," she added.

What did that mean? Having us to himself? It sounded too much like a kidnapping attempt to me. Was he trying to steal us after all this time? Stephen still hadn't spoken.

"Look," she said, now turning the volume down completely on the television. "He really sounds excited about treating you to something special. You would get to fly on an airplane. I think you should go. I would like you to go."

My recurrent childhood dreams had two themes. One, of course, was of pretty little girls with blond hair laughing with my father. In every variant of the dream, I wasn't seen and walked away feeling dejected. The more recurrent dreams were of being kidnapped. I would scream for my mother as some malevolent incarnate creature dragged me off helplessly. The kidnapping always happened in Seton Falls Park, a place we often played. I would wake up screaming but only voiceless grunts that failed to save me would be heard. The dreams' meanings are shamelessly transparent to me now. I had one loving parent I could depend on. I lived in fear of being separated from her or losing her. Her infrequent dates when I was very young were thwarted by my vomiting and crying with a babysitter until she returned home. She gave up on it until I was old enough to be embarrassed and could be temporarily distracted by a game of Old Maid or Sorry. I understood early on, having just one of what should be two, you need to guard it. Guarding and preserving it also meant being obedient and pleasing at all times. This time, I was forced to choose between obedience and insecurity. She wanted us to go. I had to trust her decision. I was mortally afraid of flying. No one I knew had ever been on an airplane. There was another unknown entity, my father. This time it was not just one meal. It was more than three meals and a hotel. I recalled his white Jockey shorts. It was overwhelming.

My mother was fond of the idiom: Every man has his price. Until that day in August, I never would have applied the idiom to my beloved older brother. The buyout price for Stephen was the offering of a flight on an airplane between New York's La Guardia and Dulles airport in Washington, D.C., Stephen's collection of balsa wood and plastic aircraft completed in scale models was impressive. The pleasant smell of airplane glue permeated the kitchen more often than of cooking food. A huge rendition of the Wright Brothers' double, fixed wing miracle was suspended over his bed, hanging by a thin piece of fishing tackle. It seemed he knew everything about airplanes and the science of flight.

"How long is the flight?" his first question.

My mother hid her surprise nicely. Surely, she thought, he would say no to another visit with the father he so openly disliked. "I can call your father back tomorrow and find out the details if you want to go. I'm sure he can let us know. So, does this mean you are both saying yes?"

"Sure," Stephen replied too casually. "Why not?" Every man has a price and for my brother it was an Eastern Airlines flight on a Lockheed L-1049 turboprop between Flushing, New York, and Washington, D.C.

We borrowed a suitcase from someone. I don't remember who, but it was a large, hard, fake leather, orangey-brown Samsonite with two brass hinged locks. I wish I could remember what was packed inside other than one set of dress-up clothes my father said we would need. We bravely said goodbye to Mom, and a stewardess dressed in royal blue led us into the aircraft and our seats. Stephen quickly pushed into the window seat. I focused on the strangeness of sitting in a flying tube with lush seats, heavy nylon seat belts, and the fold down trays that would be our dining tables for lunch. I had no plans to move out of the assumed safety of that buckled-in seat until the plane was back on land. We accelerated, and Stephen's excitement could not be contained. His head was turned and fixed to the right. "We need to gain a speed of 130 knots," he commented. Knots? I ignored his words and assessed other passengers. They looked calm enough, I thought. Now he added sound effects to the words. "Whoosh. Up. Swoosh. Up-up yea...go." His words seemed to accelerate with the plane. I had the feeling he was willing it into the air. Stephen had somehow helped the plane up and through the billowing white clouds and into the safety of some unseen, above-the-world highway meant only for planes. "So, we are probably at seven thousand feet now but the thrust of the engine will get us even higher," he spoke to no one in particular. Math was not my subject but I knew seven thousand was a large number of anything and in this case was more than I wanted to know. There was an announcement that lunch was about to be served. That was more my speed.

We ate sandwiches and drank Coca-Cola from small plastic glasses. The flight had occasional bumps that made me worry but not enough to affect my appetite. Stephen returned to his tour guide mode as we waited for our trays to be removed. "Barbara, look out the window. The clouds are almost gone. You can see tiny little cars and trucks that look like ants crawling on the roads."

I leaned over a bit and looked out the rounded rectangular window. Sure enough, ant-sized cars and trucks were moving along on roads as wide as cooked fettucine. I was impressed. Now that he had my attention, he pointed out green fields and what might have been communities of Monopoly sized houses. Satisfied that he had my attention, he offered to switch seats while he searched out the bathroom. "No, thanks," I replied, still intending to stay buckled in until we landed. He climbed over me and went toward the back of the plane. I waited a little anxiously until he returned. My anxiety was driven in part by the realization that a painfully full bladder was dictating my own need to unbuckle and walk through the plane. He was back.

"Wow, Barbara, you have to see the bathroom. It's amazing. I know you don't like looking out the window, but in the bathroom, you can lift the toilet lid and see right out of the plane. I just looked and thought I saw the Washington Monument in the distance. Go right now before we pass over it."

Mustering up all my nerve, I unclasped the heavy buckle and walked quickly to the little door in the back. I was relieved no one was waiting. Not only did I have to pee, I was excited to see the view from the toilet bowl. Happy to be at a smooth point in flight, I lifted the lid on the stainless bowl. In the blue-green shallow pool of water, a huge brown turd the size of a bratwurst floated and vibrated a bit with the engines roar. I knew exactly what Stephen had planned. Slamming the lid and bypassing the need to relieve myself, I returned to my seat. Now, instead of his head being fixed to the right, he was looking at me. "How was the view? Did you see the monument or maybe just a shit sandwich?"

"Ha ha, very funny," I said. "I'm telling Mom when we get back home." I looked straight ahead. The day had just begun. The plane landed and taxied to the terminal.

We were on terra firma now. It was hometown advantage for me, even in an unknown city. I was uncomfortable in the air, but Stephen was even more uncomfortable with our father. Our last visit was a mélange of lobster, borrowed jackets, and suicidal stepdaughters. But my desire to be here now was not based on the limited opportunity to fly on an airplane but on my need to find the missing father in my life. I looked forward to the day ahead.

We stepped off the plane and into his almost familiar double-armed hug. I was reminded of the crane-claw game in the penny arcade in Long Branch. For ten cents, the player got to position the two-pronged claw above a prize and lower it in hopes of clenching a treasure. My father had landed a double headed win. We stayed in his clutches and waited to be released, aware of his power in this anomalous setting. We walked to a car and waited for him to speak first.

"How was the flight guys? Did you have lunch up there in the clouds?" He looked at both of us. I recalled my brother's shit-sandwich remark. Neither of us answered. He continued. "We are staying at the Carlton on Sixteenth Street (which meant nothing to us). We will be passing the White House on the way. Do you think we should stop by and tell President Eisenhower that you are in town?"

Stephen didn't dignify the remark with a response. My response was more cordial and predictable. "Do you think we can really go in for a tour later?"

"Unfortunately, those tours need months of planning, and we are really short on time here. But after we check in to the hotel, we can take a walk and see the White House and the Washington Monument, maybe the Lincoln Memorial. We have dinner reservations at five and then tickets for a concert at eight in the evening. A tight schedule but things you'll enjoy." Why hadn't he asked what we wanted to do? The only concerts we knew of were the boring piano concertos my mother loved to listen to. Wasn't Rachmaninoff dead? I hoped it might at least be a singer, but not Mario Lanza.

There were so many new sights and sounds. We rode in an elevator to a high floor in the impressive huge building. I knew it was expensive. There were huge brass chandeliers and dark red carpeting covered all the floors. Stephen and I shared a room. Our father's room was adjoining. He could walk around in his white underwear in the privacy of his own space. That other memory flicked quickly in my mind's eye. The beautiful view of the city immediately replaced all thoughts of lumpy bulges in tight white Jockey shorts. I thought instead of Cissy. Is this how her life would be if she were a real young woman? Suitcases, hotels and airplanes, taxi cabs and concerts? I had never thought of these things as I changed her into a mink coat or high heels. My treasured doll belonged to a world I didn't belong in. A world I didn't know existed. His knocking on our door interrupted these thoughts. "C'mon kids, let's go see some sights before it gets too late."

Street vendors lined the park-like streets. The iconic structures of white marble and granite took a back seat to stands and booths offering colorful souvenirs. I quickly forgot about a White House tour as I considered small scaled replicas of the landmarks plated in shiny brass or silver. Colorful postcards and fluttering flags overshadowed the pale gray-and-white background I no longer cared about. "Can I have a souvenir?" I asked hopefully.

"Of course, you both can. Look around, there are all kinds of things you might like. Take your time." Stephen studied all the miniature buildings and picked up a white plastic replica of the Washington Monument. He studied its simple shape, and I wondered why he picked that one. My father watched. "Do you know what they call this kind of structure?" he asked his son.

Stephen responded without looking at him. "Of course I know. It's an obelisk. The ancient Egyptians were the first to build them. They thought the shape looked like a petrified ray of sun, and they worshipped a sun god named Ra."

My father said nothing else. Did the civil engineer feel curiosity or annoyance at his son's knowledge? Was he impressed or challenged? Stephen was a fact collector. Our compete set of World Book Encyclopedia was his favorite reading. The white, faux leather-bound omnibus was opened and referred to every day. Stephen was momentarily ahead in this tilting match. He added a few more facts. "It's the tallest building in Washington, D.C., at five hundred fifty feet. The building codes make sure it stays that way." The sparring match was interrupted when I asked to go to another vendor. The souvenirs in other kiosks were more appealing to me.

Stuffed teddy bears and eagles wearing American flag tee shirts hung and swayed from the edges of the next stand. This vendor specialized in a menagerie of patriotic plush toys. A few wore no stars and stripes. I found my choice immediately. What better symbol of our nation's capital than a two-foot long alligator made of plush leopard print fabric? He must have been a leftover from some carnival, and it was love at first sight. White felt saw-teeth lined its opened mouth. The red opened maw was smiling and not threatening. It was huge and cuddly and one of a kind. "That one," I said assertively, "I want him."

He happily paid for the atrocious pet. Pleased with my apparent joy, he asked, "What are you naming this alligator?" My father smiled benevolently, perhaps lovingly.

"His name is Charlie," I answered without hesitation. My father grinned as broadly as his namesake.

Charlie the alligator occupied the fourth seat at our dinner table that evening. "The little lady will have a Shirley Temple to begin with," he told the waitress. My brother had already ordered a Coca-Cola. I was delighted with the mock pink cocktail complete with a maraschino cherry impaled on a cellophane ruffled toothpick. He encouraged us to order something new and suggested the *Canard à la presse*—pressed duck. Instead, we ordered chicken cutlets with wild rice. When his meal arrived, I was alarmed to see the flattened carcass of a legless duck floating in a syrupy amber sauce. My developing aversion to foods with whole spines, intact carcasses, and exotic names were the legacy of my father's need to impress and immerse me in a world I could visit but not live in. Now, it is difficult to accept the cruelty of boiled-alive Lobsters or asphyxiated duck served in a sauce of its own blood and liver. I am outraged at the sight of banded and doomed crustaceans trapped in small bubbling tanks of water, waiting to be boiled alive. The indignity of flattened birds stewing in their own blood saddens me. I am unimpressed by their cost and angry at their suffering. Anger that makes me consider the disproportionate level of this outrage.

Charlie and company sat in the first row of seats encircling the grand piano. The room was dark and the musician famous. My father was animated and kept squeezing my hand as we waited anxiously for Erroll Garner to sit at the piano and perform. I had never heard of him. We were the only children in the audience. As Garner played his most famous tunes, I fidgeted with my reptile's teeth and tail. To the tunes of "Misty" and "Autumn Leaves," my head bobbed, Steve sat splay-legged and resisting sleep. The music continued. Before the concert ended, Erroll Garner was facing a leopard print alligator and two sleeping children, a most unusual audience. Eight hours had elapsed since we had stepped off the plane.

11 Intermezzo

What had I learned in the collective eighteen hours spent as his daughter? The fourth of those encounters yielded more clues in the never-ending mystery of my father. We had shared grilled cheese and a tour of my empty school building. I'd tasted vichyssoise and strolled a Japanese garden. We shared a lobster and the details of a broken stepdaughter. And last, we considered great jazz and flattened duck in a city too far from home. There is the then and the now of my understanding. And there are always the what ifs and whys.

Should I pursue my cause with objectivity and only primary evidence? Does it make more sense to view this through both subjective and objective lenses, each polished by the distance of passed time? It is impossible to separate the two. The first four visits took place in the full daylight and innocence of childhood. They were prepubescent years of Cissy dolls and stuffed animals.

Those were still years when magical thinking was appropriate and hope overshadowed reality. The two-year difference in siblings was the difference between hope and resignation. We absorbed our mother's narrative of betrayal and abandonment differently. Stephen was thrust at jet-engine speed into the role of male protector in his father's absence. Her outrage nourished his anger. Her hurt was his shared pain. Charles's failure was the fuel propelling Stephen to be better, always better. He basked in his role, unaware of its concomitant burden. A father suddenly staking some claim to legitimate interest in the nation-state of our small territory was met with a defensive young militant. I leave the obvious Freudian aspects of the relationship to speculation or experts who would chase this one path too aggressively in my opinion. I understood then and do now that my father had lost his son forever. Maybe it was no irony that Charles's return to our lives coincided with my brother's preparation and completion of a Bar Mitzvah. He was coming of age and assuming accountability for his actions. According to Jewish law, the elevation to adult status includes obligations. Stephen had unconsciously assumed obligations having little to do with morning minyan and more to do with evening the score. That is the *now* of my understanding. It is how I want to leave it.

If I remember the *then* of my brother and father, I think I can acknowledge I was not unhappy with my brother's resistance. It finally cleared the path for me to be a favored child. Stephen was the older, smarter, more confident child. He was handsome and would be a great success someday. He had inherited the best of the combined gene pool, in spite of rejecting half of the elements of the colloidal mixture. I was not unhappy to try my father on for size that first summer. There was nothing to lose except hope.

In contrast to the cured cement that was Stephen's mindset, I was bright green moss crowning through winter's frost. Resilient, yielding and eager to fill and encroach upon any dark and unlikely space available. Wanting only to survive and move forward in time. The *now* of me loves this analogy. I was eager to explore the unknown landscape occupied by men called dad. The seven year gap in his presence was not a factor as I considered the physical likeness we shared as his car door opened to reveal him that first outing. I was timid and unaccustomed to being the daughter of a man, any man. But here was a man who looked like me and had claimed an interest in knowing me. I do not need to reconcile the then and now of our intentions. I'm sure they were evenly matched. And now, I understand, a huge crevasse of time apart is not simply bridged in a single leap. Not even by tenacious moss that clings to but is never a part of the rock.

Those collected visits are best remembered for the strangeness of foods I didn't like and parents in tandem even more repugnant than the food. If I try to remember the dynamic of those visits, what is etched too deeply are the visions of my mother's graceful full skirt dancing between and around her long legs and my father's muscled thighs. They are memories laced with sexuality and tension my ten-year-old mind registered and rejected. My adult mind understands that my father may have hoped for more than reclaimed parenthood or passing curiosity about his offspring. This was a time of turmoil for him. He had destroyed the second of his marriages and had violated some cardinal rules. Second chances would not be found in second marriages that included betrayal and semi-incestuous affairs. Perhaps he thought second chances and redemption lived in his biological link to the Bronx. My mother was having no part of it. If there would be another visit after his revelations over lobster, he would need to prove his intentions on a grander scale. But first daughters were capable of second and third and infinite chances extended to the one father now a reality. I hoped my mother's anger would subside. I hoped the broken daughter and her sisters were firmly and irrevocably planted in the past. It took more time and more chances for me to understand the finite nature of patience and infinite restlessness of my father.

Was Washington, D.C., the grandstanding he hoped would turn the tide? It was only weeks after the catastrophic lobster luncheon. He had not given up on us. He was traveling for work. Was he inferring there was a new and better job? Could she trust him? He was offering to care for his own children for more than just a meal. Did this mean he felt confident he could resume the responsibility of being a parent? He was dangling airplanes and hotels and concerts as barter. For whose benefit, I wonder now. Had he asked her to join us on that trip and merely settled for his children as a good faith offering? My guess is she had resolutely rejected him but welcomed the rewards of his newfound financial security. The price of consistent child support and alimony payments meant humoring him with hope. That hope might initially have included her but was eventually reduced to fatherhood only. I came home from the trip hugging a stuffed alligator and belief that I had a forever father. The next time I would hear his voice or see him was four years later. By then, I had passed through the innocence of childhood and had embraced a metamorphosis exclusive of fathers. Three years without sun or water can kill even the hardiest variety of moss.

12 Metamorphosis

By the time I was fifteen, we had both changed, and traded old wounds for new and more promising adventures. My father was absent for the challenges of first bras, first periods, a serious crush, middle school drama, and my mother's return to dating and the workforce. I was absent from his third attempt at marriage. I was unaware then of the birth of another daughter and later, another son. That shocking information wasn't gleaned until I was thirty-two, in 1980. I learned of his death and their lives when it was too late to matter. It was impossible then to care about or project what might matter as time slid away. Immersed in the beginning of marriage and motherhood, an imagined leap forward twenty or more years was as remote as crow's feet or being a grandparent myself. It helps me now to understand that my mother's return to work and independence coupled with the finality of his other children and abandoned responsibility to us marked the end of childhood hope. We took divergent paths without caring. It is the woman-me of now who asks if I was loved by my father. Had the obstacles to being my father been too much for him to overcome? The younger me could never articulate what it was I had hoped for. Why should it matter now? It seems I need to resolve the past before moving forward, even at my age. There might even be a need for doling out redemption to the man who denied me hope.

At seventy, there is an urgency to set the record straight. It seems to me now, those first dinners so long ago were visits to a foreign land. I'd been to a place of sharply snapped cloth napkins and exotic foods, an airplane ride and the strange sight of a grown man's body, and the stranger feeling of his larger hand grasping mine. I wondered at and welcomed it all hopefully—then let it go as we mutually abandoned the hope in time. It was as natural and predictable as teenagers letting go after a summer romance. He was just my ill-fated father. I know that now.

But, those four years of yesterdays were a time I was wrapped in layers of adolescent survival and self-involvement. The relevance of parents of either gender was eclipsed by more immediate problems. He became an inert element having neither positive nor negative impact in my life. Lost opportunities are not a consideration associated with youth.

13 Learning Loneness

The battle lines had been drawn and divergent paths taken several months after the weekend in D.C. There was never a formal war or a war room on either side where strategy or plans were formulated. In fact, there were greater forces in play than either of my feuding forty-something-year-old parents had considered. By then, he was on to other romantic liaisons. But seismic shifts taking place in the Northeast Bronx had a more profound impact on the landscape of my life. It literally was a changing landscape. The first of two events that shaped my future.

A forty-eight acre parcel of land bordering our neighborhood park was purchased by the New York City Housing Authority to construct the largest low-income housing project in the city. The Edenwald projects were an ambitious collection of forty high-rise brick buildings about to be home to almost six thousand low-income families. Those six thousand were mostly below poverty level and almost entirely minority. The first families arrived in 1953. By 1958, it was clear that a middle school would need to be constructed. The students filling the new school were the residents of the "Project" and from two existing elementary schools now configured to end at fifth grade and feed into JHS 142, the John Philip Sousa Middle School. Mine was the first fifth grade class graduating from PS 68. Before that year, children in our school graduated at eighth grade. Our little neighborhood Seton Falls Park was overshadowed by the development. Our neighbors, the Italian-American working middle- class families were horrified. Shortchanged an additional three years of grade school and forced to be a white minority in their own backyard did not sit well. My two best friends, my only friends, were quickly enrolled in Our Lady of the Blessed Nativity for the 1958-59 school year.

"But Mom, I don't see why I can't go to Nativity with my friends," I pouted and pleaded throughout the summer. "I don't have to take religion with them or go to church. I can skip that part."

"Because," she snapped back, "you are Jewish, not Catholic, for one reason. Do you really want to be the only Jew in the whole school? You know they think all Jews killed Jesus. No way you want to be there."

"So, I will be the only white kid in the all-Black school," I answered. "What is the difference? I'll still be the only one of something. At least I have friends in Nativity."

"Mimi calls them *mulinyans* (Italian dialect for melanzana). That's Italian for eggplants. She says they are going to beat me up every day. Maybe it's better to be with the Catholics than the eggplants. They don't allow fighting or hitting at Nativity."

She sighed deeply and offered another reality. "You have to pay tuition at Nativity. Where is that money coming from? You will be fine at Sousa and will make new friends. It's a big and new school. Everyone will be excited to be in a new place."

In my mind, I partially believed my mother loved the idea of anything named after John Philip Sousa. Military marches, Christian Hymns, Mario Lanza, and Rachmaninoff were respected musical formats. All had equal respect in her world. Perhaps she thought racial tolerance and integration were as simple as liking *The Star-Spangled Banner*.

It is entirely possible that as I ate lobster claws just eight weeks before with my father, the maple floorboards of the new gym in the new school were being racked out, resting in place and acclimating to their environment before being nailed down, sealed, and polished. Installing a gymnasium floor takes about eight weeks. It is an involved process. Maple is the wood of choice, chosen because it is resilient and shock resistant. It is most resilient to environmental change. Our neighbors possessed none of these qualities. Was I like a maple tree? Was there even the luxury of considering such a question? The local church proved to be maple-like in its response to change. Our Lady of the Blessed Nativity quickly expanded and added classrooms to its building to accommodate Catholics fleeing urban poverty and minority status in the new school. Would I be as resilient and resistant to shock?

I was an easy target at Sousa. I was never a good student, but seemed to have excellent survival instincts. I quickly discovered the art of being invisible at school. Never be the first or last to leave a classroom. Even if lunch was the next period, it was smart to blend into the crowd as they exited in small groups and engaged in animated conversation. Get to the bottom of any stairwell quickly. Random back of the head slaps and not too gentle pokes to your back were common practice if the staircase was crowded. I'm not sure if it was adolescent boredom or a touch of bigotry. The head slap was occasionally accompanied by a snide remark. "Hey Princess, move faster," some snickering, nothing hurting anything more than my self-esteem. Mimi was wrong. I was never beaten up or threatened. My biggest fear in middle school was the music teacher. I hated Mrs. Messiah. Reading musical notes was as impossible for me as learning to multiply or divide. Crazy lines and letters and meaningless symbols I just wanted to turn into more interesting designs. Treble clefs and bass clefs and notes that looked like dismembered body parts of ants climbing up and down steps. Mrs. Messiah and my mother shared a love of Hymns and marching music. "Come Thou Almighty King," "Rock of Ages," and The Marine Corps theme shared equal billing. How was this better than a daily "Our Father"? The music room was a small amphitheater. I sat in the top tier last seat believing it to be the most inconspicuous space in the room. Was it the obvious hiding place or my skin color that prompted the mean, Black woman to call on me every day to name or sing a note on the scale? She was skinny, dark skinned, and wore thick glasses. Mrs. Messiah always held a long wooden drumstick that she tapped in time to notes or slammed down on the desk in annoyance with wrong answers. The psychological scars remained from fourth grade. I feared Mrs. Messiah. In a small nod to mercy, she immediately went to the next student when I shrugged and remained voiceless. I could now claim a mean teacher in either color. Music was twice weekly and right before lunch. It was the one exception to my waiting for a class to empty before leaving.

The cafeteria was another challenge. Unstructured time was unsafe time. Standing in line for food, I learned to engage in no conversation and to behave as if I was deaf. The girls were louder and tougher than the boys. They reminded me of dogs that bared their teeth and growled but never bit. I'd wait for mac and cheese so thick the steel serving spoon stood straight up between servings or hamburgers that looked like small hockey pucks. I'd listen while waiting my turn to select the lesser of two evils most days. Their conversation and slang were foreign to me. "Girl, I'm gonna kick Kendra's ass after school. Thinks she's all that. Hmphh, see her later. Fucked up!" The girl turned her head from side to side for emphasis and affirmation. I felt compelled to nod in agreement. I had to choose between a hearing impairment or being agreeable. Agreeable seemed a safe bet. Just a slight up and down nod and I was rendered invisible but safe. I wondered if she was really mad or just acting tough. Many of these kids had expressions and behavior I'd never known. I observed them from the safety I found within an arrogant bubble. Loneliness was softened by imagined responsive words. I discovered the pleasure of bubble thoughts that spun off the fragile surface of my invisibility. A version of my uncle's throw-away letters. Amusing ramblings meant never to be read or heard. An excellent survival technique I have carried with me forever. Two of my most valuable life lessons were learned in John Philip Sousa Middle School: being the only one of anything in a crowd is never easy. It is a vulnerable, lonely place. Lesson two: our private thoughts are our first religion. We know them to be true. They offer what we need most to survive. Salvation can be as simple as comic relief or as complex as an irreverent verse, a mantra to love. I still missed my friends. I was not missing my father. I never even thought about him. I had begun to develop a talent for loneness.

In perfect contrast, my brother was traveling by two busses to the High School of Science. His journey to the West Bronx was the reward for his brilliance. Laden with textbooks, he had to navigate through a notoriously tough neighborhood. Villa Avenue was home to low-level Mafia members and lower middle-class laborers living in small, clapboard, wood framed homes. The narrow, single street existed as an anomaly between commercial car repair and body parts shops and the Grand Concourse, the Bronx's version of Paris's Champs Elysees. Lined with art deco buildings, its glory days were fading, but most bus routes stopped on it. Survival for Stephen meant sprinting as quickly as possible past Villa Avenue to escape teen gangs for the safety of a bus. The short street was never more than a poor person's dream of home ownership. The small houses stood shoulder to shoulder in decrepit solidarity. Poor Italians living there were as closely linked as the houses. Statues of the Virgin Mary lived behind chain link and bad boys hung out on front stoops waiting for an opportunity to protect their turf.

"Hey Genius. Hey Jew-boy, why you running? What are you afraid of?" they called to Stephen as he ran not quickly enough past them. He had also learned the lesson of silence and continued to run without responding. "C'mon, show us your books. We can help you carry them." They laughed and kept pace with him. Still, he did not answer. They were feeling more empowered by the minute as they finally caught up. Still, he did not speak. They overtook him and slammed him forward to the pavement. His books flew out beyond his reach. His nose hit the ground and he felt the blood flowing out to the street.

"Leave me alone. I just need to catch a bus," he explained.

"Ha ha ha, catch my ass! This is our street and you need permission to be here." A punch to his back, a kick to his side. More laughter. "Get the fuck outta here, genius." Stephen turned over hoping to stand. A final kick to his crotch. "Okay, you can go now. Think you missed the bus." They laughed as he stumbled to his feet, found his books and tried to walk in silence to the Grand Concourse. He had missed the bus. He collapsed on the street.

There were hysterics and rage when my mother received the call from the emergency room at Misericordia Hospital. The police were called, He was taken to the emergency room and released with ice packs and instructions to rest. He never cried as he recounted the story and tried to remember what the assailants looked like or which house it happened near. He wasn't sure if he wanted to return to school unless he could be driven to school or find a different route home. My mother had recently begun working in the telephone company. She could not drive him to school and be at work on time.

We were moving. Westward ho! A job, a steady income, two miserable children, and sheer determination propelled her. Charles had stopped sending money. She hated the cold apartment where she had once had dreams of a different life. She was as miserable being different as were her children. Divorced, Jewish, suspiciously beautiful and lonely, it was time to move. I'm not sure my father would have known how to reach us if he suddenly opted to visit. But he never tried. He had disappeared into thin air. It had been close to two years since we last spoke of him. An emerging independence in all of us would have been unrecognizable to him, anyway.

His greatest gift may have been his absence in those years. In and because of his absence, I learned to be independent and thoughtful and resourceful. I learned how to reach inside for solace. Is there some credit due him for that? Is this currency I might add to the emotional bankbook? Is it offset and negated by distrust and insecurities that are born of the same benign neglect? I'm the dreamer. I am an impossible optimist. I've decided to put it in the plus column. Thank-you, Dad!

14 Bagels, Knishes, Hot Dogs

There was a strategy when it became a choice of neighborhoods. It had to be affordable. It had to be walking distance to the Bronx High School of Science, and it would preferably be Jewish. This time, cultural changes and demographics worked to our favor. White flight was rampant along the elegant buildings of the Grand Concourse and was seeping into surrounding neighborhoods of closely packed pre-war apartment houses in the West Bronx. The Jews were usually the first to leave, followed by the Irish and any stray Italians. They moved to surrounding suburbs if they could afford to. Many people opted for the huge concrete towers known as Co-Op City. thousands and thousands of fleeing Caucasians were the first inhabitants of this vertical gray city. The diaspora left affordable vacancies in what was once an unobtainable dream for my mother. The oldest and poorest Jews now shared Mosholu Parkway with newly arrived Puerto Rican and Black neighbors. Jews were still a decided majority in 1960, the year we moved to our one bedroom, third floor apartment in the back of the elevator building. The shared bedroom was at eye level with the Number 4 elevated subway tracks. Trains rumbled back and forth every ten minutes, shuffling passengers to Manhattan or other parts of the Bronx. The pigeons on our fire escape had relatives living under the guano-encrusted canopy of the tracks. They had nests and babies and cooed and we fed them rice. I loved that view! I could see the people sitting on the train. The lights inside the train anxiously flickered as it moved. At night, it was a comforting sight. I loved the noise. There was not a landlord to fight with for heat or a lace panty bearing pervert idling under our kitchen window. It pulsed with life and anonymity. Stephen and I hated sharing a bedroom.

"That's it!" he yelled. "You are a slob. You have dirty underwear and candy wrappers all over the place. It's disgusting."

I sat on my matching unmade twin bed. In contrast, his bed was neatly made with a blue cotton corded bedspread. He had a bookshelf along the wall that ran the length of his bed. His books and a few still boxed and unconstructed models filled it. All were neatly stacked. He picked up one of my thick white bobby socks, held it away from his scrunched-up nose as if it stunk, and flung it across the room. It landed on my shoulder. I snapped it back at him like a slingshot. It landed on his shelf. He leaped across the room, now screaming. "Mom, she's a total filthy pig. Do something."

Her first solution was a piece of blue masking tape placed along the floor that officially demarcated sides. That worked for a week. Eventually she gave up the luxury and privacy of the pullout sofa in the living room to Stephen. I had a new roommate. Mom as roommate was not an enviable state. We managed like that for a year. White flight continued. It freed up a two-bedroom apartment on the sixth floor. We were thrilled to move up in the world from the third to the sixth floor. There was now a view of the street. Car horns replaced the more calming rhythm of elevated trains. I was thrilled. It was heaven. I'd arrived.

It was my version of a biblical rapture. I'd ascended to a place that smelled like kosher hot dogs, pickles, and fresh hot bagels. I could travel vertically to our own space. It was not *lesser than* anyone else's from the vantage point of dark brown painted doors identified only with a letter and number. We were 6E. I loved 6E. We had cockroaches that traveled in their own elevators, the dumbwaiters that no longer worked. We had colorful neighbors and *yentas* (gossips) who rested their heads on their folded arms in kitchen windows. I had never seen the lower half of many of these women. It was fun to imagine their fat bottoms. The hallway smelled of cooking all the time. Brisket stewing in onions and stinky cabbage was somehow appetizing. I missed the smell of basil and garlic simmering for tomato sauce, but now these scented hallways welcomed me to my lobby and hallway and tiny elevator. They were the building's smell and belonged to all of us, including my family. I wasn't a visitor. These were the smells of my home.

I had new friends, lots of them. They were Jewish and Greek and maybe atheists or Christians No one talked about religion. No one went to church or synagogue. Three of my first friends had no fathers either. I don't know why. No one cared. We cared about sitting on a front stoop or meeting after school to sit on a park bench. We all loved Jerome Avenue. It was the bazaar a block away. Under the train tracks there were stores that felt like extended family we visited just to keep up with change and news. There was something for everyone there. Teen Lane Clothing sat next to Yetta's Corset shop, and the David Marcus Movie Theatre had flashlight-bearing ushers who kept us quiet. The fruit markets were works of art, colorful produce stacked in tiered boxes exploding with color. Three kosher delis were all filled for lunch. A Chinese restaurant was there for special occasions. We checked for cockroaches that may have died in the Subgum Chow Mein. It was not unusual. Montefiore Hospital was two blocks in the opposite direction. The doctors and nurses seemed to share our love of Jerome Avenue and elevated its social status as they shopped and ate there so often. Their presence somehow assured me of my logical future in their ranks. Within a year of living with my hospital neighbor, I joined the staff as a candy striper each Wednesday. On weekends, we took the number four to Fordham Road to window shop at Alexander's Department Store. If we traveled further, we passed directly in front of Yankee Stadium, and because we were elevated could see the scoreboard and bleachers as we passed. None of us could afford a game. We were happy to watch the crowd and experience the occasional joy of hearing a roaring crowd pleased with a play. We bypassed Grand Central and rode straight to West Fourth Street for an exotic hour in Greenwich Village which might have been the only place better than Jerome Avenue.

I was finally in a place where I belonged. I may have failed Algebra, but I excelled at friendships. Our apartment was the hub of activity on days too cold to be outside. My pretty mother was always funny and joined us watching television or listening to music. My brother had made new friends also. There were superficial flirtations between our friends and casual hanging out before dinner. My mother befriended the building yenta and a lonely elderly bachelor named Sol who serenaded us with his mandolin. Theresa, the toothless yenta, and Sol often stopped by together. Sol the bachelor was a ghoulish looking creature with thick white tangled hair and red-rimmed lower eyelids that draped and drooped downward. He stooped forward and had an elaborately sequenced twitch that started with a full throttled snort, then a jerking movement of his head and ended with his bandy-legged knees bending in a quick dip and a hand to his crotch where he'd flip his testicles to the opposite side of wherever they'd last landed. I was embarrassed and amused by his special dance. His nimble fingers had mastered both his mandolin and testes without interruption. Our home was a happy collection of human odds and ends. The building of forty-eight families provided endless anecdotes and per-diem awareness that kept us connected. I knew more about the Hungarian Holocaust survivors and their bakery or Mr. Murray, the alcoholic who beat his wife and kids most Friday nights, than I knew about my father. The building was a community of tolerance. We were settled.

Eventually there was a very best friend named Rennie. Her older sister was my brother's friend. Our mothers were both smart and funny and became friends as well. Her family was intact and her father, Leo, was a handsome, athletic, and attentive father. He loved his family, played handball as often as possible, and washed his new Chevy every Saturday morning. They frequently invited us all for weeknight dinner and shared holiday meals. The Shermans became extended family. If I could have chosen a father, it would have been Leo. His birthday was July twenty-fourth and I have thought of him on this date for all of my seventy years. My father may have been born on December nineteenth. I only learned that with the letter bearing the news of his death. I am still not sure. Leo allowed us to laugh at his hypochondriacal symptoms and humored his wife's awful culinary skills. He kept tight reins on his daughters' whereabouts but looked the other way when too much makeup or hidden cigarettes were in question by their mother. He was the perfect balance of strong and sweet. When the family planned a car trip to Miami Beach, they asked my mother if I could join them. They laid out every detail of the AAA itinerary and assured my mother the girls would be carefully watched at all times and would share a room adjoining theirs. As their guest, no expense money was needed to send me. I had just turned fifteen and was ready for adventure and a real vacation with my best friend. I was prepared to see palm trees and pools but not my father. Images of flamingos carrying calligraphed letters to a mailbox no longer mattered. I had not seen him in four years. Was it only a coincidence that the Aztec Motel was steps away from the Castaways on Collins Avenue? I had not thought of or spoken to my father in four years, but communication continued to exist between my parents during that time. The extent and nature of their communication will remain an informational black hole in my data base.

15 Castaway Dad

Who was responsible for creating the vacuum that sealed the fate of our relationship? Was it a conscious or passive decision? I had stepped tentatively into the cold water of a shallow pool as a ten year old. I was willing then to believe the risk was worth a happy outcome. But now I was fifteen and unrecognizable as a near woman emerging from some soundless depth into a vibrant world, which I could navigate happily, without a father. Exploration was not a tentative thing anymore. Full of the confidence and bravado that accompanies adolescence, I had entered a new era of invincibility where tentative things live in the deepest recesses of the mind. I had dismissed him from my thoughts. Had both my parents miscalculated? Did either of them understand the important collective of transformational days they'd dismissed so casually? That critical period of time was their missed opportunity. Do I assign blame to one or the other? The advantage goes to my mother. Always available and sharing the days unselfishly, she is held near blameless. There is too much evidence to suggest otherwise. But, by 1962, my father had a new daughter named Rebecca. There was her mother, Nancy, his third wife. There must have been a three-year period of gestation associated with these events. During that gestational pause his first daughter had lapsed into young adulthood. I think he is responsible for the irrevocably closed door. Still, decades later, I tug at it from time to time in thought just to be sure it really was firmly shut. I need to be certain we were equally guilty of abandoning the relationship.

"You know, Barbara, that your father's hotel is right next door to the Aztec," my mother offered casually a day after accepting the Shermans' offer. That was a confusing statement. Did he live in a hotel? Did he own the hotel? I assumed he still lived in Florida, but the details of his life there ended with images of a young woman flying along the edges of a pink stucco building and landing in a fuchsia colored hibiscus bush. Somehow, I had added technicolor to the memory and those colors never faded. I can picture it now. The fuchsia flowers crushed under her weight. Her arms and legs also splayed in an impossible pose.

"So what?" I snapped back. "I really don't care about him or *his* hotel. Does he own it or something?" Could I still be influenced by an imaginary fairytale ending?

"No, he doesn't own it, but he did design it. It's a pretty famous place, and I've seen pictures of it. It is just beautiful! It's built on a little spit of land they call Fantasy Island." My mother certainly was impressed. She began to describe the sweeping roof and celebrity guests. "The Rat Pack goes there all the time. Can you imagine bumping in to Dean Martin?" she said dreamily. I disliked Dean Martin and his contrived "oily" voice. She was near swooning, I thought. She had obviously been following my father's career in Miami if not his personal life. She might have assumed he was available. She might have considered options for increased child support. My guess is that she was living vicariously and was impressed with his success. I was not impressed or interested in seeing him again. She persisted. "I already let him know you would be in Miami for a week. He really wants to take you out when you get there." She waited for my answer. I had no words. I was older now and felt no obligation to please her with an answer. "I'm going to Rennie's house for dinner. See you later."

We drove to Florida, tightly packed into Leo's two-toned red-and-white Chevy Impala. He had the same New York license plate for every car he ever owned. LS-581 drove along I-95 South at breakneck speed. We made the obligatory stop at South of the Border Hotel in South Carolina. This landmark highway oasis was a high point in the trip. Leo let us buy small souvenirs in the gift shop. We left clutching keychains with dangling miniature sombreros. We continued along, collecting memories that have lasted a lifetime. I was fascinated by fields of growing cotton plants, their brown stalks and clingy fluffy bolls like no plant I'd ever seen. We opened windows to inhale orange and grapefruit groves. We stopped at a gas station that still had separate "colored" and "white" bathrooms. I was an eyewitness to history most will only see in old photographs. We finally stopped to sleep at a cheap motel.

The five of us slept in two queen beds and groaned when Leo woke us up at daybreak to resume the trip.

"Sorry girls, no time to brush your teeth or comb your hair. In the car for the last leg." He whistled and punched the end of the mattress for emphasis. We feigned annoyance and giggled for the next hour of the trip. We had a bad breath contest and no one won. I loved Leo and his make-believe military discipline. We arrived at 163rd Street and Collins Avenue before the sun had set. I had not once thought about my father.

The pool seemed enormous, the sunset remarkable for the size of the orange moon over blue-black water. We lay perfectly still at poolside the next day and applied liberal doses of a baby oil and iodine mixture which turned us an unnatural shade of burnt sienna. We studiously turned from side to side like chickens on a rotisserie spit to insure an even burn. I explored the lobby on my own and flirted with a portrait artist working in pastels. His name was Juan Carlos Diez-DeLaVega and he was at least thirty. Without ever speaking, he began to sketch and then color a very flattering portrait of me. Flattered by his attention and the enhanced likeness, I returned for a short time each day and watched his progress. The clandestine nature of our unspoken tryst was flattering and frightening. By the third day, a suspicious Leo followed me to the lobby. A random check on my departure from suntan duty alerted him to the danger. Without speaking, he assessed the artist and his subject and asked the artist if he knew my age. "Okay buddy, nice picture. She's fifteen. It would be a good idea to throw that out before you get booted out of this lobby for good."

The handsome and charming artist handled it well. "You have a beautiful daughter, sir. Please accept this gift for allowing me to capture her."

Leo looked at the lovely, albeit matured version of my likeness and accepted the gift. He took my hand and marched me out of the lobby. I never returned to that lobby and settled for romantic ruminations of what might have been. I thought about how good it felt to be called Leo's daughter. There was another lobby I intended to explore the next day. The Castaways seemed as frightening as the unknown future with a handsome older artist.

My mother called every day to chat. She told me my father would be calling me to meet him before the end of the week. I had a day or two to prepare myself. It was a short walk to Fantasy Island and the Castaways lobby. I crossed a bowed footbridge and looked at the impressive façade. The grandeur of the faux Polynesian building and tropical foliage were completely foreign. Everything seemed to be make-believe. Even the warm sun and longer days were pleasantly unsettling. This was my father's world. It was beautiful and fancy and fake, just like him, I thought. I entered and sat in a chair that looked like a tufted flower, considering the lines of the ceiling and expansive windows. *He must be rich and famous if he did design this*, I thought. I was impressed and intimidated by that thought. I looked for his name on cornerstones and plaques that buildings sometimes had. All I found at eye level were planters and small tables. Anger now dominated my feelings. Who cared about this place anyway? Not me! Remembering my newfound "father-protector," I left before Leo missed me at the pool again.

"Your mother's on the phone," Rennie announced. "She's talking to my mom about you going out with your dad I think." She rolled her eyes dramatically. Rennie knew I didn't want to see him. We wore matching turquoise terrycloth cover-ups over wet bathing suits that now soaked the end of our bed. Annette handed me the phone.

My mother's familiar but too chirpy voice was in my ear, in the room. "Sounds like you're having a great time. Nice and sunny. So, I spoke with your father yesterday. He is going to pick you up at the hotel for lunch tomorrow. Expect him about one in the afternoon." I was being told, not asked. This was nonnegotiable. Not wanting to argue in the presence of Rennie or her mom, I robotically agreed. I handed the phone back to Annette. Rennie and I left two large, wet, half-moon impressions on the bed and walked out of the room.

"Well that stinks," Rennie blurted out, assuring me of her ally status. "You can tell him you have your period or something. That will gross him out. Tell him you have cramps and need to go back to your room to lie down." The problem with that was the ridiculous thought of telling any man, especially this one, that I had my period. Ugh, not an option. I would just have to go and waste an afternoon of good pool weather on him. It didn't matter where we went, what he had to say about his life here or what he wanted to know about me. I was determined to speak as little as possible. No famous hotel or exotic food or offer of a gift mattered. My days of interest in him or hope for a future that included him had passed. This was an obligatory visit orchestrated by parents with agendas that had out-of-date expiration times.

Wearing the only dress I'd brought, I waited with Annette and Rennie in the entry of our hotel. How strange it must have been for him to reconcile a fully grown teenager in a spaghetti strapped, floral mini dress and strappy gold sandals with the pudgy, flat chested eleven-year-old he had last seen clutching a leopard print alligator. He looked exactly as he had four years before. This time, he wore short sleeves and khaki pants. He smiled broadly as he approached us. Unexpected feelings welled up at the sight of him. There was that surprising familiarity of shared features I remembered so well. No denying he was my father. He wasn't as handsome or strong looking as Leo but I had to admit to liking how he looked. He was a handsome man. So what? Borrowing a favorite phrase from my mother, I thought, *That and fifteen cents will buy you a subway token*. The days of subway tokens and mending fences were long gone.

He greeted Rennie and her mother with self-confidence and insincere familiarity. "So nice to meet some of Barbara's favorite people. And I am so excited to get to steal her away for a few hours to show her Florida." I felt like he was, in fact, stealing me away. "I will have her back before dinner. Don't worry. Enjoy the sunshine." A reminder to me that I'd be either in a car or a restaurant and not in the sunshine at all. He held the passenger side door open for me. That chivalrous gesture was as foreign and insincere as his fixed smile. *Please, give me a break*. I thought of saying, *I can open and close my own car door. I'm almost ready to drive my own damned car. And I know better than to think you're a knight in shining armor. Yep, I know that for sure.*

It was going to be a long afternoon.

Hello darkness my old friend, I've come to talk to you again.... It was almost 1963 and Paul Simon's song, "Sounds of Silence" was a hit. The iconic song of youthful alienation seemed to sing especially to me. I was sure my parents had stopped listening to or hearing me. Clearly, I had not been consulted about this outing. As long as no one listened, I could retreat to my safe place, where no one heard. I'd become skilled in the language of silent "bubble talk" since middle school. Yes, people talked without speaking and heard without listening. I would not disturb the sound of that silence. It was my opportunity for honest internal conversation while I offered audible speech that filled the space called conversation. It was age-appropriate passive-aggressive social intercourse. Defiant, cynical, oppositional and delicious offerings I served my father that afternoon.

He reached across the car console to take my now older, pink nail-polished fingers in his right hand. I was aware of the cool air from a vent blowing on our hands. The gesture was more repugnant now than foreign. In the absence of ploys like an errant lock of hair or a desire to please, I allowed it to remain there in dead fish posture. He glanced sideways at me with a benevolent smile. "So, my dear, where would you like to go?"

My dead fish hand matched my flat voice. "Up to you, I guess. I have no idea." The having no idea response was accompanied by a strategic and exaggerated shoulder shrug, which elevated my arms and lifted my hands to an upturned-palm questioning mime. My left hand was finally free. Where would I like to go? Speech bubbles were now active. I laughed at the image of air bubbles streaming from a big mouthed bass. *I would like to go back to the hotel,* I thought. *I wouldn't mind sitting in the back seat or going to a beach.* Instead, I offered a more acceptable option. "Where do you live? I'd like to see your house." He was quiet, and, I thought, pensive. I began to chip off my pretty Ballerina Pink nail polish while I waited. It was a perfect way to keep my left hand out of range. Really a shame since it was still in perfect condition. Little pink flakes landed on my thighs.

He looked straight ahead now as he answered. "Oh well, actually I live in a garden apartment in North Miami. It's not that close to here and nothing much to see."

I knew he lived in North Miami. That was where his return address was posted in the upper left corner of those air mail letters. I had stopped considering how he lived, and just assumed it was luxurious. I adjusted the image now. A garden apartment was like Alley Pond Park in Queens. Better than the Bronx I guess, but not really luxury. I imagined Alley Pond Park with Palm trees and hibiscus instead of hedges and stunted evergreens. "You pick," I finally said.

"Okay," he said, "let's do this. I think a drive through downtown Miami. We can go to Jordan Marsh if you want. I designed their parking lot. It's a pretty great design, twelve-foot ceilings, double helix spiral on a six percent grade."

Bubbles again. *He really is weird. What is a helix? And grades are in school. It's a parking lot. What is Jordan Marsh?* "Sure, who is Jordan Marsh?" I asked.

He liked my answer. It made him laugh. "Jordan Marsh is a nice department store. Its big like Macy's. We can walk around and see what they have."

Bubbles again. *Does looking mean buying? I'd really rather shop with Rennie, not this guy. What would I like if I could buy something here? Is he rich or poor or in-between? Would my mother be mad if I came home with a gift from him? Does he shop here with his girlfriend or the wheelchair daughter? Nope, I'm not shopping with him.* "I don't really need anything. What else is downtown?"

We exited the coiled snake parking garage and faced more pastel buildings. Everything was pastel or bleached white. Laundry in my house was divided between whites, pastels, and darks. Miami was missing a key component in its living color scheme. It was clean and fake. Where were the shadows and contrast? Did anyone even have a black car?

"I have an idea." Now he looked happy with his idea. "Your grandmother works just a few blocks from here. We can stop in and say hello. We can eat lunch where she works. She really would love to see you."

Bubbles, giant, full, almost bursting bubbles formed. *Holy shit. Was he talking about his mother, Nora? Now this was a curve ball. Big tits? Mom's nemesis? The reason I inherited psoriasis? The wicked witch of the South and North and probably the East and West. Is she really still alive? Is this what he planned all along?* There were no memories of Nora. I don't know if she'd seen me as a baby or toddler. She was, inherently, a woman I held in contempt by default. There were a few bizarre photos in a box stored on top of a closet. She wore a flapper dress and cloche in one and a tank style bathing suit in the other. In both, her breasts were impressively large and disproportionate. There were the stories I grew up on. Hiding whores in her house, smoking cigars in Cuba, and owning a Chow dog that ate poodles and cats. And here and now, I was being offered a chance to meet the legendry bitch. There was no question my mother would kill me if I went along with this. I was sure she never discussed this with him when she gave permission for him to see me in Florida.

"Does my mother know about this?" I asked.

"I don't think so," he answered. "We really didn't talk about much more than having lunch together. But then I realized that Nora works in the best kosher deli in Miami. She is their cashier. Oh, she just loves her job and it would be such an amazing surprise to stop by and meet her. I even called her to tell her we would be having lunch there. She can't wait to see you."

Oh no, no, no. This is not going to happen. I am not getting out of the car. I am not going to meet her. What a shithead he is. He knew about this right from the start. He lied to me. He lied to my mother. A sin of omission, as my mother would say. Just as bad as any other lie. Maybe even worse. Sneaky Bastard! "No, I don't really want to meet her," I said courageously. "I mean, I'm almost fifteen and never, ever met her. I think my mother would be angry with me. She really doesn't seem to like her." *Oh my God, what an understatement. She would love to hear that she was truly dead. Not just dead but dead by hanging or* being eaten alive by rats or choking to death on her own vomit, or at least being hit by a Mack truck.

"But I know you must be hungry by now. Do you like pastrami?" he asked. "They have an amazing pastrami sandwich. I like it with mustard on rye. You could get French fries on the side."

Food again? Wow, Dad, a pastrami sandwich. Really? Guess what, Dad, I can get the best pastrami sandwich in Katz's Deli on Jerome Avenue. I can get their well-done fat French fries, and I prefer my pastrami on a kaiser roll.

"No thanks. I just don't want to meet her. I just can't," I bravely offered. We sat quietly a few moments. This was not how he had envisioned the day. He had not expected a disenfranchised, oppositional teenager. But here she was. No longer a little girl at the mercy of her own good manners or unrealistic expectations. She was a force to reckon with. He was desperate to salvage the plan.

"Well, you know, Barbara. We can't very well just not show up. She's expecting us. I would feel awful. She isn't even well. Last year she became diabetic and her vision isn't too good. Who knows how long she will even be able to keep working? She may never get another chance to see you." He looked straight into my eyes.

Bubbles were now rising to the surface at breakneck speed. There was chance the bubbles would break out of their imaginary membranes and become real words. *Good, a diabetic. Mom would like to know that. Then she can be really blind. That liar! Yes, really blind and yes, hit by the Mack truck, perfect! Guilt won't work, Dad. Good try. Doesn't even work for Mom, anymore. And a free pastrami sandwich is not half as good a bribe as a disgusting lobster. Uh, Uh, you lost!*

"Sorry, Dad, you better tell her we aren't going there for lunch. I hope you understand that I would have to lie to Mom and I would feel bad." That was the most honest thing I'd said all morning.

"Okay then, I will drive over there anyway. You can sit in the car while I go in and tell her we aren't eating with her. Are you sure?"

"Yes, I am really, really sure," I answered. Our speech was mechanical and flat. It was awkward and unpleasant. I knew it would not be necessary to field his right hand on the way back. I understood the deeply embedded fissures in my life. A father and mother living on opposite sides of my life and fault lines that threatened to shift under stress. This was a permanent seismic shift. It was empowering. I lived at the epicenter of this little earthquake. I had caused the earth to shift. I had caused a fissure that could swallow the earth and people if they stood too close.

I waited in the parked car for about ten minutes. The remainder of the Ballet Pink polish had floated like tiny petals to my lap. I refused to look out the window. I imagined she would look out the window to see me. I worried she would come out to the car.

My father returned. An oily brown paper bag was placed on the console. It smelled like garlic. "Pastrami sandwich," he said. Nothing more than that. I wondered if he had included the fries. "Do you want to go anyplace else?" he asked.

I nodded my head from side to side. "I think I'd like to go back to the hotel. I have cramps." *Try that on for size, Dad—cramps!* I quickly air-kissed him on the cheek as I got out of the car. I felt sad for him and guilty for what I'd done. I wondered if I was more troubled by guilt or by my empty, now growling stomach. I had left the sandwich behind. My father had been swallowed up by that fissure. He disappeared.

16 Indigestion

We had moved to the new neighborhood when I was thirteen. The trip to Miami was two years later. By the time I met my father for that ill-fated lunch, I'd grown into a self-assured and at times surly teenager. It had been a rough start; I entered eighth grade at midyear in a new middle school and was placed in a class of twelve low-functioning students. This may have been based on my academic record, classroom census and space, or a biased assumption that John Philip Sousa Junior High School was only capable of producing low functioning students. The girls in this class wore heavy eye makeup and too-tight skirts. The boys had greasy hairdos and muscle shirts. I readily adapted and began experimenting with black eyeliner and white lipstick. The academic bar was set low and the classmates were friendly. I could shine.

"Barbara Ann, please walk twelve feet in front of me or twelve feet behind me when we are out in public. I don't want anyone to think we are together." My mother was appalled by my new "look." That worked for me. I chose walking behind her so she wouldn't be watching me if I met up with a new friend. My first three new girlfriends lived within a block or two of me. Laura, Charlotte, and Paulette were like-minded fashionistas and my first friends. We plucked each other's eyebrows, bought cheap lipstick and eyeliner, and read *Ingenue* and teen magazines from cover to cover. The friendships lasted just months. High school choices separated us forever. Two chose a co-ed high school and the other a trade school. My world and circle of friends changed in ninth grade at an all-girls public high school. Those friends slipped away. But, in that first year, I experimented with makeup, boys, smoking cigarettes, and petty larceny. I was a full-fledged narcissistic, invincible teenager.

On a quiet Saturday, Laura decided we should take the train to Fordham Road and do some shopping. What she actually suggested was some shoplifting in Alexander's, a large and exciting department store. While academically sluggish, she had a quick and cunning mind when it came to crime. "This is what we are going to do. So, all of us will wear our tightest stretch pants. We go to the junior department and bring in a few pairs of pants and some other stuff. All we need to do is slide an extra pair of pants over our own skin-tight pants and no one will know. I'll ask the dressing room lady for something so she doesn't see you guys walk out. Voilà! You will have a new pair of pants."

Laura was elated. I wasn't as comfortable with the plan. "What if we get caught? My mother will kill me. How do I explain an extra pair of pants in the laundry?"

"Don't be stupid. Do you really think your mother would notice? Just get a solid color. If you get crazy flowers she might notice. That's all." She flicked her pin-straight brown hair over her shoulder in mock annoyance, and I was convinced. Laura's own plan was to try for an oversized bulky mohair sweater over her blouse. She had fallen in love with a cable knit mauve colored sweater that she planned to acquire. I didn't question how she would do that.

I was wearing solid black stretch pants and brought a pair of plum and a pair of gray pants on hangers along with a bold floral print. We waited until the dressing room lady was busy returning stock and all slipped into separate dressing rooms. I walked out first, only slightly bulkier in the buttocks. I thought gray was my best bet. Soon, we were reunited and giggling in our new clothes on our way to the door. As we approached the large plate-glass double doors to leave, I heard Laura's voice. "Hey, let go of my arm. Who are you anyway?"

The older man in a plain jacket held firmly on to her upper arm. "Well young lady, just come with me. Seems you forgot to pay for that sweater. Don't pull away. We are just going to the office upstairs." He showed no expression.

I thought I might die. Should we pretend we didn't know her? Should we run? Did they also know that I was currently wearing a double set of pants? We froze and waited.

"Can my friends come with me?" Laura asked, now weeping.

"We might have to call their parents also if they were with you and knew what you did." He looked sternly at me and Paulette.

My mother wasn't home, and Laura's parents picked her up. She was grounded for a month. I considered myself lucky. My mother never found out about the adventure. I hid the gray pants and a pack of Newport cigarettes in the back of my closet for a week. Eventually, the cigarettes were tossed. I wore the gray stretch pants just once. There was a sickening feeling as I pulled them on. They were just uncomfortable. I wasn't proud of my escapade or bravado. I didn't like who I was when I thought of the phone call that almost made it to my mother, or even of the lady in the fitting room whom we tricked. I didn't like being a thief. I went along with Laura's plan because I wanted to please her. I hated how easily I'd been manipulated. I hated how I felt about that choice. I hated those pants. I abandoned the friends and the pants within a year of moving in. By the time I was fourteen, Rennie and the Sherman family had replaced the first friends.

That same sickening feeling happened as I returned to the Aztec Motel to find Rennie and her parents. What I had done to my father was not sitting well. It was my choice of course. I hated Nora. Well, anyway my mother hated her, and she did sound awful. She helped my father cheat on my mother. What kind of woman does that? If she hated my mother so much, well, then she was my natural enemy. Yes, I hated her. Of course I did. But did I hate my father? I had stopped thinking about him at all since I was eleven. My mother continued to grumble from time to time. But now, she had a job and she even dated and had weird friends in our building. Charles Payne had receded into the background. His importance had been neutralized. But they must have kept in touch. How else were they capable of forcing me to have lunch with him? Why, if I was also angry at her did I do her bidding and take her side against a grandmother I didn't know? None of it sat well. I was confused. I didn't like myself. It was another bad choice. I wondered if I had decided to please him how I would have felt about lying to my mother. Either way, it would be other people who mattered most. Not doing what I thought was right for me became a recurrent conflict in all matters concerning my father. A conflict with no resolution. It gnawed and growled from time to time and reminded me that I wasn't feeling just right. The visit to Miami marked the beginning of indiscriminate choices about my father I would come to regret decades later. It was so much easier to appease the mother I loved and lived with. Sometimes, even now, there is a queasy feeling that reminds me of the oil-stained, garlicky brown bag I left in the car when I think of my father.

I try to retrieve some truth from the archives of abbreviated visits in my formative years. Miami marked my declaration of independence from needing to please him, maybe needing him at all. I had taken a stance. He may have appreciated that there was no longer a sweet little girl he could salvage from a long-ago marriage. After all, he was relieved of his responsibility if he was rejected. It was perfectly timed. In the same year that I had stepped in and out of his car and life, a new daughter mysteriously had arrived. Rebecca S. Payne was born in 1962. She was eighteen in 1980, the year he died from his mysterious injuries. I was thirty-three and the mother of two young boys. The strangeness of learning he had died, and that he had fathered two other children passed quickly and casually by in my busy life. I dismissed news of Rebecca and her younger brother, Charles, then an eleven-year-old, as if that news was as unimportant in my life as a minor event in a foreign country. A lawyer's letter had also confirmed his alleged poverty and the absence of assets at the time of his death. This offset any motivation to pursue his other "unfortunate" offspring. I believe now that the modest garden apartment in North Miami, which he did not take me to, was probably where he lived with a new wife and baby daughter. The truth I own and accept is that he probably never designed the Castaways, he never lived in luxury, and he may have entangled himself so badly in a trail of betrayal and failed relationships, which he struggled to keep afloat, in his own poorly designed cesspool. Am I, in retrospect, to forgive him for abandoning his responsibility to us if he actually could not support us? That is difficult to do after a lifetime of resenting the myth of his wealth and experiencing the hubris of lobster dinners and luxury hotels. What am I to think of my Cissy doll, a flower-faced wristwatch, and a leopard print stuffed alligator? Those were treasured tangibles. I long for a truth it may be too late to know and impossible to retrieve. There are living half siblings who might help with that truth. They might know who he was, although we shared him in separate lifetimes. I suspect their father and mine had little in common and so did our lives. Had that ill-fated visit in Miami been an attempt by him to reconcile, a need to do right by two daughters who shared his genes? The advent of ancestry kits came years later and well after I had resolved to forget about him. Had I ever done that, though?

17 Summer Season

White flight was good for us. The oldest Jews in the building reached their expiration dates and left their apartments for nursing homes or their final resting places. We were the beneficiaries of their misfortune or patience. The same winter I'd so irreverently parted with my father in Miami, we moved to a two-bedroom apartment in the building's front. The passing commuters on the elevated tracks and the cooing pigeons were replaced by a view of the street. This was an advantageous position for checking out which friends were hanging out. Alternate side of the street parking and limited spaces also made this a perfect sentinel's perch to monitor available premium spots on Tuesday evenings. Wednesday was parking on either side of the street—no garbage pickup—and meant a chance for a coveted space in front of the building. At fifteen, I finally had my own room. Stephen had a bedroom, too, and Mom continued to sleep on the convertible sofa in the living room. There was a sea change in my life, an awareness of my place and power in the world. I hung cheerful yellow wallpaper in the room. The huge white flowers on a wicker trellis against the bright yellow background made me feel like it was always sunny. A large framed print of Picasso's Petite Fleurs hung over my bed. I hung cheap bookshelves and bought a hideous but comfortable canary-yellow pleather lounge chair from a bargain furniture store. A weekly babysitting job in the building financed this undertaking. I loved my room. I loved my new friends from high school and most of all my friend Rennie and her parents and sister. They were extended family. We were officially just ordinary people. I enjoyed my Wednesday afternoons at Montefiore Hospital as a candy striper. My confidence in the future grew there. I didn't just fill water pitchers and deliver flowers and cards. I sat with patients when I could and chatted. My low professional status on the floor was an opportunity to be invisible. I used that invisibility to read patient charts and listen to the conversations of the nurses and doctors. This was as much a learning lab as it was a mission of mercy. I offered to straighten out the storage room and wondered at the science of drainage tubes, catheterization trays, and intravenous fluids. I never doubted my future as a nurse. After all, I could eventually pass any course, even if it was as a second try in summer school. I had seen firsthand how my mother's tenacity and patience had delivered us to this better place. The spring of 1963 was filled with the same false self-confidence and energy as a fledgling sparrow. There were false starts and misguided choices, but I owned and learned from them. No one could shake my confidence. Not even my mother.

"Are you looking forward to working in Woolworth's?" she asked from time to time when she signed failed tests or report cards better hidden in a small brown envelope with a string binding it firmly closed. "Looks like you will get to choose between selling lipstick (a dig about my white lipstick) or learning how to type."

Her threats did nothing to erode my self-confidence. There was no need to worry, I thought. I would be a nurse. I had two parents who had unwittingly created a determined, hopeful, and self-reliant young woman, one by his absence and the other by her miscalculation and low expectations. Gratitude for my father's absence is not disingenuous. Navigating the rough sea of having only a single parent in adolescence is an unrecognized benefit of divorce. My academic failures were met with resignation rather than the stern reproach a father may have provided. I had once been vulnerable and hopeful for his love. But now, there was no room for compromise or misguided hope. My optimism sprang from a silent, slow trickle of understanding that I was not vulnerable if I was in control. I expected to never see my father again. My mother accepted my pathetic destiny selling lipstick. That left me free to move forward at my own speed. The spring of 1963 was a season bursting with self-confidence and enthusiasm. White lipstick and black eyeliner were abandoned. I was a free agent. Free as a bird.

The consistency of my inferior academic track record even gave me confidence. I knew how to fail then pass. It was a skill set. I failed Algebra One and Algebra Two as well as Geometry and then passed each of them easily in summer school. I passed the New York State Regents Exams that were partnered with them. I failed Spanish One. I could have avoided that failure if I'd not succumbed to an easy fix on a final exam. Perhaps my self-confidence needed reigning in.

God, I hated Mrs. Vogel, my Spanish teacher. She was humorless and, I thought, especially unattractive. She never smiled and she made a pretty language sound like she was speaking about math or strange plants. She was dogmatic and flat and had short curly gray hair. We learned nouns and pronouns and verbs and tenses. She was methodical. I sometimes created a bubble thought in Spanish to pass the time. *"Creo que te paraces a una vieja vaca o un pollo."* (I think you resemble an old cow or chicken) I needed to pass the Regents, however. There was only one way I could do that. It took a great deal of time and effort and a fine point pen to write as many verbs and nouns and adverbs and rules on just the plantar surface of ten fingers and the palms of both hands. It was an impressive graphic design. I finished the test in record time and waited confidently for the class to end. With just ten minutes left after collecting the exams, Mrs. Vogel began reviewing some questions. *"Niñas, permite revisar la prueba. Algien me puede decir la respuesta correcta a una pregunta?"* ("Girls let's review the test. Who can tell me the answer to the first question?")

Well, I thought, *I know that one for sure*. My hand flew up reflexively. It wasn't every day, or any day, in reality, that I knew an answer. It felt good. A few seconds too late, I slapped my hand down, remembering my handiwork. "Aah, *Señorita Payne, venga aqui por favor.*"

(Ah, Ms. Payne, come here, please.") She almost smiled as she called me to her desk. And so, I added Spanish to my summer school success portfolio. I got an eighty-eight on the Regents and learned that I was a visual learner. That humiliating experience was the beginning of using carefully constructed notes as an effective way to study, albeit on index cards and not my hands. It was especially helpful throughout nursing school. Nothing could spoil my momentum in that second year of high school. Not failed exams or a disappointed mother or missing father. I was happy to have just one disappointed parent. My self-confidence grew. I was as sunny and optimistic as the garish wallpaper that wrapped the walls of my bedroom. I'd never once considered that my bedroom window faced an ugly solid brick alleyway. I never once considered anything but sunshine. I was as optimistic and empowered as could be.

Summer of 1963 was filled with warm, sunny days and friends. Stephen had graduated from the Bronx High School of Science with top grades and a full scholarship to New York University. Neither of us thought about the irony of his attending the same NYU Campus in the University Heights section of the Bronx that our father had graduated from so many years before. I was just so happy that we would get to begin our days to school on the same train for the first three stops every day. Of course, I was proud of him. We never competed. Each of us was secure in a custom-sized educational strata, which fit us, and equally confident of success. But before that, we had July and August for better things.

I loved the smell of Bronx in the summer. Blazing hot August days on city pavement is an amalgam of hot tar, day-old garbage, and cement wet down by afternoon thunderstorms or a building superintendent's hosing away fine, gray, gritty dirt. It smells better to me even now than pine-scented woods or briny, fish-scented ocean. It will always smell like home. The visual images are comely and dynamic. They are not of graceful, hanging boughs of hemlocks dancing in a breeze or rippling waves at the water's edge. My memories are of bare teenage knees bumping against other knees to the rhythms on a portable radio. Stoop-sitting endlessly until standing or walking was necessary to allow old people to pass or to walk to a candy store. Our language was mostly body language. There was a twilight parade of old people, bent over two-armed wrestlers with a cane in one hand and their webbed, aluminum folding chairs in the other. Their time to socialize seemed to coincide with sunset. Did they understand their timing was perfectly matched to the dwindling warmth and daylight beyond that of the sun? We yielded the front stoop to them so they could whisper about us and turn their heads in unison as we paraded past them going nowhere in particular. Old ladies in their cotton housecoats and carpenter aprons were judge and jury for fray-edged too-short shorts and halter tops. It was the finest summer resort on earth. It was a blend of soft whispers behind hands and insistent, in-and-out sounds of rock and roll. It was the crisp, strutting dance of bare legs and sandaled feet on sidewalk blocks and the slow motion folding or unfolding of flimsy chairs by gnarled fingers. It was the lifted leg of a little dog adding his own scent and sound against a fire hydrant. It was home.

Stephen spent his first summer away from home, a momentous event. Bussing tables and sweeping floors at the Spring House Hotel on Block Island was life altering for him. We had been there before with Mom for several special visits. In the 1960s the island had fallen far from the grace it once enjoyed as a vacation destination to presidents and the social elites at the turn of the century. The large Victorian hotels had sagging roofs, loose clapboard, and threadbare moldy linens by the time my mother had discovered it. Like our apartment, it was now an affordable vestige of a previously unaffordable place. Known mostly to sports fishermen, an old friend and, later, a man she now occasionally dated had introduced her to its natural beauty. For under twenty dollars a night, we shared a room at the Oceanview Hotel and looked out at the endless Atlantic from the wraparound porch. We all loved the rolling hills, meandering stone walls, and craggy cliffs. Steve was especially enamored of its beauty and the tight-knit group of seasonal workers and more fortunate natives. This summer was his opportunity to be a part of the inner circle. He had been away only once before, to a Boy Scout camp in upstate New York when I was sent to a Jewish sleep-away camp. That adventure was for just two weeks and under adult supervision.

While I enjoyed the bounties of the Bronx, he enjoyed a new independence, a romantic liaison with a Block Island native ironically sharing our own last name, and he returned home reluctantly. An angry oozing laceration on his right foot seemed to match the ugly mood he brought back home that Labor Day. He suddenly hated everything about our street and home. Nothing was spared his vitriolic criticism. "Holy shit, I forgot how ugly this street is. Even the people look disgusting and decrepit," he added.

"Nice to have you home, too," I answered sarcastically.

My mother ignored his anger. She must have understood the stark contrast in his physical surroundings and loss of his newfound independent life style. He had mentioned the cute girl he intended writing to and his plans to go back to visit her before next summer. My mother listened patiently and tried to distract him. "Well, you are about to have a very exciting adventure in college. Looks like taking sixteen credits and meeting new people will be a good distraction. The first semester will be a perfect way to keep busy. I bet there will be other pretty girls flirting with you soon enough."

That, of course, was a misguided attempt to help distract him from his miserable state. He spent the next few days with his two closest guy friends and rarely emerged from his room. Summer was officially ending. We had no idea how this Labor Day would mark not just the end of summer, but the end of life as we knew it.

18 Falling Leaves

It was an insidious change, like the fall season itself. The delicate shift between summer and fall is, at first, barely perceptible. But that gentle tilt in the planet caused a wobble away from the guaranteed warmth we embraced without enough gratitude. A little less daylight each afternoon, a bit of yellowing mixed with the deeper green of our beautiful maple and oak trees. Soon enough, long sleeves covered bare arms, and we succumbed to wearing socks. It is a sad metaphor for the aging process each of us will realize with shocked disbelief in our fifties or sixties. But at fifteen and seventeen, that was as far away as the sun was.

We always left the house together that school year. Steve had a few extra minutes of formal goodbyes to our parakeet, Bubbie, who adored him. While I fussed with my hair or changed my mind about an outfit, the bird sat on Steve's neck and nibbled affectionately on his earlobe.

With thumb and index finger he oh-so-gently massaged the feathered, delicate neck of the bird. Bubbie would lift her tail in delight and we laughed at the possible sexuality of the ritual. On the way out, one last turn to look all the way up six floors to the kitchen window from the building's front courtyard before running down the street revealed a tiny white form running back and forth on the windowsill. Our albino parakeet was almost as devoted as a dog. She watched us leave and seemed to know when he would be back. Surely, she did not spend her day on that drafty perch, but was always there to chirp hello and dance along the two-inch strip of runway when we came home. We adored our little feathered pet. Her life ended dramatically that October. The absence of our greeter on the windowsill was strange. But sometimes, if we waited just a few seconds more, she could be seen climbing down the paint encrusted chain of the window's sash pulley. I imagine even a one-and-a-half ounce feathered creature needs to entertain itself while waiting for a loved one to return.

We burst through the front door expecting to be almost smacked in the face by our flighted little sibling but instead were greeted by a crying mother. There was no need to ask why she was crying. In her hands she cupped the tiny, still, conical form. Bubbie was obviously dead. "Oh, I am so, so sorry." She gulped and shuddered and let snot drip and mix with her tears, some landing on the bird. "I was just opening the window for a minute to get some fresh air and...and...and I had no idea she was at the top of the chain up in the corner. I never saw her. She never goes up that high. I am so...." More sobbing as Steve took the bird from her. We all cradled her and burrowed our noses into her neck feathers. I don't know how many people know the smell of feathers or even care to know it, but it is uniquely wonderful. Better than the smell from the first clanking steam from a radiator on a tossed about favorite sweater that smells just like yourself. A fragrance that is you and something else to absorb your scent and soften it into comforting feedback. Bubbie enjoyed a well honored bird burial tradition of being shrouded in a sweat sock and encased in a shoe box before being interred under a tree in a deserted area of Mosholu Parkway. We grieved and missed her enormously. There was, in time, another albino parakeet we learned to love as we had also learned to let go of our first beloved Bubbie. Just as surely as we had let go of long, hot summer days that are not really endless at all. Nothing is endless.

19 Winter Encroaches

We bolted out the door and race-walked to the steam-filled bagel shop on the corner of Jerome Avenue and Mosholu Parkway every morning. Whoever got there first got to choose the still hot bagel of that day's breakfast on the train. Pumpernickel for me and salt for Steve. Brown bag in hand, we bolted up the concrete steps of the elevated train station, happy with the unlikely sound of an echo from the rock-hard surface of the steps in the narrow staircase. We kept our subway tokens in a small pink ceramic bowl, which sat on top of a bookcase, in the entrance foyer. Four little brass coins with the hollowed out *Y* of NYC and embossed *Good for one fare,* were doled out each day and were deftly slipped into a turnstile slot without missing a second between pushing our bellies against the hard metal and continuing our run up another set of stairs to the platform. There wasn't much conversation as we rode high above the street and passed the familiar landmarks and buildings of Bedford Park and Kingsbridge Road. The fifteen-minute long clattering ride forward while sitting sideways was crudely meditative. "Bye" was probably the single word most uttered. We were still chewing those dense bagels and already thinking about the school day ahead. Many days, we returned home separately. Race walking was not a part of going home. He was always faster, anyway; I could saunter home at my own pace.

Our birthdays brought in November. I was born on November first, All Saints Day for Christians. Stephen was born on November second, All Souls Day for that same religious group. As children, I loved the association with the celebrations of all known and unknown saints. That was an honorable and fortunate group to belong to. In contrast, All Souls Day is a somber and soulful affair. Remembering all the dead and departed souls is certainly sobering and sad any way you consider it. We have celebrated our birthdays as one event every year of our lives. As the weather continued to get colder, a shared birthday always brightened the start of the month when dark was threatening at five o'clock and rain could be hard ice pellets as easily as water.

That November was slated to be special. A Sweet Sixteen party was scheduled for me at Rennie's house (her apartment had an actual dining room and no one slept in her living room). A few boy and girl neighborhood friends were invited, and I had a new and lovely pale blue dress I loved from Loehmann's, the best store ever for discount designer fashion. It had a narrow white yoke threaded with baby blue ribbon. A photo of me in that dress is my second ever favorite photo of myself. I was a beautiful sixteen-year-old. Long brown hair loosely caught in a high ponytail coiled into a grown-up bun and thick bangs, which offset very large and round hazel-green eyes. In the year since my father had seen a more grown up me in Miami, the soft edges of my face had sharpened and I'd grown confident in my female body. I had settled into a comfort zone he was unaware of. In just a few more weeks, he would have an unforeseen opportunity to experience my new comfort and self-confidence.

Stephen's eighteenth birthday was significant for his fabulous grades at NYU and first driver's license. He looked forward to borrowing Mom's car and going on a real date with Bobbi Tufts, the pretty Greek girl from the next block who had made him forget about love on Block Island. It was supposed to be our best birthday year ever. But I am now forced to consider the misfortune of being born on All Souls Day. Ridiculous of course to lend credulity to fortune telling songs like "Monday's Child" or birthdays that occur on holidays. Monday's child is fair of face, Tuesday's child is full of grace, et cetera is probably just an archaic mid-nineteenth century superstitious vestige of a more ignorant time in history. Nevertheless, All Souls Day of 1963 marked a change in luck for Stephen—and all of us. I'm not sure what day of the week he was born on. But if I had to guess, based on this poem it would be a Wednesday. *Wednesday's child is full of woe.*

20 Hospital

He was feeling less energetic that November. We no longer race-walked to the train in the morning. It wasn't a conscious decision of course. I assumed he wasn't in a rush. I assumed it had more to do with a flexible college schedule than his energy level. I easily adapted to a pace more consistent to my less athletic and competitive nature. He spent more time in his room reading the many books that were part of sixteen college credits. Sometimes, when I peeked in his room he was napping and not reading. *I'd fall asleep from boredom too*, I thought, *if I had to read all those books*. But the lethargy seemed to carry over to weekends also. Mom became concerned when this lasted more than a couple of weeks. The only thing she could find wrong was a persistent low-grade fever. His temperature hovered at a hundred or slightly above. She assumed it was a slight infection, but from where? She remembered the inflamed and angry reddened laceration he came home with from Block Island. But it was mid-November, and that had been more than two months ago. He had also had a bad sore throat at the start of school, which had quickly resolved. She asked to look at his foot just to be sure.

"Jeez Mom, are you kidding me? That cut was a long time ago. There's nothing to see. I'm fine, just tired from school, that's all," annoyed at her concern.

"Let me just take a look at the foot, then I won't bother you again," she persisted. He peeled off the sock with annoyance and threw it to the floor. "Do those little red spots on your feet itch? You have all these tiny dots on your ankles."

He looked at his own foot as if seeing it for the first time. The cut on the bottom of the foot had healed completely and he never noticed the tiny red dots that she was asking about.

"Let me see your other foot." He took off the second sock with less drama. Sure enough, both feet had tiny red dots around the ankle and a bit above. Too small and late in the season to be insect bites, she thought. But certainly not normal. Especially since they weren't itchy or splotchy, which could just be an allergy. "Tomorrow we are going to the emergency room to see what this is," she stated. It was her non-negotiable tone. He didn't answer. We hadn't had a family doctor since we were very little. Aside from my psoriasis and trips to dermatologists in the city, doctors were not a consideration. After all, we really were a healthy lot. Living so close to Montefiore had somehow caused us to internalize the medical center as being our resource if ever needed. I was even more comfortable since volunteering there for almost two years.

"That snide little shit. Who does he think he is talking down to?" My mother was outraged. There had been two trips to the emergency room that week. The first young resident or intern suggested she change her laundry detergent and come back in a week if he still had spots. He gave her a prescription for a cortisone cream which had not helped at all. Now, she returned as instructed and hoped for a better explanation or plan. The smug young man, not even a decade older than her son, looked at Stephen's feet and smirked. It probably didn't help that he looked a lot like her equally smug nephew Mark, who had every intention of becoming a doctor someday. "So, moootherrr," he dragged the word mother out a bit too slowly for emphasis. "This is really not anything for you to be so worried about. It could be a little skin fungus or maybe an allergy that is resistant. You could see a dermatologist if it keeps up much longer. I'd personally stop looking at his feet and stop worrying. I'm sure he would prefer to just ignore it. Mothers tend to worry more than they should."

"But Dooooctorrr," now she used his own cadence and intonation when speaking the word doctor as he had with the word mother. "Don't you think it's also a little concerning that he has had a fever for three weeks and is tired?"

"No," he flashed back. "No, I don't. He is eighteen years old. He's a college student and probably burning the candle at both ends. I do think you should stop taking his temperature and hovering over him. He might prefer that. I'll give you a dermatology referral if that makes you feel better." He now smiled in a benevolent but decidedly patronizing manner and stood up to leave. He had effectively dismissed her and ended the visit. They walked home; their quick pace was fueled by her fury. This time, Stephen struggled to keep pace with her. "That pompous prick. Sniveling little schmuck. Wet behind the ears and telling me to stop hovering? We are not going back there again. He didn't even ask if you still had a fever. He didn't even take your temperature or look at your feet. He never would have spoken to a man like that. I'm sure he wouldn't. Should have told him to shove that cortisone cream up his ass." Mom was in full-fledged fury. We knew enough to stay in our rooms that night and not fan the flames. I have no doubt she was correct about the doctor. I knew he never would have spoken like that if both a mother and father had presented a son with these symptoms. But Stephen and I did not have a father. Stephen had not seen his father in four years. I was hit with remembered resentment for my absent father. The week finished with continued fever and fewer barely audible expletives from my mother about the young doctor. She rumbled a bit like summer thunder warning of an approaching storm. The storm struck soon enough.

21 A Different Season

It wasn't the sound of thunder that stopped our lives late that November, but the sounds and images of gunshots. The nation was paralyzed with shock and grief. The assassination of President Kennedy on November twenty-second of that year seemed to topple the world. My mother had made an appointment for Stephen with a dermatologist I'd used. He was scheduled to be seen right after Thanksgiving. Stephen continued to slog back and forth to classes waiting just another week for that consult. But on November twenty-second, thoughts of school or doctors or going anywhere away from a television screen was unthinkable. I was in geometry class the afternoon of November 22nd. Everyone remembers exactly where they were of course. The PA system crackled to life. It was not a normal time for announcements at my school. We sat up in our seats and didn't need to be told to be silent. I was languidly sketching in the borders of my graph paper.

There was something profoundly pleasing about drawing long curling, curving tendrils of climbing vines that mocked the sharp angles and grids on the paper. Roses and calla lilies grew randomly along the vines. Sometimes long-lashed eyes looked out from the petals of the flowers. There wasn't a straight line in sight. I was working my way to summer school again. I stopped right in the middle of an eye and placed my pencil down on the desk. Mrs. Heffernan's voice (the principal) was somber. "Students, please be seated and silent. I have a sad announcement to make. At the end of the announcement you will be dismissed. Please collect your belongings and exit the building quietly." There was an unusually long pause, a sigh or exhale, and then her voice. "Today, at 12:30 p.m., our president, John Fitzgerald Kennedy, was pronounced dead. The president was assassinated in Dallas, Texas. Our prayers are with the family. Thank You." In the complete silence, the crackling of the microphone being shut off sounded louder than normal. No one spoke. The unnatural silence accompanying more than two thousand high school girls at dismissal was sobering. Silence had descended upon the world.

Even the number four train was silent. Students moved robotically up to the crowded platform and waited for the next train up or down town. When it arrived, the doors slid open to reveal a rush hour sized crowd. There was standing room only. Midday train cars were typically near empty. Had everyone exited Manhattan, I wondered? Was there a greater danger Mrs. Heffernan had not told us about? Why else send us home early? As I shouldered my way into the car, my anxiety grew. Normally, the source of my anxiety on a train this crowded would be the unwanted ass-grab of a traveling pervert or the more ambiguous question of wondering if the man vertically layered behind you with no space to spare was only keeping his balance by rocking back and forth, trying to romance you, or really masturbating before he got off at the next stop. Those were distant thoughts today.

People most often don't speak on crowded trains. There is an unwritten rule about eye contact on New York City trains. You read, or look out the window, or close your eyes if you dare to. It's one of those strange social constructs like not staring at or touching other people's groceries on the checkout line at the supermarket or, for men, staring straight ahead at a public urinal. But today, there was an atypical communication phenomenon. People spoke with their eyes. Eyes searched out other eyes for answers or as barometers to gauge feelings. Were the eyelids lowered as if in hiding, or wide open in fear? Were there tears in eyes? Mostly the eyes danced around the space just looking for connection and affirmation. I looked about and through the crowd for the familiar eyes of my brother. I imagined he had also left his campus and might be on the same train home. It was unlikely he would have ended up in the same car or that I could even manage to navigate through the bulky coats, briefcases, and shopping bags if my eyes found him. I wanted desperately to see him right then. We were all encased in shocked cocoons and waiting to exhale with someone we loved. When I reached our stop, the familiar name of Mosholu Parkway, I bolted from the train and ran down the concrete steps. I race-walked home alone, eager to be with my family of three. Together, we would join millions of others in grief and shock. The silence persisted for days as we watched and listened to disembodied voices talk us through the details of death and cataclysmic change from our televisions. Just a few days later, a more personal nightmare eclipsed the national tragedy. It's hard to care about an earthquake far away when the ground is shifting under your own feet.

Everyone was sad. Soon enough the anger set in. Anger helped us reject the unbearable things we couldn't change. While the rest of the country focused on an assassin named Lee Harvey Oswald, I preferred to target a man named Charles Payne. Surely, I reasoned, if he had been with his son in the emergency room two weeks before, the correct diagnosis would have been made. If only he'd been there, I thought, my brother would be spared the suffering and unknown outcome that lay ahead. But blaming my father for the cascading misery of events that began late November might have been unfair. It was always a case of *If Only's.* There are always those to call upon in retrospect. *If only*...I hadn't passed a red light, had stopped smoking, studied harder, ran faster, said something else, been born rich or privileged, or another race. *If only* is just a childish escape from the reality of what actually is. Still, would the smug young doctor have paid more attention to the set of symptoms before him if he were speaking to a man? Was this anger displaced? There was enough of it to go around. The train ride home on November twenty-second was the first of many trips in the months ahead that I took alone. A subway car is a perfect place for fulminating anger to blossom. Vibrations under and through your body displace the awareness of breath. Rocking from side to side forces your muscles to surrender to the will of the train's motion, and the off and on again view of distant objects is further challenged by the occasional flicker of the overhead lights. Your sight turns inward soon enough. You must surrender to captivity as you sit there. In that state of surrender stray thoughts find fertile pathways to the surface of your mind. Now that I rode to school alone and after that to the hospital after school every day, I could consider the *If Only's* and *Whys* as a well-practiced mantra. It was an exercise in futility. Stephen was now deathly ill. Hating either my father or the smug young doctor only added insult to injury. But in retrospect, how could I not consider either of these men without assigning well deserved blame? Particles of subconscious rage coursed through my blood as my brother's blood carried more immediate danger.

Little red dots have a real name in medical jargon. They are called petechiae. They are unlike welts, or blisters, or pustules or vesicles. They are easily distinguished from the other myriad manifestations of disease seen on skin. If they cluster and run together on the lower legs, ankles, and soles of the feet lending a red blush to the soles they should be more alarming, if not questionable. The red dots are a sign that blood is leaking from the capillaries (smallest blood vessels) that originated in a disturbance from the veins carrying blood back to the heart. Petechiae can be associated with several diseases or even traumatic events. Severe vomiting or near strangulation can cause petechiae. They are also, commonly, a symptom associated with bacterial endocarditis.

Persistent low-grade fever and fatigue are not exclusively alarming symptoms. Fatigue can be due to stress, lack of sleep, anxiety, or even, as some would say "burning the candle at both ends," too much partying or drinking or excessive exercise. Fatigue in isolation can be easily discounted or put on hold as a reason to worry. Low-grade fevers are actually another issue. Persistent low-grade fevers are elusive nuisances. They can be linked to the common cold, low-grade viral or bacterial infections as well as more exotic things like tuberculosis or multiple sclerosis or rheumatoid arthritis. Low-grade fever, persistent low-grade fever is also a presenting symptom in bacterial endocarditis.

Had Dr. Smug taken his temperature, he could have confirmed a two-week long history of low-grade fever. Had he bothered to ask about his habits, he would have learned that this eighteen-year-old was not a party animal or ever normally tired. Had he listened to his heart with the stethoscope he wore as a proud mantle around his hairy neck he might have detected a significant murmur. But the stethoscope was as useful as a pearl necklace in this case.

Had Dr. Smug ordered a simple blood test, it might have confirmed an alarmingly high white blood cell count and equally alarming sedimentation rate. He may even have had confirmation of residual streptococcal bacteria in his blood. More sophisticated tests could have offered a clinical laboratory profile of bacterial endocarditis.

Had Dr. Smug taken a minute or two longer to see if the patient's hands matched his feet, he might have noted a few more petechiae and the fact that his fingernails had an odd shape and dusky color. Clubbing is a growth pattern of fingernails that curve unnaturally into a club-like shape and are also manifestations of heart disease. The blood flow to these distal points is markedly insufficient. Nails should never be a shade of pale blue or dusky. That is a lovely color for silk scarves and twilight skies, but not fingernails. Both clubbing of the nails and dusky colored nails may also indicate bacterial endocarditis.

But Dr. Smug was either rushed, or inexperienced, or suffering too much hubris to ask another physician to consult. I am certain he felt so empowered in his white jacket and stethoscope necklace that he assumed systematic and statistical safety from error. He might have been correct under normal circumstances. After all, neighborhood people who used the emergency room as if it was their primary care physician mostly abused and misused the service. All day long, there were people with colds and flu and aches and pains and neuroses he could easily offer simple remedies and advice to. They left feeling grateful for the benediction of superior knowledge bestowed upon them.

But this one time, his arrogance was a statistically unfortunate error. Dismissing the anxious (over functioning?) mother and her sluggish freshman-in-college son was an unforced and tragic error. While Dr. Smug continued to play doctor through this rotation, awful, un-seeable, microscopic destruction was wreaking havoc in a previously healthy young body. The bacteria which had first entered his body either through an untreated strep throat or insidious dirty laceration on a foot and had multiplied exponentially in the absence of antibiotic. They had eventually spread to the inner lining of his heart and lived there uninterrupted for a time. Left to thrive, the bacteria settled eventually into other nooks and crannies of the heart. The valves, which control the ebb and flow of blood, were perfect folded, convoluted surfaces on which to take hold. A good listen with that pretty stethoscope would have revealed a strange rhythm to the normal lub-dub of the heart song. All this time, the body responds by elevating its temperature in an attempt to kill off the invaders. Eventually, the efficiency of these valves is compromised and blood flow is altered. The patient may notice fatigue from this insufficient oxygenation of the blood. Little red dots may appear as veins struggle to do their job in sending accumulating blood back to the now sluggish engine we call a heart. Fingernails respond to the swelling of tissues starved for blood. They turn inward, like cut flowers we forget to water. Microscopically, the holocaust continues unchecked. Blood clots start gathering around the damaged valves. The clots are mostly the platelets and fibrin in blood, which gather in an unholy alliance while sitting idly instead of performing normal duties. The clots are the end product of pooling blood unable to rush through the normal pattern of heart chambers and valves in an efficient miracle of feeding blood and oxygen to every living cell we need to live. The heart is a simple labyrinth that cannot overcome a closed sign in its corridors.

And those clots have no business being in the labyrinth. They are unwelcome guests clinging to land rights in a crowded, heaving community hostile to their presence. It's not long before they are unceremoniously evicted. Dislodged, they wander out of the heart and into arteries where they travel on the largest vessels they prefer to new homes in the lungs or brain or wherever luck may lead them. They can cause heart attack if they are left to obstruct blood flow to the heart itself. When a clot finds its way to the brain through the carotid artery, it is called an embolism. The embolism swiftly blocks the flow of blood to the tissues in the brain. The deprived tissue reacts by ceasing to perform its normal functions. Most stroke victims experience weakness in an arm or leg or one side of their body. There may be interruptions in speech or language, numbness, confusion, facial expression or pain are all possible manifestations of a stroke. No one expects an otherwise healthy eighteen-year-old boy to have a stroke. It is statistically unlikely. Would having a father present to share decisions or confront a smug young doctor have prevented the cascade of nightmarish physical events from happening?

22 Nightmare

We woke up to wailing sounds. Apartment dwellers are accustomed to the heated arguments of neighbors, backfiring cars, howling cats in season and in our neighborhood, screeching train brakes as well. This was not a familiar sound at all. It seemed to come from our own apartment. It was alarming in its intensity. Low moaning and crying took turns. It was coming from my brother's room. The reality struck my mother and me instantly. We ran to his room. Stephen was lying on his side but writhing in pain. He clutched his head with both hands and spoke a single word. "Help."

"Oh my God, what is it? Please, tell me what happened?" My mother's words rushed out.

"Pain, my head, help," he now pleaded.

"Stay with him. Do not let him move. I'm getting the car. When I come back, we will get him in the car and to the hospital." She was quick, decisive, and in control. I don't think she ever considered calling an emergency number. She had a plan and needed to move on it. I am sure my mother no longer trusted anyone to do the right thing. She definitely would not want him back in the same emergency room that had failed him. Speechless now, I held his hand and waited. In record time, she flew back through the front door and we supported him under his arms as we walked, dragged him into the elevator and then into the back seat of our car. The motor's engine had warmed the car very little. It was sometime between midnight and sunrise. I had no idea. The streets were deserted. "Sit in the back with him," she commanded. "Try to keep his head elevated and still if you can."

It was surreal. He looked like he might die. He didn't even look like my brother. It was not night or daytime. There wasn't a person to be seen. It was just the three of us facing a nightmare. It had always been just the three of us of course, but nightmares were usually an individual event. This time, we were trapped together in a speeding car heading to an unknown end.

"Mom, where are we going? You're going so fast, I'm scared." I was crying now.

"It's okay. I'm heading down the FDR Drive into the city. New York Hospital is on the Upper East Side. There are no lights, no traffic this time of night, and we will be there in no time. It's on York Avenue. That's as close to the highway as you can be."

She was right. We didn't need sirens and flashing lights or time waiting for an ambulance. My mother had delivered her patient to the emergency room entrance in less than thirty minutes. She jerked the car to a stop on a cobblestone circular driveway, said nothing but bolted out alone into the double glass doors marked Emergency Room. She had delivered him alive, although I was not sure of that as we arrived. He had stopped moaning but I was too afraid to nudge his still body into a reaction that may have helped confirm my worst suspicions. I allowed two uniformed men to slide him out by his underarms and then more carefully transfer him to a stretcher, which took him away from me and into his new world. There were new nightmares to consider in the months ahead. We soon returned to the separate worlds of our worst fears. Survival dictated that we find our way forward using tools uniquely suited to each of us. My brother chose courage, my mother tenacity, and I opted for anger and solitude. Anger could be momentary and transient or a longer simmering hateful thing that lurked in quiet corners and long subway rides to 68th Street and York Avenue.

There were neurologists and infectious disease doctors. There were cardiologists and psychiatrists. There were nurses and social workers and clerical staff and clergy. There were dieticians and food service people and laboratory staff to draw blood and cleaning staff happy to work as if they were invisible. There were people to transport Stephen to X-ray and radiology and procedure rooms for catheterizations and nuclear studies and specialty labs. The place hummed with activity and purpose. The grinding wheels of diagnosing and discovery and monitoring and treating and planning were set in motion. We were passive participants in a world where we held no power at all. I once believed that being poor made me less important in a world that valued expensive things we couldn't own. *If only,* I thought, we could have a new car or our own home or a real vacation, I'd be so happy. *If only*, I could have better clothing or a real gold bracelet I would really be so happy. And maybe, *if only,* I had a father who made lots of money and hadn't left us and a mother who didn't have to work, and they lived together and doted on us, well, that would be a good thing, too. But now, I understood that none of those things really mattered at all. Real power was nothing more than being healthy and in command of your body and how you spent your day. There was more impotence in illness than there ever could be in poverty. Real power lay in working in the hospital, not residing in it.

All those staff members dressed in white swirled around us like white flecks in a snow globe. We were watching from the outside, aware of our spectator status. But the swirling white flecks failed to calm or entertain us. My mother would never again submit to a passive role when it came to my brother's health. Reactive behavior was replaced by a fiercely proactive stance. This required her to be informed, aware, and involved. Doctors would have to be accountable. Her tenacity was fueled by her assumption of guilt as a parent. She had her own deck of *If Only* cards to play. *If only* she had insisted on Dr. Smug taking blood or consulting with another doctor. *If only* she had taken Stephen for a throat culture when he had that long-ago sore throat or refused to let him spend a whole summer away. Perhaps he never even cleaned that nasty laceration on his foot. *If only* she had found a real family doctor instead of going to the emergency room. She hoped it was not too late to redeem herself and to save his life.

She had used all her sick days and vacation days from work. Now she was on an unpaid family emergency leave. Once again, we had no regular income. It had been an extremely long time since a letter with familiar cursive had arrived from Florida. We were down to peanut butter and jelly sandwiches and canned soup when we were home. But mostly, we never were at home anyway. Our second little parakeet lived a life of quiet solitude in his cage. That delicate bit of feathered fluff was just another victim of our family's fall from grace. It seemed like cheerfully running home from school to be greeted by a hopping, joyous improbably almost human little form in the window and being with friends had happened in another lifetime.

My mother was at the hospital from early morning until visiting hours ended at 9:00 p.m. every day. She stood outside his room and eavesdropped during medical rounds. She called the Chief Cardiologist and Neurosurgeon's offices to schedule times she could speak with them. She accompanied her son as he was wheeled on a stretcher to Angiography for his brain and Cardiac Catheterization for his heart. She sat by his bed most of the day and left only to speak with doctors, enable privacy during examinations, or to greet me when I arrived by 4:00 p.m. most afternoons. She watched as intravenous bottles near emptied and then alerted the nurses. She knew the nurses and attendants by name and was courteous and warm to the visitors of the other patient who shared the miserable room. She was a soldier, and this was her encampment. This encampment was in the center of a blizzard complete with snow squalls and gusting winds and all kinds of challenges to survival. A force greater than her had picked up that glass orb and seemed to shake it violently. But she was a tenacious fighter. On medical rounds, she hovered nearby and waited for her opportunity to catch up with the chief resident to ask new questions. Within the first three weeks, she had learned that the blood clots, which she now knew were called emboli had damaged his heart. She demanded specific answers to her questions.

"I understand he has heart damage from the strep and the blood clots. What part of his heart is damaged? How bad is the damage? Will it return to normal after all the antibiotics? Will he have lasting damage?"

The answers were discouraging; in fact, they were disheartening. Two of the four valves in his heart were seriously damaged. Both the tricuspid and mitral valves had been severely damaged. The upper chambers of his heart were seriously compromised. The antibiotics had stopped the infection but the damage was done. Yes, he was young and many things could improve, but some would not. He would need open heart surgery in several years to replace or repair one or both valves. He would be on antibiotic and other medications the rest of his life. He may never be restored to his previous health. But, as blizzards go, it is the sudden blast of cold air from an unexpected direction that could topple trees or bring a soaring eagle to the ground. There was more.

We had taken up our normal positions in the bright visitors' lounge. Surrounded by tall Gothic-shaped arched windows that knit together in a lovely curved alcove, we sat in bright blue upholstered chairs. They were Danish modern frames but generously sized. This little vignette had become the place Mom and I sat whenever we were not in Stephen's room. I imagine that after all the hours spent in those chairs, bits of sloughed off hair and skin and bitten off cuticles and scratched off psoriasis scales, which originated on our bodies, were now embedded in tiny spaces between fibers of blue and worn places of wood that might be porous. The chairs and we had become comingled life forms. The seats became as familiar as the backs of our thighs or spines. The East River rolled south in easy view. Tugboats and barges and occasional sightseeing boats continued on their own life cycle of some destination. We hardly noticed them. We were sentinels stationed inside that window to keep watch inside, not out. It is where we sat the afternoon of my brother's angiogram. It was the second of two that week. The tests involved some risk and pain but were necessary in understanding why the excruciating headaches continued. Had the emboli taken dangerous journeys to other places? We were still digesting the prospect of heart surgery, risks, and the potential of having an eighteen-year-old invalid come to terms with a change in his life plans. But the frigid wind was relentless.

"Hi, Mrs. Payne, I am Dr. Russell Patterson. We haven't met before but I have been closely following Stephen's case and am well acquainted with every detail of his health. The other doctors have included me because my specialty here at New York Hospital is neurosurgery. They believe I may be able to offer some help. Let me say how sorry I am for what all of you, especially Stephen, have endured. I hope that together, we can get back on the right track."

He was tall and handsome and blue-eyed. He was elegant, and soft spoken and self-assured without being arrogant. He had offered up the perfect mix of compassion and professionalism. Mostly, what he offered was a bit of hope. Hope was sorely needed. He had said the perfect words. "I am hoping we can get him back on track. I am aware of every detail of his *health*." He had chosen the word health and not illness. That little nuance in selected words made her son an entire person and not just an interesting case. When getting back on track seemed impossible, he had offered that hope sincerely. My mother loved him instantly. She wanted so badly to trust and to entrust again. She had been in this fight as a solitary soldier, and now, she had an ally. She didn't know at first that Dr. Patterson was a renowned neurosurgeon currently doing a fellowship to explore new surgical techniques. Stephen's timing had perfectly aligned with the timing of the progress of his research. Yes, he was brilliant and handsome and elegant and, in fact, sincere in his hope for success. He was also warm and patient and kind. But what he was delivering was not a simple fix or encouraging news. He was delivering the next devastating blow.

That icy cold December afternoon, we stood as he introduced himself. The blue chairs abandoned as we walked closer to the tall, handsome man in a crisp white lab coat. After the introduction, he asked that my mother listen as he explained his own understanding of the situation. "And I want you to stop me as I speak to ask questions. It is extremely complex and may be confusing. Please interrupt as often as you need to. After we have discussed exactly what we are dealing with I hope to explain how it is I may be able to help. But first, let me begin explaining. How about I pull over another chair and we all sit down."

A third blue chair was dragged across the tiled floor to complete a new vignette. I imagine a tugboat may have been rolling down the river or a seagull hovering along whitecaps below, but the world had narrowed to three blue chairs facing death head on. Dr. Patterson was the antithesis of Dr. Smug. He was more patient and more kind because my mother was facing this alone. He was speaking now to his patient's parents. My mother had always been both mother and father to us. Dr. Patterson recognized that.

My mother sat at the edge of that chair. She toyed with the flexible band of her Timex wristwatch as she was prone to doing when deep in thought. Sometimes, when really deep in thought, my mother seemed to stare ahead at nothing, and her eyes blinked separately. I wondered at this and sometimes thought her brain was short-circuiting from thinking too hard. Today, her eyes were alert and laser focused as her hazel-eyed team locked in solidarity of purpose. Blinking was even out of the question. She barely nodded as he delivered a litany of bad news.

The Litany of the Saints, a Catholic prayer, is rarely recited. One exception is on All Saints Day, November first. It is a long and moving appeal for help from the many great saints. It asks God for mercy and divine protection. Lord have mercy on us, it asks of each Saint and of God. I am only familiar with it by the coincidence of sharing my birthday with this holiday and, perhaps, for those formative years that as a Jewish girl I spent my time absorbing the Catholic world I lived in. As Dr. Patterson invoked the jargon of modern medicine, I retreated to a simple place where all I wanted was some mercy from this nightmare. I silently prayed to an unknown God to make all I was hearing be a big mistake or a nightmare I'd wake up from. But God didn't seem to be present. It was just a strikingly handsome doctor who reached out that day.

"I guess you know by now that the blood clots that formed from the infection first settled in his heart. They did a fair amount of damage to a couple of his valves. The good news is, the rest of his heart is strong and young. That is important to keep in mind." He offered a small smile and kept his eyes locked on hers. "So, later on, when he is stronger and maybe a bit older, we can see about repairs he may need."

She was strangely feeling less frightened. It was good to be reminded of a strong rest of his heart and the luxury of time to consider heart surgery. That respite from fear was short lived. He continued to explain the trajectory of the emboli and ensuing damage, his department now.

"So, we are not sure how many of those clots eventually traveled, and probably a few just were small and were reabsorbed by his body. Because of the severe pain in his head, we felt the angiograms would tell us what was going on in his head. The angiograms revealed that two of the embolisms had traveled to his brain and sat in place in a couple of blood vessels for a time. These emboli caused the vessels, which are elastic, to stretch out in two places. They formed two little thinned out places in the walls of those arteries. They became so thinned that they eventually broke and released blood into his brain. That blood caused the pressure and severe pain he experienced.

The little bubbles of thinned out spots on those vessels are called aneurysms. So now, we aren't worried anymore about infection. We aren't worried anymore about blood clots. But," he gave a long pause, "I am extremely worried about the aneurysms, extremely worried. Any questions?"

She was uncharacteristically silent. He didn't have a stroke. Maybe that was a good thing, she thought. She had read up about blood clots to the brain and about strokes. She had assumed he was out of the woods aside from his heart. Why was this doctor so worried?

"If you leave them there, won't he just go back to normal? His headache has gotten much better. Do you think there is some medication that can make them repair?" She was grasping at straws. Now, it was his turn to explain the second part of his consultation, why he was specifically there and what he could offer. It was an ice flow in a shipwreck in the middle of a vast ocean.

"His aneurysms are very deep inside his brain. Surgically, they are situated in an especially tricky area and are on opposite sides of his brain. He will require two rounds of brain surgery done at separate times to access them. Each of these procedures are with significant risk because of their locations. The reason I have been asked to help is because I have pioneered a new surgical technique that should reduce the risk of permanent brain damage."

Brain damage? Brain damage? What was he saying? My mother was still silent. We were speechless. When no questions were asked, he continued.

"My procedure limits the risk of damage by stopping the blood from flowing into the brain during surgery. This is done by stopping all the blood in the body from moving and doing damage during surgery. By putting the heart and blood 'on hold' while we do the delicate surgery, we can do the repair with more precision and less damage. In these locations, damage is almost guaranteed in normal surgery. My technique uses new machinery that can cool the body to a temperature of five degrees Celsius. At that temperature, the blood is drained while the heart slows and stops. After the repair is made, we resume warming the body and circulation is restored. It is called bypass surgery. Freezing the body is entirely new and the basis of my research and its completion."

It was difficult to comprehend the magnitude of the problem and the Frankenstein-like surgery he described. Speech finally returned to her. "You are saying that his heart will stop beating. Does that means he will be dead?"

He thought about how best to answer this and opted for simplicity. "Yes, but not for too long."

Then a string of questions followed. "Have other patients had this and always awakened? Is there a risk of not being re-awakened, of brain damage anyway? Why can't you do both at one time?"

His answers were not comforting. "Stephen will be the first person in the world to have this surgery. I have no other patients who can help with the answers. I do know that trials on animals have been successful. The technique is perfected in those cases. None have suffered brain damage. There is not enough time to complete both areas in one procedure. We do not want to stretch the time parameters we are comfortable with for the chilling process. That would increase risk in my opinion. In any surgery, there is always risk of death or complications.

This is true in the simplest of procedures and is magnified with time and complexity. I do think this procedure gives him the best chance at being restored to his prior intellectual and physical function. There are risks of all kinds but there is also a great chance that there will be a complete recovery. I have no idea how long a recovery will take. If the first surgery is successful, I would prefer to do the second within two weeks of the first. He is sitting on two time bombs that can cause stroke or death at any moment."

There was a longer silence now. He waited and then spoke again. "Please allow yourself some time to think this over. We will need consent from both you and Stephen. If there is another parent or relative who can help you with the decision, I think you should call as soon as possible. Time is a factor, but I understand how shocking and frightening this is. I'm sure you are overwhelmed. Any other questions? Otherwise I'll be back tomorrow to see what you've decided."

She had one last question. "Will he be in pain at any time or aware of what is going on?"

He flashed the smallest of pathetic smiles and answered. "No, no he won't."

23 The Iceman Cometh

"I have to call your father tonight." She wasn't actually looking at me. She was back to the short-circuited faraway look with eyes blinking out of synch. A left eye slowly closed and re-opened. Twenty or thirty seconds later the right would take a turn.

Why should she call my father? I thought. Stephen seemed to hate him. I had last seen him almost a year ago when I left him and a pastrami sandwich sitting forlornly in the front seat of his car. It never dawned on me now that he would care about either of his children. He had stopped sending money, and we had been lulled back into a comfortable and independent cozy triumvirate where fathers did not dwell. Whatever was going on in his life had no importance in ours. Why should he be included in the worst thing that was happening to us when he didn't care about any of the good things? He didn't even know how smart his son was, I thought. I bet he had no idea that

Stephen was walking exactly the same paths and maybe sitting in the same classrooms at NYU that he had once occupied. I had achieved none of those great accomplishments unless summer school success qualified. There was nothing extraordinary about me, but there was about Stephen. He was smart and handsome and extremely courageous. He had been lying in his hospital bed for three weeks now and had not once cried or complained. I was sure he was frightened and in pain. I knew he was annoyed at times. He was silently courageous. I believed my brother was now a legitimately courageous man. He was no longer a boy. I had given little thought to my father this year or this month. But I knew my brother was a better man. I thought about that now as my mother told me she would call him. It was, of course, the ethical thing to do. A parent, any parent, should know that their child is facing death. He knew when his son was born, and, I guess, he should know when his son may die. Yes, it was the right thing to do. She was a courageous soldier, too. She was brave and focused on her task and was ethical as well. My mother signed the consent. She was not a gambler but couldn't risk the time bomb ticking in his brain. She feared the surgery that promised to deliver a different son to her. The probability of paralysis, speech or intellectual loss was repugnant. There was only one viable choice. Her decision was made. Now she would discuss it with Stephen. She would not discuss options with Charles. She would simply let him know the date once it was scheduled. We were forging on, fatherless as always.

My battle did not include ethical choices. I was struggling with the solitude imposed on siblings of compromised children. Instead of heading home, I headed for the number four train after school. No one was home. I had no desire to see my old friends. How could I listen to the Beach Boys or talk about boys while my brother was so sick? I didn't want to talk about him to anyone. I just wanted to be with him and my mother. They were the only people in the private world living the same nightmare. Of course, when I was with them, I felt invisible anyway. I did my homework on the forty-five-minute ride to the hospital and then walked alone the three long blocks between Lexington Avenue and York Avenue. My anger was fueled during that walk. I hated the Upper East Side of New York. I hated the well-dressed women and the men in business suits. They were all in a big rush and none of them smiled. The women all looked painfully slim and stylish. Where were the comfortable old Bronx ladies with shopping carts full of laundry or groceries? Where was a good bagel shop or kosher deli? Where did they even hide their garbage cans? The buildings were too tall and as sleek as the people. No one hung out of a window. No houseplants took in the sun on a window grate. The dogs even looked self-satisfied here, well-coiffed and groomed pedigrees walking obediently on short leashes and never daring to lift a leg or squat in public. The owners looked away in embarrassment if one broke rank and squatted in an impossibly tiny patch of grass surrounding a Gingko tree or on the sidewalk. I imagine there was an inner dialogue then. *I will check my watch and look into the distance as if to check the color of the next traffic light. I am NOT watching my pet defecate. No way.* But then they'd quickly stoop down to collect the waste in a tiny bag they could hand to the doorman. They were completely full of shit and I hated them. I bet none of them had much to worry about. Maybe worrying about a favorite restaurant or next vacation in the Hamptons could be a burden. I doubted it. I was sixteen and had a fairly well-developed sense of social class and injustice. Righteous indignation was a good fit. I wore it happily. I needed it then. It helped distract me from reality. It has latched on for a lifetime. I embrace it now as a familiar battle scar I have earned the right to and can disguise when needed. It's not much harder than applying pancake makeup to discolored skin.

Stephen was perpetually angry at my father. I can't remember a time that he didn't hate him. He was older when our father left—more disturbed and upended by the loss than I was. I was curious and receptive to his visits at ten, eleven, and twelve. Stephen was emphatic in his negative feelings. The only bit of ambivalence reared its head with the lure of air travel. He remained disengaged and unwilling to accept him. He remained angry. My anger had more to do with being marginalized or dismissed as inferior. It wasn't associated with the root cause, that same man. My father had unwittingly cast an identity of rejection and inferiority upon me. Being different and unwelcomed my first thirteen years was accompanied by the sting of poverty which persisted well after that. An evolving comfort level in my early teen years and change in environment enabled me to relinquish any need for a father or anger associated with him. I could marginalize my father, and I did. It felt right. My brother's illness forced me to confront the absence of a father when one may have helped my mother if nothing else. The return to being pathetically poor again fanned the angry flames. My mother was forced to ask her brother for financial help to pay rent and utilities for several months. I am sure she feared Aunt Dorothy's interference, but that happened later. I was returning soda bottles from the trash in the basement for the nickel returns they yielded. I used that money to pay subway fare. Pasta was standard fare for every meal not eaten at the hospital. Even there, we were careful with our choices of cafeteria food. Soup and oyster crackers or a sandwich were what we limited ourselves to. If Stephen skipped a meal, we would salvage pudding or milk or a piece of fruit from his tray before it was picked up. Complaining was a selfish and futile activity. Most of the time, I squelched the anger. I could distract myself with television or magazines in the hospital. There were hours and hours of being alone in the waiting room or sitting for short spells in his room but not talking. There was very little to say. I could save up all my anger now. I had a focal point that was more concrete than the imagined thin arterial wall bubbles on the inside of my brother's brain. It was so much easier to contemplate unleashing it at a person. That person was scheduled to visit soon. The anger gained momentum as the fear began to show in my brother's face and the indignities mounted. My father had never been a targeted source of my anger. If anything, he brought short-lived promise for three pre-adolescent years I held on to childish dreams. And then I gradually stopped needing that promise. I let go of him at a time he was needing to let go of me. Letting go at fifteen was mutually, albeit informally, agreed upon. My anger was always just a lightweight sweater I'd put on or take off in response to insecurity over little things and not directed at any person in particular. I never enjoyed being angry at that time. Now, I was angry at so many things it felt good to have a target. My father was in the crosshairs

Stephen was such a good patient. He submitted to daily blood work and painful tests and residual headaches. Very few things seemed to upset him. He was resigned to his present state. He had responded to the news of having surgery with several guarded questions and resolve. He made it clear he would not see his father, even if he wanted to visit. Again, he decreed this in a resolved matter-of-fact manner that no one dared confront. "He can't come into my room. If you need to talk to him, do it without me. You can let him know anything you want to, but I won't see him."

There was no attempt to change his mind. He was entitled to any small request he had at this point. It looked like he was in control of his feelings but that was far from the truth. I knew my brother had hated him before this. I seized upon his anger and made it my own. I was his advocate and if I could render some insult or express some rage on his behalf then I would. Our father was scheduled to arrive the evening before surgery.

That day was especially difficult. It started with medical rounds, and today there was an even larger group of physicians and medical students. My brother was a celebrity. He was about to change the course of modern-day neurosurgery. I had taken the day off from school and drove in earlier than normal with my mother to the city. We stood outside the room and watched the huge collection of white-jacketed men assemble in and spill out of the room. Most of them left within a few minutes, but a group of six young medical students had stayed behind for their chance to be connected to this historical event. They ogled him as if he was an exquisite lab rat or insensate plastic medical model. He was little more than a larger re-creation of a favorite of his own models, *The Invisible Man*. They were only a few years older than their patient, but unfortunately unable to empathize. They took turns listening to his abnormal lub-dub and bounced rubber reflex hammers off his knees. He was completely objectified. No one spoke. They communicated effectively by moving forward and back to enable the next lucky white jacket to take a turn. It was as formal and slow as a minuet. They slow danced around him never knowing that their subject had reached a final, boiling point of two hundred and twelve degrees. His blood was roiling and they would not escape being scalded.

These obviously healthy, probably wealthy, and in our minds overly fortunate medical novitiates were about to be reminded that the item in the bed was a young man who had only weeks before been an NYU student on full scholarship with his own future plans. The plans did not include a damaged heart, two craniotomies with unknown outcome, or being poked and prodded on what might be his last day on earth by a gaggle of white jacketed, stethoscope adorned contemporaries there to reinforce the cruel nature of luck. The inequity was too much to bear. Now, the square, plastic coated medical school students' identification badges with their names had morphed into perfect bull's-eyes targets. He looked no one in the eye when he spoke.

"Okay guys, thanks. Now, get the fuck out of my room. The show is over. Did I even say I wanted company? Out! Now! Little cocksuckers!" The dance ended abruptly. It was as if a stiff blast of wind had caught their white jackets and rendered them weightless. They blew out of the room looking more like loose pages caught in a snow squall than any form of humans. When the wind and anger dissipated, Steve finally wept. It was the first time he had succumbed to his fear and anger.

24 Uninvited Guests

The day was marked by unwanted and unwelcome guests and a newfound abandon and honesty in response to their intrusion on our misery. Misery, pain, fear, and degradation are intimate states of being. As intimate, I think, as their happier counterparts of love and romance. There is no need or place for a public face or contrived words on the precipice of death. The silent presence of bound hearts acknowledging only shared breath and time matter. Other voices serve only to undermine that precious peace.

They shaved his head that evening. A bizarre, one-sided assault with a straight razor that made him look freakish. His straight, thick brown hair had grown impressively long while in the hospital. Now, his head looked too much like a pair of neighbors feuding over an unkempt lawn. A carefully fenced and demarcated line drawn down the middle accentuated the overgrowth on one side and baldness on the other. I was horrified and kept my eyes averted so as not to alarm him. I imagined his shaven head might be similar to a death row prisoner being groomed for electrocution. He could not eat, and so, we sat empty bellied and silent together in his room as evening continued.

Footsteps and voices approached. Familiar and unwanted voices. "Walter. I think this is his room." The nasal, Long Island accented voice of Aunt Dorothy broke the silence. And there they were. She held a garish bouquet of dyed turquoise mums and baby's breath. They were an unnatural shade of blue mixed with purple accents. The flowers were jarring in the cool white and faded yellow of the hospital room. They didn't belong. Their bearers didn't belong. They were unwelcome. Under the best of circumstances, what eighteen-year-old male is grateful for a bouquet?

She quickly went into nurse mode. It had been decades since she'd actually practiced, but her confidence had not faltered. She was suddenly in charge. A clipboard, which chronicled his vital signs and fluid intake and output, hung off a hook at the end of his hospital bed. Dorothy quickly removed it and sat down to study the useless data. She flipped through the collection of pages as if preparing to render an alternative diagnosis or more probably, to offer her confirmation of its accuracy.

Sweet Uncle Walter made a stab at his well-worn humor. "Now Stephen, I think your haircut may set some trends. Definitely going to turn some heads with that look." It hung heavily in the air and was met by deafening silence. Uncle Walter responded appropriately by just squeezing Stephen's hand quickly and a quick pat before retreating to a chair in the corner of the room. He understood. But Dorothy continued to intrude and insert her unwelcome ministrations. She untucked his top sheet and thin-napped white blanket from the bed. They had been loosely kicked off in his restless state. She pulled and tugged first the left side, then the right, and then the bottom edge. She pulled the linens taught and tucked them under in a rendition of hospital or military cornered perfection. His feet were now tightly constrained and bound in her unwelcomed shroud-like swaddling. No one spoke. But the temperature was rising and the boiling point was nearing.

She sat a minute or two and eyed the intravenous tubing and bottle of saline hanging above him. She seemed to be calculating the drops per minute or was clicking off some calculation in her head. Her expression was cocky, arched eyebrow and thoughtful tilt of her head. This was *her* territory. There was an occasional quick nod as if she endorsed the speed of the gravity-driven droplets. There was a stillness in the air similar to the airless silence before a tornado. A vacuum of sorts. She stood up and went to the other side of the bed to look closer at the intravenous tubing and small plastic knob and stopcock that adjusted the flow. It was as if she was challenging the system to misbehave. She confidently rolled her thumb and forefinger over the plastic wheel for a moment, but then, having duly identified her authority over the mechanism, turned to sit in a chair closest to Stephen's head. "Everything looks fine," she proclaimed.

Everything was as far from fine as it could possibly be. Her nephew sported a half a head of hair and an unknown prognosis. She had managed to cow us into silence as she so often did. The voice of confidence and authority coupled with our occasional need for a handout had stolen our ability to resist or protest. But this was not a stolen coat from the donation bag or a word challenge in a Scrabble game. The misery index had changed the rules. The blood boiling point was approaching a danger zone.

My brother, now as tightly bound to his bed as if he were indeed in a funeral shroud, looked at the night table on his right and then at Dorothy. In his newly constrained posture, only his left arm was unencumbered by intravenous lines or linens. Next to him on that table was a water pitcher (now filled with purple dyed water from the flowers, which occupied space in the previously functional vessel). There was a paper cup with some drinkable water and a large stainless-steel urinal standing in wait. It had a flat side, a spout, and an elongated handle that the patient might easily grab if needed. He had become very adept at using the vessel, and its contents remained for hours until they could be measured by a nurse and documented. It was, as Stephen knew, quite surely near full at the moment.

"Would you like some water?" Dorothy asked. Of course he couldn't drink and she had tainted the reservoir with the ugly flowers but pointed at the half-full paper cup.

"No, no thank you," he said, his voice trailing off as he arced his left hand over his head and reached for the urinal. He handily gripped the narrowed neck of the urinal and held it aloft a second or two in final contemplation of his intended move. It reminded me of how a priest might hold a chalice in reverence during communion. He studied it a second and then tilted it to the right and splashed its contents directly into Aunt Dorothy's face. The smell of penicillin-saturated urine was overpowering. There was shocked silence as the impact of the tornado was being assessed.

Silence ensued as she stood and wiped her face with her sleeve. She was horrified but maintained composure. The perfect nurse. She collected her coat and her husband and retreated rapidly to the bank of elevators. My mother waited a minute or two then spoke. "Well, that was well-deserved. I'll get the nurse to clean up the bed and throw out the flowers." After she left, I enjoyed the first good laugh I'd had with my brother in the longest time. We slipped back into silence. There was another visitor expected this evening. My brother had set the stage for defiance and decadent abandon. I was ready.

The sun had set. Steve settled into a quiet reverie in his dimly lit room. I doubt he enjoyed the now twinkling city lights and graceful string of "diamonds" on the fifty-ninth street bridge. People living in Sutton Place paid handsomely for the same view. In illness, the playing field is leveled. I imagine both the Sutton Place millionaire and my brother, in grave illness, would be unable to delight in that view. My mother and I retreated to the visitors' lounge to consider our private fears. Every few minutes a soft bell announced the opening of the elevator doors. Evenings were the busiest time for visitors. I had hoped my father would just fail to show up. I understood I would have to extend myself and be sociable. Both Stephen and my mother had made it clear they were in no mood to socialize or be distracted by the man who had become a ghost in our lives. I had seen him last in Florida. That visit apparently elevated my status as his closest relative here and now.

The bell announced a new load of visitors. I looked up and saw the now almost familiar face of my father. Once again, I was struck by our shared features. The slightly bulbous nose and large eyes (his blue, mine green) the full lips and broad forehead. Like me, he was neither tall nor slim. He entered the brightly lit corridor wearing Florida clothes in a New York winter. I shuddered in response to his too-light clothing and his intrusion in our lives.

Reflexively, we stood to greet him. He hugged my mother warmly and placed a protective arm around my shoulders. As they spoke in hushed tones about the surgery, his arm patted my back to denote the need for my continued silence and his awareness of my presence. Relieved by the need for silence, I glanced around the room and noticed a very young woman hovering nearby. Ironically, she too was dressed for summer. A short coral linen shift encrusted with an embroidered neckline in brilliant turquoise might have been an expensive Lilly Pulitzer creation. A light cardigan matched the trim. She was both leggy and petite and had perfectly straight and smooth long black hair held back by a simple headband. She may have been in her early twenties, but I wasn't sure. I was sure she was somehow connected to my father. The likelihood of two seasonally inappropriately clothed passengers standing in the same room and paying rapt attention to my mother's voice seemed unlikely. This lovely young thing had braved the cold and gloom of New York with my father. Their colorful clothing and tropical tans offended me. She cocked her head a bit to listen closely to my mother's words. A shaft of perfect, blunt cut silky hair swayed in response. I had brown wavy hair that tended toward frizz unless punished into obedience and flattened with an iron or rolled on hair rollers the size of soup cans. I marveled at the grace and flow of her hair. I had an encroaching awareness that they seemed to be a couple. My mother seemed newly aware of the hovering brightly covered figure in her peripheral vision. Now, we both trained our eyes on her. My father followed our gaze to the delicate coral colored seashell that had washed up on the wrong beach. He understood the need for an introduction or explanation. We waited.

"Oh, so sorry, this is Liz." He wore a sheepish smile. It was our turn to cock heads in curiosity. "Liz, is my…"

But my mother didn't wait for him to finish the sentence. "Sorry, Charles, but I have to get back to Steve. Why don't you and Liz and Barbara get acquainted over dinner. I'll see you later." She crisply pivoted and walked away, leaving me with two complete strangers.

I wore a heavy wool sweater and bell-bottom jeans. I felt bulky and bewildered as we walked to the elevators. Who was she? I wondered. We headed toward the hospital cafeteria. I was aware of walking in the wrong direction. I did not want to leave my brother's bedside. I was, uncharacteristically, not hungry. As I walked further away from where I wanted to be and those I preferred to be with, my anger mounted. Was I the sacrificial lamb offered up to assuage my father's guilty conscience? My anger mounted with each footstep. I looked at her again. *Who are you? Why are you here?* I thought. She might have been a natural enemy under any circumstance. After all, what insecure, chubby, frizzy haired, denim-clad teenager could find charity in her heart for the fine boned, silky haired, and well-dressed specimen who had casually looped a thin bare arm through her father's arm? Few, for sure, . Certainly not me.

I knew the labyrinth of hospital corridors well. There had been too many lonely walks and solitary meals of chicken noodle soup and saltine crackers at the end of this path. It had become familiar territory. And now, the ice cream colored pair of strangers walked behind me as I led them to food and war. They followed obediently. I picked up my pace to challenge them and expend some anger. *Let's go guys, pick up your pace. I feel a power surge rising.* I could hear her high heels clicking faster and faster. *Giddy-Up-Girl move faster, almost there.* The familiar smells of stale coffee and steamed vegetables greeted us. Wordlessly, we queued up on a long line of visitors, nurses, and doctors. We claimed three plastic trays and with my father in the lead made an unhappy Barbara sandwich. Dad on my right and Liz on my left. We eyed the gelatinous gravy over gray meat and lumpy mashed potatoes behind glass as if it was an interesting art exhibit. My father chose chicken noodle soup and crackers. We shared a broad nose and penchant for noodle soup. The miracle of genetics. I chose only my favorite desserts. Vanilla pudding and a fudgy brownie were perfect energy foods. I mentally converted the calories of each into energy needed to fire twin cannon balls at them. I looked left to observe her still empty tray. She was not eating it seemed. Fear may dampen an appetite, I mused. I looked at her straight on to enjoy the fear. Her eyes were indeed deer in headlights mode. I wondered if hunters ever took a final sympathetic look into the big brown eyes of their target before firing. I turned to my father and fired.

"So Dad, who exactly is Liz?" I tilted my head a bit left to make sure he saw the target as well. I was still speculating if she was a secretary, girlfriend, trophy wife, or another stepdaughter.

He looked benevolently at Liz, not me, and smiled. "Liz is a really special friend of mine," he answered.

I turned to see her reaction but just saw her wringing a paper napkin into a frayed knot. We took our trays to a table and sat. Now, I faced her and could pin her down like a butterfly about to become a specimen under glass. I savored a spoonful of vanilla pudding before I spoke. "Liz, and just how old are you anyway?" I smiled.

She looked desperately at my father and exhaled "In my twenties. Why?"

"Well, I'm just asking because I have no idea who you are and why you had the nerve to be here." I stared at her now. My father faltered and then squeezed her hand under the table.

Yes, Dad, she would need adult help to get out of this pickle. I wasn't done yet. "Dad, it looks like you're screwing someone young enough to be your daughter. You should have come alone, don't you think?" These were the very last words I ever spoke to my father. He had no answer. I stood and left them sitting speechless in the bright light and awful smell in the warm cafeteria in a bone-chilling cold New York. I retraced my steps to my brother's room. Stephen would have been proud of me. I had delivered the final fatal wound to my father. I felt empowered but never considered the finality of my words.

There was no time for reflection or indigestion this time. There were bigger wars to fight tomorrow. Now, the three closest soldiers gathered in a quiet hospital room to share the silence.

25 Battlefield

Sometimes, I think of that hospital meal as my own *Last Supper* moment. It was as transformational in defining the future. Jesus is said to have shared wine and unleavened bread with his apostles at his Last Supper. It is believed to be the first of all communions which offer up the symbolic foods as his body and blood, in eternal life. Jews like to believe Jesus and his clan were enjoying a Passover Seder at the Last Supper. There, they celebrated the liberation of Jews from the evil repressive king. And for me, it was vanilla pudding and a fudge brownie that marked my liberation and emergence into a formal and permanent fatherless world. I understand now that the meal was transformational. It marked the last living vestige of a doomed relationship.

Regardless of who Liz was, she represented all the women my father chose above me. There was the singing cocktail waitress, and the imagined blond and braided trio of stepdaughters. There was the shattered and broken stepdaughter and other girls and wives I never knew. And there was the eventual news of a third wife and a replacement daughter and son born so many years after he left us. In 1980, a lawyer's letter helped to answer some unanswered questions. The year before Steve's illness, a daughter had been born, a son, seven years after that. There was Rebecca and Charles to replace Barbara and Stephen. He left behind four children who remained strangers to each other. He was also a stranger. Perhaps, I wonder now, If I'd not left behind a greasy pastrami sandwich or an unfinished fudge brownie I may have come to know him. I may have known half-siblings. There may have been a final opportunity on the eve of Stephen's surgery. For so many years, it never mattered. There was the business of Stephen's recovery and moving forward again through hopeful and normal life without a father. There seemed no reason to care about who he really was. We resumed being a family and force of three. He receded into some nebulous place reserved for long-dead ancestors or infamous dignitaries with no concrete connection to the present. But the present is a dynamic entity, clinging to its own ancestry in spite of us.

In the absence of a father, the first surgery took forty-three minutes. Two weeks later, the second procedure was completed in just twenty minutes. The aneurysms were repaired, his heart restarted and the sawed bones of the skull left as vulnerable soft spots on either side of his head where the dark brown hair regrew and covered all evidence of the daring intrusion. These two procedures were the genesis of all modern neurosurgical techniques.

They are considered landmarks, and Dr. Russell Patterson an iconic pioneer. Stephen's reward was continued life, not fame. For the next six weeks, we cautiously tracked his progress and recovery. Initially, we waited for consciousness to return, then movement in his fingers, feet and limbs. The fear mounted as he was challenged with following simple commands by blinking or nodding or squeezing a hand. Speech was slow to return, his chosen words at first unintelligible and disarticulate. He was aphasic. My mother remembered the explanation of stroke-like results because the parietal lobe might be compromised. I silently wondered if he would ever be able to return to school and a normal life. *How awful it will be*, I thought, *if he can think and know but not communicate*. My daily trips after school continued. My mother had not returned to her job. Our job, our vocation and our mission, was to stand vigil and be witness to the unknown outcome. Together, we willed him to improve. We projected love and positive energy and unwavering belief in his recovery. My mother was nothing short of a Herculean Goddess in her commitment to total control of this earthly setback. All other mortals and issues receded in shadow. That included long-lost fathers.

Two long months after the harrowing ride to the hospital, he returned home. His speech returned to normal, he regained some strength, but had missed a semester of school. Friends visited and his interest in the world around him returned. Some visitors continued to be a source of angst.

Aunt Dorothy and Uncle Walter waited several weeks before asking to visit. I imagine she was licking her wounds and searching for her better angels to stifle her hubris. On a cloudy Sunday afternoon, they arrived bearing an assortment of cakes left over from her Friday mah-jongg game. The grease-stained bakery box with re-tied red string held crumbs of chocolate babka and cheese Danish. It was an improvement over dyed mums and baby's breath. The Corningware percolator soon filled the kitchen with the welcome smell of coffee. Stephen rested on the sofa while my mother entertained her brother and sister-in-law. I hovered between both rooms, keen to a new formality. Easy conversation was handicapped in the absence of a Scrabble game. Those little wooden tiles had always served as a bridge across the chasm of two women steeped in differences and seething with resentment. Long minutes of quiet thoughtfulness over seven half-inch squares bearing a single letter and point value masked the underlying bitterness. It's entirely possible that their consistently high combined scores (usually an impressive eight hundred points) was fueled by the increased flow of metabolic chemicals and improved cognition secondary to pure anger. But that afternoon, Scrabble seemed an inappropriate pastime. This was a "sick" visit with an understanding of limited time constraints. We were well schooled in financial constraints. My mother understood this visit would address both constraints. Before they arrived, I questioned her.

"Mom, are you a little nervous about seeing her again?" I asked. I'm sure we both recalled the lasting image of her wiping urine from her shocked face. There had been several short and perfunctory telephone calls about the status of Stephen's health and recovery. But we had not seen them in more than a month. Scrabble games and leftover cake were put aside.

"Why should I be nervous? I didn't throw piss in her face, your brother did. Well-deserved I might add. I can handle Dorothy, don't worry," she said and returned to looking for matching plates.

But I understood that my ego-bound and too proud aunt was a formidable opponent. "Do you think she will ask him to apologize?" I worried for my brother's health and about his temper.

My mother looked at me with a trace of what I recognized as sarcasm on its way. "She won't be looking for an apology. She may be looking to save money."

I was confused. I'd known they sent money, but never considered how much or for how long the arrangement was agreed upon, if ever. "So," I continued. "They are just coming to see if we need more help I guess."

"Ha, that's funny. No, my dear, I doubt that. Your aunt is not the most charitable person. Let's just say she thinks Stephen is the dog that bit the hand that fed it." She elaborated. "Bitten on the hand, peed on her coat, whatever. It's all the same. We are no longer her favorite charity or her favorite pet."

Now, I was concerned. The absence of income and mounting bills weighed heavily on my mother. She had casually mentioned a possible return to work in the spring. I understood she needed to. She was adept at dodging the bills that, like dogs, were constantly nipping at her heels. But now, a different animal was chasing her and dodging would be difficult. She was masterful at juggling minimum payments and extending due dates with emotional appeals. She knew how to alter cutoff dates and charm the most determined of debt collectors. She danced up and down and around all the notes of poverty's fiddle in a nimble jig any Irishman would praise. Step up! Step high! Step forward, then back! Hop high! Spin around! Turn this way and that! Kick, jump high! Smile, always smile! Hold that head up high! A nimble dancer was my mother.

And I excelled at patience and understanding. I always believed poverty was transient. I understood this about many bad things. I wore the same blue denim wrap skirt to school every day of my junior year in high school. It looked like every other skirt that was the fashion of the day for sixteen-year-old girls. I washed and rotated the three cotton print shirts that were also ubiquitous and unremarkable. I could take fashion chances with eye makeup or different shades of white lipstick. I'd become skilled in the art of collecting soda bottles for deposit returns. The hours between six and nine in the evening most weekdays yielded the largest harvest of glass. That was subway fare. These coping skills are not taught in any public or private high school. They are not taught in finishing schools or in summer school. They were my own lessons. They are lessons I was privileged to have. There is more skill than shame in mastering the "Poverty-Jig."

And when humor intersects with desperation it is that much richer. On the rare occasions I asked for new shoes or a sweater or shirt, my mother's predictable response was this. "Rich or poor, it is good to have money. But right now, there is none to be had." Woody Allen put it another way in his humorous writing. *Money is better than poverty, if only for financial reasons.* We understood that. We were managing. My mother never spoke about rent or bills in my brother's presence. In fact, she had promised him that upon his full recovery, she would buy him the smallest used sailboat she could find. She secretly hoped a dinghy would suffice. But Stephen dreamed of owning a Dragonfly series sailboat. He had chosen its name already, "Aeolus the keeper of the winds." Her beloved son could once again dream of a future. She believed his recovery was linked to hope. If that hope hinged on images of windblown hair and control of the world by the tilt of a single canvas sail, it would be his. She understood that he needed to dream of more than school and grades. She was committed to fulfilling his dream. Returning to work was step one in squirrelling away bits of money toward that goal. I never doubted her earnest intent to fulfill his wish.

Stephen yawned dramatically and lay his head back on the pillow with an exaggerated thud. He was signaling the end of the visit to Aunt Dorothy. No penicillin stinking urine splattered to her face was needed. The not too subtle message was understood and their mission had now been accomplished. He appropriately welcomed the news that cousin Mark had chosen Cornell and that it would be expensive. He listened to their cheerful banter with a fixed smile. I silently absorbed the meaning of this visit. I would later recall each detail as I struggled to frame an elusive truth about their relationship to us. They kissed him quickly on the cheek and promised to visit again soon. When the door had slammed shut, my mother joined us in the living room.

"Well, how did that go?' she asked with a smirk on her face.

"Jeez Mom, they really want you to get back to work fast. I didn't know they are paying our bills, but they sure are worried about affording Cornell next year for Mark. I didn't even know that little putz was old enough for college. When are you planning on going back? I am really okay to be alone. Barbara is home by three almost every day and if you leave lunch, I'm good."

She was speechless and infuriated. How dare they burden him with worry? How dare they use him to reinforce their message? How dare they steal away his hope? The battlelines were drawn.

She returned to work exactly two weeks later as planned. The rent and utility bills were paid on time and she took twenty-five dollars out of each bi-weekly paycheck to save for the boat. *Aeolus* would be a reality. There is an old French proverb that says: "Hunger drives the wolf out of the wood." The fangs were bared. She let Dorothy and Walter know she was financially independent. Visits to their apartment in Alley Pond Park had ceased completely. A new rhythm of phone calls and rare visits to our apartment complete with strong coffee, high Scrabble scores, and small talk defined the relationship for the next decade. Her words had hurled us away from her but brought us closer to each other. Many years after that, hurtful words by Aunt Dorothy would corrupt my own core beliefs. For now, I learned the lessons of hope and determination.

My brother's greatest scar was a distillate of anger which seeped into his soul and seasoned the flavor of his relationships. He had grown up with rejection by the father he had known and loved his first five years.

Outraged at his return on the cusp of his adolescence, he defiantly ignored him. Somehow, he had overcome this anger by excelling in every arena of his life. He was handsome, smart, and charming. He was seemingly unscathed as he succeeded at anything he put his mind to. He was the hungriest of hungry wolves. He was hell-bent at proving his value. A young man without a male role model designing his own image to perfection. And just as he sat poised to launch into manhood with a bounty of blessings, the meanest of winters, the cruelest twist of fate, had reminded him of his vulnerability. He was forced to fight for survival. He was brave and determined, but he was also outraged. He was enraged. Enraged at his absent father and the presence of his well-heeled but stingy relatives. Enraged at the simple bad luck of it all. Enraged by his struggle to remember words and then what it was he ever wanted to begin with.. He survived in spite of it all. But his teeth were sharper and his patience was thin. He spared no one his charm or wit. But when it came to love and trust, the wolf took just tentative bites which he savored but often had trouble sharing. But our pack of alpha mom and her beta cubs were comfortable in our own love and hierarchy. It was time to consider a better future.

Aeolus was perhaps twelve feet long. He stenciled the letters in gold and outlined them in red enamel paint. The tiny boat was moored in an almost invisible space in a boatyard on City Island. He spent as many days as possible tending its needs and sailing alone on the Long Island Sound. If he had found first love on Block Island the summer before, he discovered the love of solitude shared only with screeching seagulls and gusts of wind that summer. It was exactly the space needed to consider there might be good fortune and better days ahead. My mother had indeed provided him with the most important part of recovery, hope. I joined him on *Aeolus* just one time. The wind was stiff and challenging. He was exhilarated. I was frightened by the bobbing and constant need to shift from side to side. I bent backward at times in an unnatural arc and attempt to stay afloat. I was soon nauseous and later more frightened than nauseous. We were nothing more than a paper boat on a rough sea. I pleaded with him to get back quickly. He assured me the winds were our friend and would deliver us to safety. I wondered at his calm belief in the wind as our ally. His command and joy at the challenge were in sharp contrast to my fear and impatience. He couldn't help but be amused at my whining but eventually caught the small sail in a gust of wind that was my friend and brought us back to the safety of the wood pilings. He had conquered a fear of the unknown and his ability to survive. He had defied the odds before and believed that Aeolus, the god of wind, the conqueror of storms, had guided him home.

26 Aftertaste

We were altered by having survived the nightmare. An angrier but more determined Stephen returned to NYU, where he maintained perfect grades and a full scholarship. There was an ever so subtle change in his persona. As if someone had adjusted a camera lens to its sharpest longer focal view, forming a sharp, crisp image of a single subject. Where there had been soft edges and indistinct blurring allowing the viewer the latitude of suggestion, there now was little room for interpretation. He bluntly stated what he thought and clearly articulated his preferences. He was no longer interested in becoming a doctor or engineer. He would not follow a path others had defined as ideal for him. He may or may not go to graduate school at all. All of his decisions were now nonnegotiable. He began dating an NYU student whom my mother clearly disliked. She was silent and sullen and looked too Bohemian. Her long dark hair and eyes coupled with a withdrawn demeanor troubled my mother. There was no comfort in the fact that she was Jewish and obviously intelligent. He seemed to have chosen the antithesis of his own mother's more playful and engaging personality. The girl's family life was in stark contrast to his. Her parents were married, financially stable homeowners from Queens. She had an older brother and live-in grandma (Bubba). Scratching the surface of this tableau revealed sex abuse, a domineering father, and constant fighting. My brother found someone who needed him. My mother had needed him. Now another young woman needed him. He immersed himself in being present for and adored by her. In her dark silence and withdrawal, he was able to navigate for both of them without question. I think he welcomed an opportunity to be in control and she found safety in the inertia of his control. They were engaged by the time they graduated together from NYU. He had become an independent, strong willed and self-directed young man. He was, ironically, more his father's son as he graduated from the same stage, which faced the iconic University Heights Hall of Fame and the Harlem River, as his father had done little more than thirty years before. My mother spent the afternoon immersed in memories of Charles's graduation when they, too, were newly engaged and her future mother-in-law took every opportunity to reject her. History was, indeed, repeating itself. Could a more learned psychologist speculate that he was conquering his father by emulating him? Was he just evolving through the stages of recovery and maturation? An argument for nature versus nurture could be considered as well. I am a nurse and better suited to more concrete problems. My father was a civil engineer. He created elaborate blueprints and designs drafted on tiny grids. Stephen had a natural ability to build model airplanes and boats in miniature scale with hundreds of seemingly unrelated pieces. Stephen could sculpt chunks of wood into lovely whittled animals. Like his father, he was charming and intelligent. He enjoyed an extremely close relationship with his mother, and now, he had become aloof and slightly egocentric. A newly emerged man now struggled to reconcile his similarities and differences. Distancing himself from both parents was a healthy attempt to construct his own identity.

There was never a conversation about including my father in the academic milestone. His name had not been mentioned in three years. His presence at the event was only a symbolic one. I wore his ten-karat gold college key on a chain which I discreetly tucked into the top of my summer dress. In tiny relief letters and numerals, the year, 1939, and words College of Engineering, New York University warmed against my skin. It somehow felt right to me to include the man I had also rejected.

The question of rejection confuses me. Did I reject him because he had rejected me? Did I reject him to please my mother? Did I reject him because it was well past the time that having a father in my life mattered? Is there ever such a time? There is no comfort I find in the power of rejection or in the state of being angry. Unlike my brother, I prefer understanding and conciliation. I prefer sunshine to rain. My mother had a favorite fable she loved to recant. She thought it described her attitude about inequity in life. I think she liked the inequity part more than the attitude part. Her version was often personalized or adapted to a current situation:

A pair of brothers very close in age grew up knowing that the older brother was always favored. He was showered with attention, praise, and lovely gifts. The younger boy lived in his shadow and accepted his family status. In fact, he loved his older brother and rarely complained. On the Christmas the boys were ten and twelve years old, a special gift was presented to them. Tethered to the white split-rail fence outside their house was a beautiful palomino pony, with a large red bow affixed to his saddle. The horse was the older boy's gift. Next to the pony was a large shovel staked into a pile of manure that had collected next to the animal. The shovel was the younger brother's gift. He clapped happily and thanked his parents. His older brother asked how he could be happy with that gift. "Oh, I am so excited to start digging. I know my pony is right there under that pile. I can't wait to see him."

Maybe I am, in essence, that younger brother, or sister.. I never completely closed the door on wanting a father. In spite of his absence and my mother's occasional disparaging references to his indifference and imagined luxurious lifestyle, I silently refused to let go. I refused to accept blanket dismissal of him as selfish and disinterested. Perhaps if I dug just a little more, I might find something. I teetered on a razor sharp tightwire where loyalty versus discovery challenged my desire to step in either direction. I buried thoughts of who he was under heavily weighted layers of everyday events. The next six years marked major milestones in my life that pulled and tugged like a tightwire into a taut blade, which sometimes forced me to act, albeit timidly. Occasionally I took a shaky foot off the straight line and tentatively tested the empty space. With each major milestone in my life as a newly emerging adult, I considered what he might think about an achievement. What it might be like to have two proud parents.

My high school yearbook shows a bedroom-eyed brunette with windswept bangs and her career choice neatly printed under the black and white photo. The audacity of that label has never been lost on me. After graduating with a bottom of the class GPA, a trail of summer school makeup grades, and an absence of awards or achievements, I was alone in believing my goal could be achieved. My mother had predicted a career behind the lipstick counter at Woolworth's or as a typist in some insurance agency if I buckled down. I like to believe she said these things to motivate me because they may have. The guidance counselor in my all-girls high school suggested night school to learn math fundamentals before considering formal applications. I was quickly ushered out of her office so she could attend to the girls with good grades, high scores on the SATs, portfolios that included service offices held and extracurricular club participation. They may also have had parents who took home all those glossy college brochures and did the obligatory visits to potential campuses. The almost three years I had spent volunteering at Montefiore Hospital every Wednesday, or my summer jobs there, had never been considered. No one had considered my absolute conviction to this single goal. Had anyone bothered to ask this graduating senior why she wanted to be a nurse, they may have shared my confidence. Had they bothered to ask, I may have told them about my brother's illness and what it felt like to be completely powerless in the face of death, pain, and physical incompetence. Being sick was worse than being poor. Both robbed you of choice and dignity. I completely understood the power of the people wearing white uniforms. Their position in the hospital provided immunity it seemed. They were respected, financially stable humans who also could help others. Had anyone probed further, I may have told them about my aunt Dorothy. I often disliked her, I sometimes feared her, but I completely respected her authority and self-confidence. My mother called her opinionated and cocky. When she won a contentious game of Scrabble, my mother said those exact words to her. "Ha," she chuckled and clucked, "But you are wrong. It's not cocky, its confidence." My mother was quickly silenced, and I had years and years to consider that statement. I loved her retort although I was never sure if I loved Aunt Dorothy. In the absence of anyone asking why or how I would achieve this goal, I was launched with greater amounts of optimism and determination than confidence.

I watched *General Hospital* every afternoon. I continued to volunteer on Wednesdays, and I attended night school four nights a week to take remedial math courses. My classmates were other people with inferior pedigrees. They were high school dropouts and immigrants from countries I'd never heard of. They were hairdressers and the lipstick counter girls from Woolworth's. We did equations and fractions and math word problems and practical math and square roots and powers and any other thing you could do with numbers to elevate their status in importance. I hated every digit in any of its forms. A curvy eight or sinewy two or serious straight-edged one or four were all just meaningless symbols that I would need to manipulate into compliance and commit to memory. And so, I did. And when I did, they rewarded my obedience with a grade enabling me to apply as a non-matriculated student in a community college. And when I proved there that I could manipulate and discipline my own mind into dedicated thought, I was again rewarded with perfect grades in English Composition 1 and History 1, and yes, Basic Math Skills 1, and I was admitted to Bronx Community College School of Nursing as a full-fledged, full-time nursing student. And two years later, I graduated from that nursing school with a near perfect GPA of 3.96. Organic Chemistry prevented me from graduating with a perfect 4.0 GPA. And when I graduated, my mother and my brother watched proudly as I received my Associates Degree, earned a nursing cap, and easily passed my Nursing Boards that August. Had anyone bothered to ask what I was thinking four years after leaving high school, I might have told them I believed in the power of shovels staked in shit and what might be found there.

Incomplete. I didn't think of that word until several milestones later. But it was the first time I entertained the thought of contacting my father to share an achievement. We no longer had an address or phone number for him. I imagine it would not have been difficult to find him. Facebook, the internet, Google searches and Ancestry DNA kits were not yet a part of American life. An old-fashioned White Pages telephone book or personal detective would have been the starting point. I was unaware then of the existence of his new children. By then, the oldest, Rebecca, was six and the youngest, Charles, was about to be born. I was twenty-one. That knowledge would have been liberating. Surely, I would have understood that my existence and achievements were as relevant as an outdated driver's license to him. But I thought then that we were his only children. "Mom," I asked after passing my boards, "do you think I should try to let my father know I'm a nurse now?" I reflected on my fiery last conversation with him, ironically in a hospital. Was he angry enough at my behavior then to finally forget about me, about us? Did he ever find out that Stephen had survived and finished college? Had he ever written to or called my mother? I assumed he had not. It hadn't mattered until a subliminal awareness that my own fruition was not a solitary achievement had entered my thoughts. The "Now," I reasoned, was a product of an inversely timed sequence of past moments in time. It was the present considering its own past. Time, which included all the people and events that had aligned by intention or accident to bring me here. Somewhere in the convoluted and tangled place that brought me here was my father. The subliminal slid from some foggy place to sharp clarity that pierced the peace I'd lived with. It was as if I'd been staring at my own image in the soft comfort of a fogged-over bathroom mirror after a steamy shower. The door had cracked open an inch or two, letting cool air push into the smaller space, the fog became small rivulets that ran in unpredictable paths and yielded snippets of clarity. The emerging image less forgiving. "Mom? Should I try to call him?"

"Do what you want," she responded with the caustically casual flick of her head I recognized as annoyance. "Why not? Of course, why does he deserve to know anything about either of you? He really does not deserve the time of day. What did he contribute to your success for God's sake?"

I was silenced. I was rendered instantly ashamed and guilty for even suggesting he be rewarded for his absence by good news.

"Of course, Barbara, it's totally your decision," she added. "I don't want to influence you. If it makes you happy to let him know, then go right ahead."

I instinctively closed the door to the small fissure that offered clarity at the expense of losing the warm comfort of fog that blurred and softened the edges of reality.

Was this the epitome of Jewish guilt? There are so many genres of guilt. Is there a special category for children of divorce, or of single parents? Maybe there is even a category for about to be emancipated young adults who have the audacity to offer up something culturally repugnant to the parents who spent years imbuing their offspring with values they assumed were permanently instilled. Maybe, in my case, I won the trifecta and could claim all of the above. But, of course, I countered, in the storm that was my mind, she is right. Had he ever been there long enough for anything that mattered in our lives? Did less than a forty-hour work week worth of visits and dinners stretched out over a few years count? Of course not. How could they? There was not even a question about what the right thing was to do. I was sorry I had asked. I was sorry I had hurt her. This was a firmly tied knot on one end of a tightrope that spanned the next eight years of milestones. It was anchored at the other side by the final tautly pulled and immovable twin leading me painfully to its end. I could dismount in 1980 when the end freed me from choice. The death of my father in that year ended all question of what to do. I learned then of his other children and the strange circumstances of his death. He had been stabbed to death and died leaving no assets other than four children who were perfect strangers and a legacy of unanswered questions. I felt strangely empty. There was no longer any need for guilt or anger or decision. There was an empty space a father should have occupied. A space better filled with grief than indifference. It was his final betrayal and my lost opportunity.

27 A Father's Daughter

There was a new void where old questions had lived. Who was my father? I believed he had loved me once then left. I thought that before there was a new family and another set of children, he had reached out in feeble attempts to recapture his role of father to children who had become strangers in his absence. He may have tried to be this daughter's father. I embraced the chance to know him then. In spite of the disparate worlds we lived in, I was less impressed by airplane rides or vichyssoise and lobster dinners than by the nasal softness of his voice which I think I always knew. I was taken not by the vision of pagoda rooflines and a faux Polynesian structure in Miami Beach but by the understanding of a familiarity in the potential of a blank page and promise of a pencil or paintbrush in my own hand. His lust for luxury and determination to possess his share were always the same as the forces that drove me. My mother was content in the belief that her wealth of knowledge and appreciation for luxury were gifts she could settle for. Gifts that put her in a superior position but which, I believe, ate away at her self-esteem and sense of fairness. Those gifts brought her more anger than pleasure. My father understood that he was the rightful owner of the luxuries he loved. I am my father's daughter. My brother is his father's son. We have spent our adult lives emulating his patterns in the absence of having him as a present role model. We collect the art and furnishings we love. We write books and try our hands at painting and sculpting and crafts that come and go on a whim. We are his children.

We are never, ever practical. We consider debt a reasonable alternative to not owning the painting we fell in love with or the finer silk rug over a more affordable facsimile. We don't consider settling for less until we hit a wall that sobers us for a short time. We are greedy for what we believe we are entitled to by virtue of loving it more than we can stand. We are unapologetic for our lust. Martyrdom or apology are not in our DNA. Our mother was practical and self-sacrificing and martyred in that role. She gave us security and knowledge and lots of laughter. She gave us books and adventure and a love of nature. She instilled empathy in us and intellectual curiosity. She modelled what commitment to family and practical choices were about. But there was always more that existed in our germinating path to maturity. There was the unknown and incomplete part of the whole that couldn't be denied. It would rear its head from time to time and confront me with its reality. In those early years of remarkable milestones, there was a small voice that snuck out from some dark and hair-like fissure and called to me in its soft and nasal voice. It called out and asked me to acknowledge it. I responded with my own feeble attempts at being a father's daughter.

All the world's a stage, and all the men and women are merely players. They have their exits and their entrances. And one man in his time plays many parts. Shakespeare's comedy, *As You Like It*, succinctly defines the seven ages of man in the voice of a melancholy Jaques. In playing our parts, I wonder, how tethered we are to the past or aware of a future. Our adult lives and roles shift around ever-changing desires and casts of characters. It is a subtle shifting without a closing curtain or dimming of lights to warn us of last chances. Is melancholy avoidable?

Seen in retrospect, I can demarcate my own transformative exits stage left or stage right. Awareness at the time was as elusive as capturing a breeze as it slipped through my fingers. I realize now, that in Acts Two and Three of my life, full of desire and success and evolution, I played my role with devotion to my part as my mother's loyal daughter, Stephen's loving sister, then as a young mother and wife, with a set determination to goals. I consciously chose to ignore the breeze that gently nudged me from time to time. I had prompts, which may have stirred me to act, but with each opportunity, with each milestone, it was so much easier to enjoy the soft comfort of a gentle breeze and ignore voices that nudged me to consider their sound. I turned a deaf ear.

Over the next decades of reaped rewards for hard work and collective second and third decade milestones, I claimed my bounty with the casual confidence of a farmer's wife gathering the fragile and variegated eggs she owns and then shares as a matter of course. I was completely in control of how and with whom I shared my gains. Only rarely did I consider my father's rightful place in the audience of recipients. Engagements, a wedding, and impending motherhood were the formal prompts that offered islands of clarity in the soft blanket of fog that embraced me. Clarity which I occasionally acknowledged and casually dismissed.

"Henri Bendel? Really Barbara. A wedding gown there will cost twice as much as it would at Fontana's (our local bridal salon)." My mother was appalled at my choices. I sported a three-karat diamond engagement ring set in platinum. Fortunately for me, an elder cousin of my mother's with a Madison Avenue jewelry store had tired of the bauble and offered it to my fiancé at its original wholesale cost. I felt entitled and fortunate. I was my father's daughter after all. I was also a mother's daughter and had grown up surrounded by classic books and poetry and cheap reproductions of fine art in flimsy wood frames. I grew up on a steady diet of obscure Scrabble words used awkwardly in contrived conversation. They fit like rented patent leather shoes matched to a single evening's tuxedo. I grew up with a mother who befriended a talented seamstress. I studied the pattern-filled white packets with drawings of dresses by Chanel or Dior. I watched the patterns come to life in fine fabrics I learned the names of as if required vocabulary. I came to know and revere the importance of French seams and fine tailoring. The straight broken white lines of chalk marks on an inseam or hem held the promise of destinations more exciting than any road map. I traveled to Europe through the romantic movies my mother insisted I adore with her. *My Fair Lady* and *Gigi* and *The Sound of Music* were revered opportunities for sightseeing. No detail was left unexplored and was supported by historical information she felt compelled to add. The origin of a beret or construction of the Eiffel Tower. The fragrance and delicacy of edelweiss. The brutality of war and skeptical hope for happy endings. Her ability to live vicariously and absorb facts was incredible...and always struck me as pitifully unfair. I would not live vicariously. All her beauty, all her knowledge and understanding, filled her with unending angst and an undercurrent of outrage at being denied. She was an aristocrat by proxy. Her entitlement ended with the reality of poverty. The ugly plastered walls of Bronx apartments and real income that afforded travel to work and not the larger world gnawed at her spirit and shadowed our lives. Now empowered by my own appreciation instilled by her and lust for finer things inherited from my father, I considered the future. I would not be denied the things I loved, even as I acknowledged the underbelly of that want. I was, undeniably, also my father's daughter.

I imagined an undeserving father whom I imagined enjoyed a life of luxury denied his first family. He was educated and ambitious and selfish. I assumed he was wealthy and well-traveled. How else would he know about Hilton Hotels, live jazz and vichyssoise? I considered his lack of responsibility. He took what he wanted to have in this world. He left what he had tired of. That was the narrative I was raised on. The narrative I never questioned until I understood that, like him, I would have what I wanted because it was better to act on ambition than to lament its elusive nature. I loved my mother but would reject the legacy of being a victim. I could not know my father to love him, but I would not hate his ambition or reject his infusion of self-directed mobility that lived in my own marrow. I was the daughter of two people, one I loved unconditionally. Love that tethered me with a need to please and compensate and the other, unloved parent that covertly begged for recognition and crept from under the long shadow cast by mother's sadness.

"This is the dress I'm buying. Look Mom, the Alencon lace is patterned like lily of the valley. It's exquisite."

"Do you think anyone will really notice that detail?" my mother responded and flicked her blond bangs away in annoyance.

"Who cares? I know they are lily of the valley and that is worth every penny of this three thousand dollars." That was a significant amount in 1970, perhaps not insignificant today. "This is my dress," I proclaimed with finality.

"You are your father's daughter. Sometimes I can't believe how much you sound like him. Why do you feel so entitled to this ridiculously expensive choice?"

"Because Mom, I am entitled to it. I understand the details others may not notice. I love the fine lace and simple style. But, because it is my money. I have worked hard to be a nurse. I have saved some of my salary to buy this dress and that totally entitles me to it. I am its rightful owner." That moment of clarity through fog shined brilliantly. I was now contributing to household expenses at home as a grateful and dutiful daughter. I felt no guilt for my choice. Unlike my father, I was not selfish, but, like my father, I would have what I wanted, rather than only wish for it. I was the rightful owner of beautiful things. I would not be denied. I would not be practical. I would not be sorry.

Weeks before my wedding, I revisited a question I had presented three times before, albeit timidly. "Mom, do you think my father should know I am getting married?" I had posed this question when I graduated high school, nursing school, and when I got engaged to be married. There was a part of wholeness I missed. Unlike my brother and my mother, I could never sustain the hatred and resentment of a man I suspected of being more than a villain. In my collective set of memories and knowledge were images of a man with my features taking me out to dinner and sending letters with words that looked like dancing ribbons. There was a man who could design fairy tale buildings that were little more than whimsical facades. It was hard to dislike beautiful things, even if they were only facades.

The question was always answered in the same flat-toned manner. "You are a big girl, Barbara, it's totally your decision. If you want him to be invited, go ahead." A pregnant silence would be followed by a more elaborate response. "Of course, he doesn't deserve any credit for raising you. He doesn't deserve to have any pride or pleasure in the event. But, if it makes you happy, go ahead." Sometimes, she would offer more specific details of her struggle as a single parent or of his presumed indifference to where we lived, what we ate, how we dressed, our childhood diseases, my miserable psoriasis, Stephen's brush with death or her refusal to introduce another man in her life because we deserved her undivided attention. She would offer speculative details of swimming pools and indulged new families living in perpetual Miami sunshine. I never opted to extend an invitation. I never even considered writing him to share news. How could I consider such betrayal? It was just easier to dismiss the random thought as easily as brushing away a stray hair blowing across your face. My mother held enormous power which she now exerted. Was she evening the score for how vulnerable and powerless she felt all those years before?

And then I became a mother. The question of contacting my father, of telling him he was now a grandfather, receded into a backdrop of joy and juggling the details of my life. I was now more mother than daughter to anyone. I may have considered a call but not too deeply. Was it too late? I was thirty-three in 1980. I was the young working mother of a one- and three-year-old set of my own sons. I was, as Shakespeare might offer, a busy soldier committed to my cause and making my mark. The stage and cast of characters were set in delightful frenzied motion. I understood there was time ahead and other acts to follow. How could I have known that the role of father would be written out of the script? There would never be an opportunity to know who the grandfather of my children, my absent father, my mother's unfaithful husband, and the man who looked so much like me was. I could never know if he ever loved me. I could never know if he tried to be there or really didn't care. I would never know if he, too, was sad. Was there a narrative about his leaving I never heard? How fortunate

I was that he left when I was just three. There might have been at least a year preceding that of a torrid affair and long absences. So, I was perhaps less than two when his presence mattered. All I may have ever really known was a loving mother. I may never have uttered a single word in his presence. He may never have read me a story or carried me on his shoulders. My early and only memory of him is of a swinging foot and crossed-over leg. I liked to sit at his foot and hear his voice. I do remember the smell of cherry pipe tobacco. These are snippets of history I own. That rudimentary anchor was surely easy enough to pull away from and move on. I don't own much of the history about him that nurtured me. I never really owned being abandoned. My brother, at five, grieved the loss of a father he must have needed and loved. My mother must have raged at being left to raise his children alone. But I was the lucky one. I had no need for grief or anger. I had no reason for it then or need for it later. Initially, I felt nothing about his death. I was dispassionate. How could I grieve what I hadn't had? How could I be as joyful as my brother or mother when I'd never for a moment hated this stranger? The letter brought no more than shocking news about a near stranger. I marveled at feeling nothing about a father's death. It was just news, but it brought information that I would speculate about for the remainder of my life.

28 Just Desserts

The phone call came first. It was dinner time on a Tuesday evening. Bath time for the kids, dinner on the stove, and a collection of matchbox cars and colorful plastic nesting toys or shape sorting pieces scattered across the floor. "Hi, are you busy?" Mom's relaxed after-work voice on the kitchen phone.

I navigated the twelve-foot cord to peek around the corner and check on the kids. "Yeah, but I just have a minute, everything okay?" That question was always first. I worried about her. She had survived an aggressive form of uterine cancer just months after my first son's birth. His first nine months of life are memorable for Mom living at our house. Strapped in his car seat, my eldest son joined us as we drove to Mount Sinai for months of chemotherapy, preceded by daily trips to an Upper East Side radiologist for weeks of radiation. In between and after those trips were weekly visits to a psychiatrist to help her cope with a combination of depression and anxiety. Mark, at less than a year old, was a sweet and mellow baby who hummed and lulled himself to sleep in the car. By the time he celebrated his first birthday, she was both physically and psychologically healthy. She returned to her own home and her job part time during treatment. She had faced her illness and recovery with resolve, but her illness had created a new element to our relationship. I lived in fear of losing her but also about her recurrent anxiety and depression. I wanted nothing more than to see my mother happy and healthy. She visited our home several times a week. She was helpful and loving but intrusive. It was a strange dynamic of having dual roles. I was demoted to being a child in my own home. Daily decisions about childcare or food were dictated by her, but I was the mother of a fifty-nine-year-old fragile woman who spoke of death and illness frequently. At just thirty-three years old, I was as insecure about losing her as a toddler might be on a first day of nursery school. Surely, this exaggerated response is not uncommon with most children raised in single parent homes. Do those rules apply to grown-up children also? Overdependence seems a logical response. If I were born with a single kidney, I might guard and overprotect the remaining lifeline most carefully. I took my cues from Mom. If she was happy, I was happy. If she was worried, I worried as well. If she was angry, then I would try to share her outrage or opinion. I was hurled back in time. And now, she was so excited to share some news on the telephone.

"I need to come over and show you a letter I received today." Her words rolled out with a rapid and upbeat tone.

I immediately thought of a monetary windfall. A Pavlovian response to an impoverished childhood based on no logical rationale. "Can you tell me over the phone?" I asked. I had not planned on her for dinner, was busy with chores, and anxious to hear her news.

"Okay, I guess so. Why not? So I got this very thick letter from a law firm in Florida. It seems they were hired by a private detective to find me." She halted dramatically, I thought. Private detectives? Looking for my mother? Why? The wheels spun in my head without gaining ground. She paused. I heard her sigh and thought about Florida. That could only mean Charles Payne. My only link to Florida. She continued. "Well, I guess this is shocking news but not really. Your father is dead."

My mind went back to her first statement. "I guess so. Why not?" she had said. Why not? Why not? And as casually as a discussion of what she was having for dinner, I learned that the clock had stopped for my father. It was a nonnegotiable and simple fact delivered casually in a rushed phone call.

The next day, she came over. She had called my brother the night before as well. We spent the following evening reading and digesting every detail of that five-page letter. The intent of the letter was to have Stephen and me sign off as legal claimants and heirs to a worthless estate. There was so much information to digest in the letter. We processed it like a rich dessert we should savor. Delicious, decadent joy with little thought to consequence. Those first bites of information took hours of meticulous analysis and yielded predictable conflicting responses.

"That Bastard, he's even screwing us over from his grave," my brother pronounced after assessing the stated value of his estate. "Bullshit, to his piece of shit old car and a few hundred dollars. That's a lie. Why do we need to sign off on our rights if it entitles us to nothing? They must think we are stupid. Yeah, right. They hired a detective and a high-priced law firm just to be fair?" He had been pacing in circles around my classic white lacquered Chinese Chippendale dining room set covered in polished chintz. The ornate eight-armed antique iron pagoda chandelier with cream colored silk shaded lights did nothing to alleviate his agitation. The softness of the light and elegance of the furniture the wrong backdrop for his knife sharp, white lightning–like response.

"So like your father," my mother added with an affirmative nod to my brother. "I *can* believe he died *intestate* for sure. Why have a will or think about taking care of anything but your own immediate needs? It's entirely possible he died with nothing. One of your father's favorite sayings was, 'It's important to die owing someone money. That's the way to win the game.' This was a big win for him. He loved to *borrow from Peter to pay Paul.*"

I listened to the words that were in fact a litany I'd heard many times before. I needed to change the direction of this meeting. "Mom, are you inferring anyone might consider being stabbed multiple times and dying days later in a hospital might be considered a winning situation?"

This only rekindled Stephen's rage. "That's just what he deserved. I'd call it Karma. Isn't that a *ten-dollar* word he liked to use? I think I remember that and the word metamorphosis in one of his bullshit letters." Those words and other *ten-dollar* words in his scarce letters were indeed read aloud to us sardonically by my mother. Stephen wasn't done. "God, I hope he suffered a lot first. I like to think it was painful. Maybe he got a couple of stabs in his neck and face."

I hadn't actually considered any of these gory details. I had some difficulty reconciling having anyone I knew, even remotely, stabbed to death under unclear circumstances. It was sensational and too foreign to consider as relevant. I sat quietly through the continued rumbling and growling of this thunderstorm.

Stephen erupted again. "Well, fuck him and his lawyers. He's not screwing us again. It's our turn to collect on his debt. I am sure there is money hidden somewhere in some bank account or investment that we will uncover. Nice to know his other family thinks we can be written off. We will hire our own lawyer and find the hidden money. We will have the last laugh." He looked at me and our mother as if he was a freshly coined war hero commanding obedience and respect. He assumed we'd be willing to fall in line. But my mother's strange response was more confusing. "Jeez, he died a couple of months after his fifty-ninth birthday on December nineteenth. He never made it to sixty."

Until that day, I don't think I ever knew my father's birthday or considered his age. Was her reflection one of sadness or glee? I imagine it was a bit of both. If his theory of cheating someone at the end to be a winner was valid, she may be considered the victor in the game of time as an asset. My silence continued until it became notable as it bridged the competing cacophony of angry sounds and became the completing portion of a discordant symphony. There was a strange triad of reactive themes. My brother had focused on potential assets and retribution. His lifetime of repressed anger now had a vehicle and path forward for vindication. He found power in his plan. Power that might alleviate some old pain. My mother considered the money, but quickly became preoccupied by the more intimate details of a birthday and lost time. She had little to say that evening beyond reaffirming his lifetime of irresponsibility and indifference and, I suspect, finally punctuating it with a winsome thought of what might have been. The frayed edges blunted by a greater misfortune.

What were my thoughts? What, in those five pages of details and dates and legal-speak stood out to me? In all the images of rusted-out cars and bloody stab wounds and mechanically whooshing, life sustaining ventilators and intravenous bags or Bahamian bank accounts or a newfound date to mark my father's birthday or a potential inheritance, what struck me most were two names of newly existing people in my world. Listed as impersonally as addresses, social security numbers, bank account balances, and the assessed value of an old model Mercury were the names of his surviving children. It was 1980. I was thirty-three years old, and I was not my father's only daughter. We were not my father's only children. There was a daughter, Rebecca. She was then eighteen years old. There was a son, Charles Jr.—he was eleven years old. I was well past the childhood imaginings of blonde or flaxen-haired braided beauties who had displaced me. I was well past the jealousy or speculation or rejection that plagued my childhood. I was a mother, a wife, a nurse, a homeowner. I was successful and settled. And yet, the names of Rebecca and Charles unsettled me and unleashed a curiosity and desire for something more elusive than a Swiss bank account or thoughts of what might have been. My father's death marked the rebirth of a crucial and unanswerable question in my life. Who was my father? Who was Charles Payne? Did my father ever think of me? Did my father ever love me? How had Rebecca and Charles fared as his children? Did they know there were others before them? Why did I need to know? Before they existed, the question of Charles was mine to casually consider in a nebulous future. Until the arrival of that thick envelope, I assumed the answer would be revealed in time. I imagined eroding sands washing away at evening's low tide and uncovering fragments of seashells and rounded pastel stones, smooth and comforting to hold then claim and collect as my own. I randomly imagined him a somber old man seeking closure in his final years. But time had run out.

29 The Chef Suggests

There would be no more internal conflicts about including my father in the milestones of my life. I was free to have complete allegiance to my mother and brother. The first test of that allegiance accompanied the letter. "We have to begin by finding a lawyer who has offices in Florida and New York," my brother suggested. "They have to have access to all his business records and possible holdings. You can be sure there is money tied up in either his wife or children's names. Even if he had no will, he had a home and what about life insurance?"

I dismissed the importance of that possibility. His life insurance may have been significant, but probably didn't name us, a hurtful thought. It was just this hurt that convinced me to go along with hiring a lawyer.

Within a week, we had hired a law firm, each of us agreeing to a shared retainer fee of two thousand dollars. My mother would not be named or responsible for fees or legal action. We held the unsigned request sent by the Florida lawyer and waited patiently for news of our windfall. I imagined the hotels and office buildings in Coral Springs and North Miami (his last residences) that he may have designed. I tried to calculate what twenty-five percent of a million or two might be. It took almost two months to hear back from our own lawyer.

My brother speculated about how he might best spend his money. He was also married with two small children just a couple of years older than mine. He seemed to think the found money would best be spent on luxuries. The choice a genetic irony not lost on me. I occasionally thought about the windfall and how I might also share it with my mother. I continued to think about an eighteen-year-old half sister and her younger brother. Were they aware of the letter which identified the existence of half-siblings? They were young enough to have been shielded from all the probate and money matters. Were they so traumatized by a murdered father that they were protected from the sequelae of the death? They may or may not have known at a time before or after their father's death that they were not his only offspring. That would equal the playing field in my mind. Were we all kept in darkness? It opened a door to imagining new possibilities and new choices.

My brother was correct. Charles Payne had continued to slight us even in death. Our investment returned only confirmation of the existence of his heirs and his pathetic list of debts greater than assets. They were unable to unearth hidden bank accounts or property in children's names or proof of life insurance. We were both sure our lawyers hadn't tried hard enough and were livid at losing a thousand dollars each. This was *insult to injury* as my mother would remind us. It was a turning point in our lives. There was silent agreement that my mother was proven right. Our father was a selfish and irresponsible man no more capable of thought than a bee spreading pollen from one flower to the next. She was vindicated, her martyrdom and sacrifice etched permanently in granite. I was happy to be on their side of historical truth. I gave little thought to my father or half siblings for the next decade. Occasionally I would wonder if we or my children looked like them. If I passed Rebecca or Charles as adults somewhere, would I recognize the set of our eyes or shape of our lips as familiar? Would a broad forehead or slightly bulbous nose have come from that same busy bee? I imagined scenarios of who they were and how they lived. I was able for now to dismiss thoughts or judgement of my father. After all, he was dead.

But if other children existed, what were their lives? What was their history? Who was their father, if not mine? I could entertain as many scenarios as I liked. I could choose offerings to suit my mood on any given day. I could deny them happiness or his love. I could resent their indulged childhood filled with swimming pools and travel or private schools. I had a permanent menu with broad choices. I could stretch all the way back to childhood jealousy of imagined blond curls and blue eyes. Then it made me happy to believe it had turned to mousy brown by now. I could imagine his affairs with other women during their childhood and angry fights between parents. I could imagine he was murdered by the mob and that they'd spent their childhood hiding in shadows from gangsters or police. On my busiest or happiest days at home or work, I gave it little thought. I may have generously conceded they had a worse childhood than ours with an older and even less interested father. On unhappy days I dwelled on how the older Charles was finally embracing fatherhood and hung on their every achievement. The choices were mine. "What will you have today Madame?" my internal waiter inquired. Today I might have a decadent denial of their happiness, or, if already satiated, I might choose no thought to dessert at all. The problem was the presence of a choice. The existence of other progeny I could not deny kept him alive. As long as they lived, there was more to resolve. He was not simply dead and gone from my life. Four people claimed him as their father. What, if anything, did we share of his legacy? If the borders and shapes of these peopled pieces could be fit and aligned in the puzzle, would a sharper visage of a whole man be revealed? Firsthand knowledge of my father's character remained a mystery. Could he ever have been a good father? For most of my life I unconsciously and knowingly at times longed for facts to be unraveled or revealed to me. Early on, I was unconsciously unable to hate him. My brother's illness and teenage angst made it possible to hate the world including him at the tender age of sixteen. But I welcomed my brother's restored health and my ability to relinquish hate and enjoy life after the nightmare of his illness.

I always believed my mother withheld some bits of history I was entitled to and needed. Had she really not known about a second or third marriage and other children? What was the reality of his work and income? My father's death ended his ability or mine to satisfy this need. I would not speak of him again to my mother. I accepted her love and sacrifice. I accepted her need for a narrative that helped her through a difficult life. It was the best selection on the menu of our lives and functioned very effectively. But there would always be the unanswered questions and the reality of feeling still just a little hungry for facts. Do parents understand the empty place that truth must fill? Obliterating historical facts masks pain at the cost of identity. There is a logical need to understand the causality between a parent and what he produces; who we are. And now I understood there were four of us denied the truth. What truth would I want if I could select the facts that enabled me to let all of the past just slide into an acceptable narrative? Would that truth be a man with a limited proclivity for responsibility but the greatest of intentions? I think I could be content with good intentions. Maybe his four children were expressions of the same creative ability responsible for fantastical roof lines and imaginary promises in buildings, which paid homage mostly to his ego. That was who my father was. I was content in assuming the missing pieces of truth were no more devastating than his inflated ego and irresponsibility. Could his other children offer proof of this theory? For many years I secretly hoped to find them. But, a vestigial allegiance to my mother and busy life dampened this enthusiasm. It was another family member who rekindled my interest in the truth. Her toxic impression of history served to disrupt any hope I'd harbored for a palatable outcome. Suddenly, I was unsure of either parent's identity. Which parent had withheld the truth? Who was I to believe? Who was I supposed to love or forgive? Who were they? Who was I?

Part 2

30 Burnt Offerings

Aunt Dorothy wore five-inch high spiked heels with sharply pointed toes. When women's fashions transitioned from skirts to slacks, she wore five-inch high wedges or platform shoes with pointed toes. They looked impossibly painful. She was never seen barefooted. "She can't take off her shoes because her heels can no longer reach the floor. Too many years of wearing her shit-kickers," was my mother's disdainful assessment. "That's my sister-in-law, the fashion plate. Guess it helps her look less dumpy," my tall, slim mother added. There was no love lost between them in spite of a well-practiced façade built on Scrabble words and Danish pastries.

Aunt Dorothy's heels were airplanes in perpetual flight, unable to land. Her chubby, pinched toes fought for space and survival in their half inch of space in the narrow point. She was a shoe warrior engaged in daily battle with her own feet, her discomfort and irritation driving her to bilious victory that necessitated occasional vitriolic verbal release.

Our family was not unlike her shoe problem. An uncomfortable accessory to her fashionable, socially stable, upwardly mobile marriage. She wore us well, mostly. There were the challenging Scrabble games she often lost most ungraciously. But my mother's superior vocabulary could always be countered with bits of casual conversation about a new car or planned purchase. Just a subtle reminder of having a financially superior position.

Then there was her smart and handsome nephew. Stephen was handsome and charming. His chiseled features and graceful build in sharp contrast to a pudgy and socially withdrawn cousin. Cousin Mark was smart and blessed with all the resources necessary for eventual success. Fat camps in Maine, SAT prep courses, a competitive school district that dictated the guidelines and narrowly defined choices ahead. Of course, he did go on to acceptance at Cornell University and later to Mount Sinai Medical School and eventually to a lucrative medical practice as a radiologist in the affluent Five Towns of Long Island. It was pre-ordained. His slim and pretty wife and he settled into a wealthy Long Island community, had two beautiful children, and the programming was completely successful. But there were those unknown begrudging years of Stephen's acceptance to the Bronx High School of Science and a full academic scholarship to NYU. These years predated Mark's academic trajectory. Fate would negate a need for Dorothy's subtle status reminders. Stephen's brush with death and hospitalization, perhaps, she thought, divine intervention, had enabled her to quell her desire for an occasional snake bite. Perhaps she believed he would not eclipse her son's success. Had she even entertained the possibility of minimal brain damage and an intellectual fall from grace? Her visit to the hospital on the eve of his surgery is vividly etched in my mind's eye. Dorothy in officious nurse mode asserting a position of authority and self-assurance as Stephen considered his last hours of life. Her urine-splattered smart gray cardigan and confused husband wordlessly boarding the elevator. Stephen had reflexively thrown the nearly full urinal at Dorothy to end the charade. It was a moment of truth.

A month later, another moment of truth ended the agonal breaths sustaining the pretense of a close extended family. She may still have been silently fulminating at the indignity of a splash of urine to her face. To add insult to injury (a favorite expression of my mother's) there was their continued financial support to our family. The amount of money begrudgingly metered out remains a mystery. I don't imagine there was an honest dialogue between my mother and her brother and sister-in-law about the parameters of the help. How much and for how long were questions that might have been hesitantly asked in the face of trust and good will. There was little of either commodity in their relationship. And so, truth, painful truth, crashed through the façade of family fealty on a visit that late winter of 1964. The details of the visit are more vividly recalled as I consider her intent years later. The distance of time and liberation of age free me to remember the day. I replayed the details as any old woman might ruminate over and fondle a photo retrieved from storage. Aunt Dorothy would settle for insensitivity for now. The visit I so clearly recall was only a prelude to the ultimate revenge she sought.

Stephen wore his uniform of blue plaid flannel pajama bottoms and white tee shirt. He looked like any other nineteen-year-old college student casually relaxing on a Sunday afternoon. His hair had grown long and hid the semicircular scars above each ear. He gingerly probed the depressions where bone had been removed to feel a weak pulse in an unfamiliar place. The protective cover of temporal bones now left room for potential swelling or surgical re-entry if needed. A casual observer would not be aware of the vulnerability he was reminded of with each tentative swipe with an index finger. He read new issues of *Scientific American* and seemed distracted and detached from the content. He watched a few episodes of *The Fugitive* and otherwise took naps or rested in deep or no thought at all. We let him be. His presence in his own bed, in his own home in his own blue plaid and white uniform were reasons for gratitude. We fell into a slow rhythm of little rituals of recovery. I left for school comforted by the thought of my brother at home, my mother tending to him. It was the same elementary school security one had knowing mother was at home and the house would smell like ironed cotton or fresh coffee when you returned. She made simple meals for breakfast or lunch and called him to the kitchen. She sipped a second cup of coffee and weighed his mood. She measured her words according to the weight of that mood. Sometimes silence kept the scale perfectly balanced. On days when he seemed engaged with the minutia of the flavor of a favored soda or the weather or news of his friends she waded into tentative conversation. On those days, the dark lifted and mottled sun cast dancing shapes on the off-white walls of apartment 6E. It was a delicate balance. We were all testing the waters before stepping back to reclaim our previous lives. We were moving forward together, aware of the delicate nature of balance. A simple nudge too far to either side could topple the building blocks. Our army of three guarded a magnetic field that repelled negative energy. Aunt Dorothy and Uncle Walter broke through that barrier in spite of our best efforts. As I remember the visit now, the details are in knife sharp focus, readied for war.

Dorothy came with tortured feet and sharpened fangs. He had been home close to a month and they wanted to visit. Not an unreasonable request. A request that implied concern and thoughtfulness. My gentle, graying, slightly paunchy uncle entered first. He made me marvel at the full spectrum of neutral grays or beige. His light gray winter slacks were topped by a charcoal V-neck sweater and his shoes were marshmallow soft leather oxfords in dove gray, laced in charcoal. *His* feet were surely comfortable. The neutrality of his clothes matched his position on family loyalties. He loved my brother and me. We adored his corny jokes and genuine interest in our lives. He cared about his divorced sister. He worried for our finances and secretly slipped silver dollars to us and small checks to my mother hidden in the pages of old magazines. He also loved, respected, and feared his wife. It was a difficult balancing act. He may not have felt the strain of regular help while my mother took leave of her job. He may have written checks during those months without consulting his wife. But neutrality was no longer an option. Mark would be attending college (hopefully an Ivy League school) in just another year. There was legitimate cause to review their expenses and savings. There was legitimate cause to question continued help. A month of recovery seemed a good time to address the issue. But the new delicate balance of measured words and welcomed silence in our home was unknown to them. The patterns of conversation as delicate as Battenberg lace in this Bronx apartment. The loosely assembled set of rules could easily be upended by a whisper of poorly chosen words. The sound of clicking high heels couldn't disguise the underlying aura of an impending assault. In the rarified air of apartment 6E, all the senses were heightened. Clacking sounds and the smell of fresh coffee couldn't diminish a pervasive atmosphere of impending doom.

"Well, finally, we get to see you at home." The door flung open as they rang the bell, sending the positive charged ions in the atmosphere into frenzied activity and imbalance. The vacuum seal of safety breached. They bypassed the kitchen and my mother on their right and rushed down the narrow hardwood hallway to the living room. Steve reclined in pajama bottoms and tee shirt against the narrow spindles of our Danish modern sofa. A salmon and brown knit throw casually propped up a book on his lap. "I'd give my one good thumb to be able to grow hair like that," Uncle Walter joked. We all knew his other thumb had been blown off in rifle practice during World War II. "Dot, look at him, good as new, sitting up and studying, ready to go. You look great." The stage was set. He had not asked, but told Stephen how he looked and felt. His intention to prop and cheer was not in the new playbook of delicate balance. Uncle Walter tousled his nephew's too-long hair in affectionate play. A loving gesture of the past, now unwelcome and misunderstood as invasive. Out of character, Dorothy hovered silently and observed the exchange. She smiled and assessed the mood. She was gauging the atmosphere and timing. Uncle Walter was determined to engage and entertain the nephew he loved. "Are you hoping to catch up with the spring semester or just ease back into summer or fall courses? I'm sure you'll eventually catch up either way."

Stephen didn't offer an answer. The silence hung heavily in the invisible lair. My uncle looked to Dorothy for help or a prompt. She knew the time to strike was now. Clearly Walter had no appetite for more concrete questions or casual banter that would fall flat. This was not the same nephew who delighted in guessing punch lines or talking about school. He would not make any suggestions. Dorothy was charged with delivering another moment of truth. But she believed in truth, even when it hurt as much as her pinched toes. She had hoped her husband could at least bring up the subject of college costs in his conversation. They must have discussed the most graceful way to break the news. Ultimately his neutrality and conflicted loyalties rendered him an effete messenger. The shit-kicker shoes stayed on but the gloves came off.

She sat gingerly at the end of the couch and lightly patted Stephen's foot. I sat quietly in a chair in the corner. "We are so thrilled to see you recover this quickly. What a horrible siege. It really is a modern-day miracle that you are almost completely back to normal. Really, it's remarkable how resilient you are." She looked earnestly at him, studying his expression. His affect was flat. She had no clues. In fact, Stephen understood and remembered that his heart had also been damaged. He lacked the will or courage to think about the valve replacements that faced him in the months ahead. The imagined surgery, its outcome, and his future were topics we never discussed. They were balance tipping subjects repelled by the positive magnetic field we had established. Dorothy also preferred to deal only with the present. She felt a present urgency to be freed from indefinite financial support to her sister-in-law. After all, it didn't seem as if Stephen wasn't well enough to dress and feed himself. Lounging about and reading did not necessitate a nursemaid or companion an entire day. Charlotte could and should return to her job at this point. It might even be healthier for him to be more independent. A return to normal routines and sources of income seemed a positive move. Dorothy may have believed her theory. .

"You know Mark is not far behind you in thinking about college. We had a great time visiting campuses he was interested in last month. I can't believe he is finishing his junior year in a few months." She paused, hoping Stephen might ask where they visited. He slightly nodded his now damaged head a bit to the left to denote listening. "He has to work pretty hard to get the good grades he needs for college. But so far so good. Looks like he is hoping for either Cornell or Tufts. He also likes Binghamton as his *safe* school. Secretly, we really want him to end up at Binghamton. State University tuition would be a godsend." She seemed to be rambling and rolling forward in her litany as if there was a finite end she was about to crash into. This was the preamble to the truth she needed to lay out as if it were a congressional bill that must get passed. Yes, she needed him to understand they had high-ticket items in their family shopping cart. It was belt tightening time in their own household. The budget could no longer include charitable handouts to extended family.

"So, we were thinking that maybe the timing is really perfect for your mother to get back to work." She glanced over at her husband. He cleared his throat and forced a phlegmy plug into his mouth. The self-inflicted gag worked. She would have to continue speaking for both of them. She placed her right hand back onto Stephen's bare foot and gently stroked his toes. He wiggled them out and away and met her eyes now. She had his rapt attention. She took the cue and sat poised to strike. In the sunny yellow kitchen, my mother rummaged through the white, painted metal wall-mounted kitchen cabinets trying to find matching coffee mugs and the ceramic cow pitcher she liked for cream. She was pleased to hear the muffled sounds of conversation. She thought it sensitive of them to have not brought Mark.

"The truth is, we really can't afford to help out anymore. I know how much Mom worries for you, but it will be healthy for her to get back to her real job and friends at work." She looked at Walter and now glanced over at me. I had been sitting silently in a distant corner, pretending to be filing my nails. We were expected to affirm her benevolent suggestion. Silence followed her remarks. She didn't seem to understand the healing nature of moments in time as thoughtfully strung together as amulets on a shaman's necklace. Our days were built on quiet moments and simple routines. The clanking radiator pipes brought heat and comforting familiar sounds. The regular rumbling of the elevated train or an occasional distant car horn were reminders of the sanctuary inside our three rooms. A shared television show or meal brought us together to speak or not. We understood each other's fears and hopes because they were the same. I was happy to return to school knowing in more collected moments and days we would all return to *before*. My mother would return to her *before* when she was confident that her son could envision not just his *before* but the courage for his *after*. Our moments were leading to that time. A finite or abruptly imposed date and time offered a jarring reality.

"So," she continued, "I think if you suggested it to her she might be so pleased you are feeling ready to be left alone during the day. That is a sure sign of progress. Really, what guy wants his mother hanging around all the time?" She forced a shy smile suggesting mischief he probably wasn't even capable of. He forced a smile in return. Pleased with his response she elaborated. She really did value truth. Unvarnished truth and legitimate facts were surely the best foundation for a close relationship. Timing and intention were secondary factors.

"Sometimes, we just have to push ourselves a little harder. Run it by your mother when you think the time is right. We think another week or two of us helping out should do it. Truthfully, I think you will be ready to get back to school in no time." She gave a final quick tap to his now, pulled up to his chest foot and stood. "Wally, how about some coffee and cake. It smells great." They stood in unison and left the room. The foul odor of truth lingered in the room. How Dorothy must have hated holding back other truths – truths she would unleash in the future.

The last coffee cup was washed and my mother closed the door behind them. She was thankful that the visit was brief and uneventful. There were no references to Stephen's anger in the hospital or questions about future plans. She was even absolved from a quick Scrabble game. This seemed to be a simple attempt to resume contact and check on things. She walked to the living room to join her children.

Stephen did not waste a minute to ask his question. "When were you planning on returning to work?"

My mother hesitated, her curiosity piqued. "I don't know. Maybe next month. Nothing set in stone. Why are you asking?"

He was as honest as his aunt right now. "Well, for one, I had no idea they were supporting us all this time. I thought you were getting some benefits from work. But aside from that revelation, they wanted me to tell you that two weeks might be the perfect time for you to go back. They think it might be the *healthiest* thing for you and me. Oh, and by the way, as soon as you do return to work, they won't be helping us financially. Jeez, I had no idea. Anyway, they are worried they won't have enough savings for Mark's college if they continue to help." There it was, the message had been delivered. The room was silent. Only a gentle clanking of radiator pipes disturbed the silence.

"That bitch! So rather than ask me when I was going back, they asked you. What cowards. How dare they burden you with these things? As if they can't afford to help." She was outraged at being manipulated. Even more offensive was their breach of her cardinal house rule. This sanctuary was free of financial stress and concrete plans. "Well, anyway, two weeks is perfect. That brings us right into April. A nice time to get back."

The subject was closed without further discussion. April first brought my mother back to her *before*. Stephen's would come months later. There would never be a return to the *before* of our extended family. Visits and regular calls fell off the grid. Several years after my grandfather had died in 1963, my grandmother moved from New Jersey to a small apartment in our building. A few years after that, she became blind and entered a local nursing home. Walter and Dorothy and my mother met there every weekend. That was the new normal. The next decade before my grandmother died in 1977 brought dramatic change. Mark was a doctor. Stephen was a high school teacher and I was a nurse. We were now all married and had children of our own. Dorothy was wrong. Truth and concrete facts never brought us closer. Her brutal honesty failed. We remained only formally connected and shared news of important events from a dispassionate distance.

I considered the nature of honesty because of my aunt. I missed the closeness of our visits. I missed my sweet uncle and opinionated aunt. I missed the smell of fresh coffee and feisty exchanges over obscure Scrabble words. I missed the thought of Sunday afternoons being family days. I missed all the people who defined my childhood. Whose fault was it? Looking back, I understand that my aunt and uncle were probably not as wealthy as my mother suggested they were. They lived in a garden apartment in Flushing, not a private home in a greener Long Island suburb. Perhaps the fat camps and nice clothes and furniture were their well-deserved luxuries. Why would they have to assume responsibility for another family for an indefinite time? How much had they helped or not helped? My mother never revealed how much she made at her job or how much money they had given at any time. Her sins of omission about them paralleled all I never knew for sure about my father. Had they all shortchanged us? I grew up resenting my father's imagined wealth and luxuries and my aunt and uncle's begrudging help as they enjoyed better. It was the implied truth I accepted without facts. It created distance. It fostered a lack of self-esteem. Still, I was never able to hate them. I considered the things I missed about them and the curiosity I harbored about my place in their hearts. The curiosity about their place and intention in my life gnawed at me. A similarity about my father first surfaced before the rift with them, when the phone rang in 1957 and the nasal male voice of my father asked if I could join him for lunch. The question of my father's love remained unresolved. Eventually, I was able to reconcile my aunt's intention and ability to love me. She delivered her shit-kicking final blow with ice cold precision and abandon. Aunt Dorothy could not have loved me. Her hatred consumed any available space where love may have existed. Her hatred altered my life.

31 Best-Laid Plans

The best laid plans of mice and men often go awry. This famous line is taken from a 1785 poem by Robert Burns. It represents the futility of careful planning. No matter how much we plan, something may still go wrong. Cousin Mark had met and even surpassed every dream his parents had nurtured. A lucrative practice, a pretty wife, a sprawling ranch home in the five towns, and a grandson and granddaughter. But as those children entered adolescence, the pretty wife fell out of love with her smug and predictable husband. Affluence was not enough to hold her commitment. Dorothy and Walter were outraged at her lack of gratitude and for the scandalous affair she was having with an actor she hadn't intended to fall in love with. During the dissolution of their son's marriage, my aunt and uncle began visiting us again. In the absence of young children or aging parents who drew them to necessary rituals, they took to an occasional visit every few weeks. They also called my mother just to chat. Mostly, the conversation was about the evils and shortsightedness of Mark's wife, Paula. My mother was a good listener and served as a sounding board rather than participant. Secretly, we all considered how easy it might have been for the pretty and outgoing Paula to have stumbled into the less traditional role of life with an actor. Uncle Walter wrote and read aloud cryptic and cutting poems about Paula. Aunt Dorothy's venting stayed on a narrow path of single word epitaphs. I suppose Mom was a perfect outlet for them. She had been *a woman wronged* herself. More importantly, there was a candor and comfort level with her that might not be as easy to assume within their more elevated social set. She served the role of sounding board and her tacit silence may have been interpreted as agreement with their opinions. Over the next few years, the anger abated as did the frequency of their visits. Mark eventually remarried another attractive woman whom his parents didn't care for. She was a former patient, divorced and with older children. Perhaps she was an opportunist. She may also have loved him. We were past caring. Stephen and I had little to no contact with our cousin and kept up with news of our extended family only through my mother's infrequent phone calls to her brother and sister-in-law. Mark's children remained close with their father and paternal grandparents. We gave little thought to these children or our cousin until one had come of age. It was time for a Bar Mitzvah.

A simple cream-colored, deckle-edged invitation arrived. The return label bore the familiar last name but only the first name of Paula and an unfamiliar address.

Paula was apparently celebrating the event independently from her ex-husband. A few days after the invitation arrived, my mother received a warm phone call from Paula asking if we would help represent the children's father's family. She added that she had not been invited to the larger celebration her ex-husband had planned but was inviting all relatives on both sides to share in the happy milestone.

"Of course we will be there. I think it is lovely that you want us to attend," my mother answered. "It seems mean-spirited to exclude you from the larger celebration, but I guess Dorothy is holding a grudge. I'm not surprised. I know they are having a large event at a country club. I guess their invitation will be here soon. I'm sure Barbara and Stephen will get back to you. I imagine we will all be at two parties. Well," she added on a lighter note "lucky boy will get to party twice, why not?"

The invitation came a week before the more elaborate glossy black and silver heavy stock packet, which included invitation and smaller cards pertaining to the festivities, arrived. I couldn't help but reflect on my cousin's Bar Mitzvah thirty or more years before at the elegant Roslyn Country Club. My memories were of crystal chandeliers and royal blue and gold carpeted lounge areas, a ballroom decked in gold tablecloths and tall centerpieces of creamy long-stemmed roses in golden cylinders wearing black bowties at their necks. It was the height of my white lipstick, black eyeliner phase. My large eyes were ringed in heavy-handed black eyeliner and mascara. My hair was grandly teased and coiffed to add three inches to my height. I wore my first pair of high heels. They were low but white satin with pointed toes Dorothy would love. My mother allowed me to put eye makeup on her as well. We were, after all, attending a black-tie affair. I have a group photo of the family at the event. My mother and I stand out for looking as if we had been severely beaten up about our faces or as morning-after whores. We both managed to laugh at the image many times. I returned both invitations with a positive response. I imagined an updated version of the country club event. My brother opted out of attending either event. He held no loyalty to any of them. In contrast, I felt compassion for both Paula and Mark. The ripple effect of divorce is rarely addressed as an important loss to children. The cousins and aunts and uncles and other peripheral family undergo a changed dynamic. There can be divided loyalties or complete loss. In the case of my own parents' divorce, I was only denied the pleasure and influence of a cigar-smoking, colorful grandmother with breasts she could throw over her shoulders and who is said to have owned a pet monkey. My father was an only child. Grandmother Nora, my mother's nemesis, remained a collection of sordid and colorful tales. In telling me this shady history, my mother managed ironically to create the image of a storybook antihero I proudly have related to and love being genetically linked to. I imagine the *truth* of who this woman really was is another of those losses that are an unfortunate part of divorce.

The call from Aunt Dorothy to my mother hoping to get positive feedback on the elegant invitation came days after the first call from Paula. "Hi, Charl, how is everything?" And without pausing for an answer she had a classic "Kvelling" (Yiddish for basking in good news) moment. "Did you get that gorgeous invitation? Oh it's going to be amazing. The Swan Club for God's sake! We couldn't be happier. Sharon (Mark's new wife) really has excellent taste. They had us go with them to select the menu and look at the room setup. By the way, poetic justice. He is not inviting Paula or her parents."

This was, of course not news to my mother. "I know. Paula told me that," she answered. The prolonged, underwater-like silence was when the final reset button was pushed.

"Paula called you?" a simple question that triggered the explosion.

"Yes, she wanted to be sure we got the invitation to the party she is having for David. She feels hurt at being excluded. I guess she knew it might be a delicate situation for us." In Dorothy's shocked silence, my mother continued. "I guess she had no choice. After all, her family and relatives will be at the service. I think she planned it with David in mind. Two parties in two days."

"And you said NO of course!" Dorothy bleated.

"Actually," my mother answered, "I said yes. It makes sense for us to be there. Why should he feel we don't like his mother? I know the kids really aren't close, but I couldn't say no. I've always liked Paula and thought it was best for everyone to stay neutral." My mother waited. Dorothy had retreated to a hate hole deeply formed over many years.

"You will call her back and tell her you made a mistake. How dare you let her use you to strike out at us? Are you so stupid you don't see what she's doing?.."

My mother thought about this a second or two but believed Paula had sincerely wanted her party to be inclusive. Now she wasn't sure. It was too late, anyway. She had assured Paula she'd be there and had mailed back the response card. It was now irrevocable. "Dorothy, I can't do that. I already said yes. Really, what's the big deal? Do you really think she used me for revenge? That's pretty far-fetched."

And then, Dorothy played her final card. "Yes, I think she hates us and doesn't give a shit about you. She never has. You are nobody to her or her children. You are nobody, NOBODY! Choose which party you are going to. You aren't welcome at both." The word *nobody* resonated long after the receiver was placed back on the phone's cradle.

Choosing sides, too often the primary rule in the game of divorce. Divided loyalties, small rewards, subtle threats and hidden truths are the extra cards to be played. Now, there was doubt about Paula's intentions. Even worse was the possibility she didn't care about or respect my mother, and by extension us, at all. Had she intentionally weaponized a trusted relationship? My mother was experiencing the conflict usually reserved for the children of divorce. What was the truth? It wasn't much different than my lifetime of conflicted loyalties. "Mom, should I invite my father to graduation, my wedding? Do you think I should let him know he is now a grandfather?" and always the stock response. "Do what you think is best, but he doesn't deserve to know. He doesn't deserve the honor or privilege of being there, but it is up to you." Was it really up to me? I could be loyal and grateful or I could hurt and disrespect a lifetime of her love and sacrifice. His absence and lack of support were the only facts I had to weigh in my decision. Other than the less than thirty hours spent at dinner tables with a virtual stranger, a pretty wristwatch and fabulous doll in a steamer trunk, there was nothing concrete to guide me. It was never that difficult to decide, but it was often painful. I had always considered the missing information, the what ifs. Was there a father who thought about me? Had he kept track of the passage of time and been curious about milestones? Who was he, after all? Now, the adults played the guilt and doubt divorce game usually reserved for children.

I expected the call from my aunt. My mother was still conflicted, but equally as angry. Surely, Dorothy had intended to strike out and inflict pain on my mother. Of course my mother would be incensed. How dare Dorothy issue an ultimatum? She was not a child to be threatened or manipulated. My mother was still agitated when she'd called me. "You do what you want Barbara, but I've made my decision. I am going to believe that Paula does want us there and I responded in that belief. I am not going to the other party."

Well then, I thought, *here is another "Do what you want" moment.*

I had not yet thought it through when Dorothy called. "So," I guess your mother has filled you in on the Bar Mitzvah problem." It was dinnertime and my nine- and eleven-year-old sons and five-year-old daughter, aware of the situation, were all ears. I walked into the formal dining room for privacy and continued with a simple "Yes, Mom told me."

She picked up on my hesitancy and launched her assault full throttle. "Paula is a bitch. Your family means nothing to her. Your mother is just trying to get back at *us* by going to her party." I wondered if my mother *was* getting back at her. Maybe that was true. Dorothy's behavior through the years was questionable. Mom never forgave her for using Stephen to stop helping us financially. My mother thought it revealed the worse character flaws of greed and cowardice. All those contentious Scrabble games and always the subtle condescension. Perhaps Dorothy was aware of an underlying motive. I hated to think my mother was vindictive. Even as I questioned the truth behind my father's absence as an adult, I had not considered the situation as anything more than a nebulous history of unfortunate circumstance, selfish pride, and ineffective parenting. I put thoughts of my mother aside as I finally spoke. "I know she has decided to go to Paula's party. We will also be going. The boys are looking forward to a weekend of events. It does not mean we are choosing sides, Aunt Dorothy. We are trying to be gracious and supportive. I hope you understand that." I waited…. The pause seemed too long. Still, I waited…and waited. And then.

"Well then, let me tell you something about your mother. Something you probably don't know." I felt off-balance. This was unexpected. "You don't even know *who* or *what* your mother is." I didn't answer. I couldn't. "You think your poor mother is so innocent. Hah! Let me tell you something you should know. Let me tell you the truth!" Dorothy was a hissing snake about to inject a venomous poison into my soul. The aftereffects of the poison, a blurred impression of my own identity and insistent urge to rub away the undulating, ungrounded beliefs I had lived with for half of my projected lifespan. Dorothy wasn't finished. No sense in leaving an amputation incomplete. "Do you know, your father was a really nice guy? I bet you never knew that! Yes, we liked your father a lot, a good guy. You should have known him." I could hear her exhale through the phone. Had her conscience caught up with her mouth? Or was she finally exhaling her own stored up poison? "Your father didn't want to leave. I have nothing else to say to you. Don't bother coming to our party. It's not necessary."

32 Food For Thought

My father was a nice guy? He never wanted to leave? These words were the genesis of my thwarted journey to find another truth. I'd spent almost four decades wondering who my father was, now I wasn't sure who my mother was either. If neither parent had a clearly defined identity or history, who exactly was I? There was now a before and after. Before Dorothy's revelation, I believed my mother was the victim of a philandering husband and malicious mother-in-law. I'd grown up on stories about my paternal grandmother that were not all just colorful or exotic anecdotes that offered vivid images of naughty pet monkeys and even naughtier escapades in pre-Castro Cuba. I chose to keep those images in the forefront of my memory bank. They lent unique drama to my life story and a bodacious bent I hoped had trickled into my own DNA. There were other stories I chose to forget. My mother recounted a harrowing drive down the West Side

Highway of Manhattan. It was dusk and a challenging drive on the serpentine, two-lane highway leading her back to the Bronx. She was alone in the car, and I imagined she either had no children yet or had left us at home. Suddenly, her 1948 black Studebaker Land Cruiser was being forced to the side of the road by a larger black sedan (of unnamed model) driven by a sneering Nora Payne. She describes Nora as yelling and laughing at her as she edged her ever closer to a retaining wall. With each telling of my mother's version of this incident, it is understood that Nora's intent was to drive her off the road into a serious accident. The thinly veiled implication was that she wanted my mother dead. My mother often stated that Charles was nothing more than a "Mama's Boy" who never could cut the apron strings. Because he was a late in life only child and the product of a loveless marriage to a much older man. Nora found her son to be more companion than son. He was, according to my mother, indulged, spoiled, and arrogant. He could have anything he wanted. When he had tired of his wife and children, Nora was there to facilitate the disposal of that family. According to my mother, Nora harbored her son's mistress in her apartment. The much older, wiser, and worldly cocktail waitress he'd met in Poughkeepsie got along well with Nora. My mother also casually remarked that they had "whoring" in common. It was much too long a ride for Charles to visit her in upstate New York. Nora was happy to facilitate the extramarital affair that would free her son from the burden of his wife and two young children. A litany I had decided to remove from my memory bank and colorful family history. I preferred less malevolent tales.

In spite of believing most of what my mother told me, I chose to relegate these uglier tales to a deep and shadowed crevice in my brain reserved for ephemeral facts not worthy of deep analysis or real estate space in the forefront of my brain. Ugly Nora stories lived with those of vengeful gods and wicked witches. I preferred considering the tropical colors of Havana to visions of feuding black sedans at twilight. Now, I needed to reconsider everything. Now, both sides had evil characters. The protagonist and antagonist shared center stage. Why had Nora tried to hurt Charlotte? Had Charlotte done anything at all to deserve that wrath? They dueled for a victorious and benevolent place in history. There seemed to be no such thing as simple truth. There was no one left to trust.

It was so much easier to be the child who wanted even the bad people to be worthy of redemption. I always understood who the bad people were. They were the father who abandoned his responsibilities and the pleasure seeking, amoral grandmother who helped him. But it is never that simple. Even villains can have a reason for their malevolence and can be endearing. Villains can be cool or misunderstood or misguided. Literature and theater are full of characters we strive to understand who may not be completely sinister. The Grinch had an unhappy childhood after all. I wanted a father capable of loving me even as he may have loved other children more. I preferred an irreverent version of a grandmother to the less likable whore or killer my mother offered. Other than the four dinners shared with my unknown father and the confrontation in a hospital cafeteria, I could silently consider who I would have liked him to be. I could allow myself the guilty pleasure of hope. I could build an internal language that identified my mother as unfortunate victim (noun) and my father as a dangling participle that might be modified. Years later, when he became the victim of a horrible crime and was deceased, I needed to alter the narrative I'd wanted. Truth and hope were abandoned. The irony of his death being another exotic mystery immersed in drama is not lost to me. I could spin even that anomaly into a colorful tale. Other fathers left home. Other fathers died or became ill. My father was special even in death. He was murdered on a Miami street by a "crazed Negro" (the archaic language of 1979—always an uncomfortable fit) for no apparent reason at all. This was better than shit-flinging monkeys or paralyzed stepdaughters. More dramatic than Cuban rebels, perhaps Che himself or even the Pagoda-like roofline of an iconic Miami motel. I could continue to embellish my paternal history in the most exotic and palatable version, as my mother remained the constant heroine of my story. She was beautiful, funny, intelligent, devoted, and self-sacrificing. She devoted her most vital years completely to raising us. We adored her. She did the best she could to instill cherished values in the absence of a husband and in the face of poverty. She chose celibacy and solitude over opportunities to date and remarry. She reminded us from time to time that men she had met would not be interested in the burden of her children. We understood we were her choice and her sacrifice. We accepted her decision with an abundance of gratitude and guilt. We were loved in a uniquely special way that other children were not. We were loved more specially. Could that security have enabled me not to consider hating the father responsible? Could an abundance of love offset the need to hate? I was content with a mixed heritage of colorful scoundrels and single parented sacrifice. The formula worked for all of my childhood and most of my adult life. My father's death eventually freed me from the need to speculate about the other daughter and son. If he was a better father to them, so be it. He was lost to all of us now. Would I have felt better or worse about him if he provided for them as he had deprived me? By the time I was almost middle-aged myself, it seemed irrelevant. I was settled in to motherhood and was grateful for my mother's continued devotion to the next generation of children. But there came a time when words uttered in a fit of anger would test my ability to render the past as dispassionately as I had before. Now, there was the question of who either of them was. There was the question of truth. I needed to know their individual truths, but suspected it might be a bitter pill to swallow.

33 Bitter Truth

I had been happy with a life of selective memory and cognitive dissonance. The lies we tell ourselves to accept an unwanted reality worked for me. I avoided the tension of conflicting beliefs and behaviors or truths. Overcoming cognitive dissonance requires challenging accepted beliefs or avoiding information that conflicts with beliefs. I chose to cherry pick the stories I loved about an unknown grandmother. I adored stories of shit-flinging monkeys and her torpedo sized breasts tales better than the Cruella de Vil version of Nora. I liked believing my father was a famous architect rather than a failed civil servant. I liked the romantic version of an unknown paternal grandfather who rode throughout New England as a train conductor on the New Haven Railroad better than the story of how he had once propositioned his pretty daughter-in-law (my mother). When a letter arrived in cursive script and fountain pen ink, I wanted to believe my father really was strapped for money and not just lying to cheat us. After all, that is what his words claimed. Yes, the envelope rarely contained a check, but the words existed and the check did not. When he asked to visit me and have dinner together, I believed he wanted to know me. He wanted me to love him. He loved me in his own way. I rejected my mother's theory that he was between women and feeling insecure. And when he was finally absent from my life through either my rejection or, finally, his death, I preferred to believe it never mattered. I chose to extinguish all lingering thoughts of preferred children or possible fortunes denied us even in death. I resolved the tension between truth and belief by bringing down the curtain on the play that was my father's life. It was now a darkened and silenced place in my heart. I could go forward secure in the reality of the life lived as my mother's daughter. That was concrete. The memories of her running alongside my bike as I abandoned training wheels or getting lost for fun car rides were real. The trips to Long Branch to visit Grandma and Grandpa and sit with her at the beach were as real as the smell of hot dogs and suntan oil I could recall. The endless board games and the prayers before bed had happened. The rented row boats and squirmy bloodworms on a fishhook she threaded for me happened just as I remember. The trips to skin doctors and a fight with a terrible teacher were as vivid today as if just yesterday-real.

And then, just a few words later, an ugly cognitive dissonance reared its ugly head. Suddenly, long suppressed alternative truths presented themselves at the previously shuttered window where I had thrown the unwanted beliefs. I had neatly rejected any memory or errant thought that tainted the preferred image of my almost perfect mother. The single person I could trust was sacrosanct. How dare anyone intrude on the sanctity of my dissonance?

I began my descent into the pitch-black truth tunnel methodically. I wanted to consider the ways of finding truth as if it was a four-credit core curriculum course. I hoped there would be a reconciliation of my chosen memories with the stories I'd lived with that were my mother's memories, my mother's viewpoints and the newly hatched narrative of my aunt. Of lesser importance, I thought were the repressed memories I imagined might surface just to confuse me even more. I had read Oliver Sacks's (the British neurologist and author) book *The River Of Consciousness* that addresses the scientific nature of memories. Sacks speaks of primary memory and secondary memory. Our primary memories are those with the direct stamp of our own experience. The secondary memories are those experiences transferred to us by reading or listening to stories or things we are told by others (parents?) that become embedded as our own in time. With each repetition of the information, it becomes more firmly fixed. That may account for why siblings remember historical facts differently. But if secondary memories are constructed rather than experienced, are they truths?

Was Dorothy's belief that my father was a good guy a truth? Maybe she just identified with him because they were both better educated and more inherently arrogant than my mother. Her belief that he didn't want to leave may have been her own preference for him and desire for him to remain in the extended family. But, what if her words were truths? I thought about what having a different point of view meant. It meant everything, I guess. Everyone has a point of view, but why do some overwhelm others? I thought about another favorite book, *A People's History of The United States* by Howard Zinn. Zinn retells American history from the point of view of Native Americans and African Americans and factory workers. He interviews farmers and field workers and all people at the grassroots level. Our romanticized, politicized, and cleaned up version of American history is suddenly dispelled as largely a fictional interpretation. It's a point of view not a truth.

I wish I could have just unremembered her words. It was simpler not to consider the repressed memories, which continued to surface, after her indictment of my mother. There were the half-siblings I could search for and get their points of view. I had their birthdates and names. We now lived in a world of technology and genetics that could enable me to contact and question them. I searched for them on social media sites and search sites. We had come a long way from hiring private detectives to find people. What would I ask them anyway? Was he a good father? Did you know he had other children? What do you think happened to his first marriage? Was he rich or poor? Did he have other affairs? How did he really die? And what I would get from them would be nothing more than other points of view. I didn't need another point of view. I needed facts. Hoping that some facts would surface, I spent the next two decades attempting to find them.

My mother was never aware of my search. She was old and comfortable in her sanctified status. I searched secretly and informally. The half siblings had no social media presence. Old phone numbers and addresses proved to be outdated. Letters were returned to sender, phone calls not returned. It was futile. I let them go. Finally, the imagined girl with long blond braids, the much-loved replacement daughter, disappeared as if she were a wispy cloud pushed off by the winds that were my unsettled mind. I wanted only primary facts and my own lived memories. They were the ground I could stand on, not clouds to dream about. I began with the most destructive of Dorothy's words. I knew I had heard those words. They were a primary memory. "You don't know *who* or *what* your mother really is." I would not ignore that ugly memory. I would consider it. I would allow myself the painful struggle of bringing up memories I'd thrown out the window. I would struggle against the sticky, debris-clogged sashes of the shut window and force it open to recall those facts.

34 Buried Treasure

Who or *what* she is? *What she is?* Yes, she said those words. She said *that* word. What: The interrogative pronoun or adverb which requests further information about the identity, nature or value of an object. She had objectified my very human mother. The verbs or nouns I automatically linked to her innuendo were whore or slut. Why had my mind gone there? What other objects or nature of things could she have meant? A liar, a thief, a malingerer, a philanderer? What led me to other thoughts? What repressed memories or thoughts had bubbled to the surface? What had I chosen not to remember? If I acknowledged the words I reflexively chose, I needed to consider the issue of men in her life and mine beyond my father. It was time to throw the window open. I understood there were dark clouds that gathered on the other side of an invisible and protective glass barrier. It would soon be raining ghosts of men.

It was time to recall the ghosts of the men in her life and by extension mine. Strangely, the first memory is not of a man at all, but of a little girl named Kathy Coughlin. Maybe it was the word *what* that made me go down a long-forgotten path and find that memory first. "*What* your mother is!"

I was mostly comfortable in the neighborhood of my first thirteen years. We lived on the second floor in a railroad flat apartment of the ugliest lime green asphalt shingled house on the street. We were the only renters, the only Jews, the only single parented family and the smallest family as well. There were two other large, old, frame, single-family homes and a row of brick attached homes. Everyone else belonged to intact large Italian American Catholic families. The differences were felt by me but went unnoticed by my two closest friends, Mimi and Alexis. I went to church with them on Saturdays for confession. I liked confession and the scent of the dying votives in Our Lady of the Blessed Nativity. I waited in a pew while my friends entered the confessional. I worried I might exhale the scent of burnt wax or lingering Frankincense when I got home so did deep breathing and exhaling on the walk home. I worried the infusion of the scent might even make me Catholic, which my mother would not approve of. I liked the paint colors of the statue of Mary and her benign gaze toward me. It was a soft blue and creamy white paint color not found anywhere else but the sky. I loved my friends' siblings and they loved mine. I am sure they gave little to no thought to our differences. Mostly, I gave it little thought until middle school. We went to Public School 68 together and shared every after-school moment engaged in play. The missing father in my home was my normal.

When I was nine, the one empty lot on the street, next door to Mimi's house, was sold. We were a little saddened that the ungroomed square would no longer be available for collecting odd-shaped pebbles and pieces of colored glass. We used these as currency in our make-believe store (a fallen log with flattened top, the counter). It was also a good place for hide-and-seek. In just a matter of months, a new single-family home was constructed on the site. It was unlike any of the existing homes. Built of sturdy red brick, it had a long concrete porch above the stone staircase. Decorative wrought iron grillwork flanked the steps and perimeter of the porch. An oversized plate-glass window looked over the porch and street. This house seemed grander and innately different from its neighbors. The inhabitants of the house were different as well. Not different like my family, but different in a new way.

Kathy was the only child of this Irish Catholic family. She wore a gray plaid and navy school uniform with pleated skirt and attended a Catholic school in a neighborhood east of us. Her father wore suits and ties to work. The other fathers owned bakeries and pizza shops or did construction. She was exactly our age. We gave as little thought to her differences as they had given to mine. Soon enough we were all friends. In fact, it was for a short-lived time.

Kathy's mom wore slim capri pants and pretty ballet flats most days. She sat on her porch reading magazines and observing her new neighborhood and her daughter at play. My mother said she seemed to be full of herself because she avoided even casual conversation with the neighbors. She may not have spoken but she was listening and watching and assessing every watchful minute. Looking back, I can only imagine her horror at hearing the evening ritual loud call of Mimi's aunt Lena every night. "Pasqualina, Mario, Pepe, get here NOW! It's time to eat." We were all loud and unsupervised children. She watched over Kathy like a hawk. Soon, she accommodated this by arranging play and snacks in her own driveway. We adapted easily from our dirty lot to homemade Toll House cookies, a blow-up swimming pool and a child-sized picnic table. She had elevated the social status of our playtime.

It took Mrs. Coughlin only a short time to learn that one of Kathy's new friends was not only a Jew but had no father at home. She was unhappy with this alliance for her daughter. Things soon changed for the four little girls. A new dynamic evolved, orchestrated by the slim woman in capri pants and shiny ballet flats.

It was an especially hot summer day. The blue blow-up pool adorned with orange and pink fish was filled and sat ready for four sets of wiggly toes and giggling girls. Kathy called from the height of her cement front porch. We had been jumping rope on the smooth surface of our freshly paved street. "Mimi, Alexis, get your bathing suits on and come over." I hadn't noted the omission of my name. I was so enamored of her loopy beige terry cloth bathing suit. Its bodice was a dark brown dog with long loose ears that swayed when she moved. Its halter top was tied with a facsimile of a red leash. We scrambled home to change. In minutes we were in front of her house.

"Not you!" she shouted at me. "I didn't say you. I only said Mimi and Alexis." I stood in shocked silence, waiting for the tilted world to right itself. "You are too fat. You are a fat, dirty Jew."

Mimi and Alexis looked at her and turned to face me. They stood still and seemed to be studying me. I thought they were confused and trying to see something about me that was new or different, something they'd missed before. It seemed like a long time but probably was not. Kathy came down the steps as Mimi and Alexis stepped forward tentatively toward the blue oasis. In my confusion, I stepped forward also.

"I said no. You can't use my pool," she screamed. "You are too fat and all the water will come out. You are a dirty Jew and will make the water dirty. Besides that, my mother said your mother is a 'prostituter.'"

My confusion turned to shame and my shame to red hot rage. It was an emotion I'd never felt before. It hijacked my brain and settled into my hands. In seconds, I stepped onto the bouncy tubular edge of the pool and felt the escape of cold water over my foot. But my hands were still red hot and wanting more than water. They had a plan of their own. They grabbed the limp brown wet hair of the ponytail at her neck. The little red bow of the leash stayed neatly in place. The mousy brown string of hair was attached to her head which led her unresisting body over and out of the bouncy edge of the cheerful pool as I yanked it toward me. I noticed the floppy dog ears bounced up in mock surprise as she was jerked up and over. I had gone mad. It was the first and only time in my life to be driven by blind rage into a hateful and violent response. With the ponytail now in a firm two-fisted grasp, I spun her body as if it were a shot put. Her bare legs scraped in circles on the hot pavement. The energy dispelled as quickly as a summer thunder storm and in a stuporous cloud of ozone rich air I sauntered back home. There seemed to be an unnatural silence behind me.

"Mom," I asked. "What is a prostituter?" I was now calm. I was not wet or in any way appearing distressed. My mother looked casually up at me from a crossword puzzle she was working. "The word is prostitute, not prostituter, no *R* at the end. Why would you ask that? Where did you hear that word?" She was now looking at me with interest.

"Well, Kathy Coughlin called you that word. What does it mean?"

Still, she studied my face then gave her answer. It was short and abstract and left me satisfied that she hated Kathy as well. "A prostitute is a name for a woman who does bad things. Wow. That's great. I bet Kathy even learned the word in her fancy private Catholic school. That little bitch. I bet she called you a dirty Jew too." She looked intently at me after that. My mother was so smart. How did she know exactly what Kathy had said? "So, you can't play with her anymore. Shanty Irish Bitch in her capri pants. Stay away from them," was her final declaration. I wanted to ask what Shanty meant also but was done with new words for the day.

And now, I considered Dorothy's single word and why I'd linked it to the oldest of deeply buried memories and another long forgotten word. The word *what* somehow conjured up another word that stung: *prostitute*. Long after hearing this word, I'd come to know its meaning. It had no relationship to my mother. I was sure of that. She was always at home. She did not date until I was ten years old. Still, I retrieved that memory. It was where I would start. The memory moved forward slowly, like a lazy, rain-starved river. Fine sediment and small rocks rested at the bottom. I reached down into the cool stream and tentatively stirred the bottom. Happy images were first to rise. The two best friends, the empty lot before the new house and hateful people replaced it. I dug deeper to recall the shame and rage. It was still hurtful. It was deeply embedded but retrievable. Her word was a seed that now germinated and grew. This early assault on my mother's character now forced me to remember Dorothy's innuendo. My mother was something or someone other than the woman I most loved, needed, and respected. I was unable to dismiss the creeping distrust of who she was if not that woman. I'd spent so many years trying to reconcile and reconstruct a palatable version of my little-known father. Now, I realized I might have to redefine both parents. Still, Dorothy's words were only an opinion, a point of view. I shouldn't count on her opinion or choice of words. I had to retrieve my own memories. I needed to remember the men that had been in my mother's life. These were men I knew and remembered. These were not the men in my family. I looked forward to closing the window of doubt that had been cast about my mother. She was very much alive and nearing seventy when I began to dig out these memories. I spoke to no one about them. I felt as if I was betraying her. This was so much worse than the guilt I felt each time I asked her if my father should be made aware of a milestone.

35 Baker's Dozen

Did my own identity hinge on knowing the truth about my parents? Every experience that molded my childhood and contributed to defining me was affected by their behavior and decisions. Our poverty and social status, my relationships with men, my own self-confidence, my values and character had not happened in isolation. Blame was never my objective. I knew I loved her unconditionally just as I knew I never hated my father. In finding their truths, I could let go of everything but understanding them and myself better. There was no need for forgiveness. But it was my right to know all of the truth. Then, it would be my privilege to pick and choose the pieces I wanted to use to construct my own story. I wanted to build my history on a foundation of truth. If a truth was too painful, it was my right to bend or bury it. It was not my aunt's right to build that narrative. I forced myself to remember the men I never liked who had been casually foisted on me by my mother. Through the lens of maturity and love, I hoped there would be little need to bend the truth.

I lean toward removing my father from this memory quest. Memories of him are the origin of this truth crusade. I have neatly filed those well-documented primary memories in column A and all of the secondary memories and opinions, including my aunt's words, in column B. I am resigned to never finding those half siblings I had hoped could support additions to either of those indexed columns. But he was the first man I shared with my mother. If I were a scientist and not a nurse or a writer I'd label Charles Payne, Specimen Number One or Exhibit A. Perhaps I can only conclude that Exhibit A represents a failed attempt at marriage and commitment and the generous benefactor of half of my genetic pool. He represents my earliest impressions of men as extraneous beings to my everyday reality.

There was the grandfather I knew and loved. Grandpa Philip. The Philly cigar smoking, tall, white-haired man we visited frequently in summer and for all major holidays. He was not a part of everyday life, but I loved him. My mother loved him. Everyone seemed to love him. To this day, I love the smell of a stinky cigar. A warm and protected feeling envelopes me in a smoky cloud others may find offensive. He didn't speak much. His job was to watch the news and monitor all things political. When I try to recall his whisper soft but gravelly voice, I can only remember one word, an utterance really "Shaaaaa" meaning be quiet. No one was allowed to speak when the nightly news was on. I understood our safety and well-being depended on his ability to keep current. I don't remember being hugged or kissed by him or my mother being shown affection. It was more a matter of respect. But he was there for shopping at the corner store for penny candy and change for the penny arcade at our beloved boardwalk. He was, most importantly, a symbol of a respectful and committed marriage to my grandma Sara and his children and grandchildren. I knew many things about him. Things my grandmother and mother told me. He left Poland to flee religious persecution as a Jew and had been trained as a synagogue cantor. His family made bricks and sent him to New York in 1912. He became a tailor and eventually a coat maker in different factories for the remainder of his working life. He fell madly in love with my grandmother, a Russian immigrant, and married her in 1913. She was twenty-seven and considered old, in fact a year or two older than him. Their first child was born exactly nine months later. Philip was smart and religious and serious. His wife was salty and irreverent and loved the less cerebral things in life, like playing Gin Rummy and Bingo. They complemented each other perfectly and were unquestionably in love the entirety of their almost fifty-year marriage. My mother once told me she had asked her father for money to help buy a small co-op apartment in a better neighborhood when Stephen and I were very young.. He had reportedly told her, "You should meet a nice guy, get married again, and let that guy take care of you." My mother never forgave him for not helping but never stopped loving him either. He lived in the margins of our lives, but I loved that he existed anywhere in my world. I will discount my mother's anger as her own. He made me believe in the possibility of an unwavering male presence and the importance of politics.

He was family. My uncle Walter was family. These men existed in a world unscathed by sexual energy. They could not be linked to Dorothy's words.

Uncle Walter was the most present man in my childhood. There was nothing about this man that even hinted at sexuality. His domineering wife created a costarring role for him. He dressed in her choice of neutral colors and slouched his six-foot frame into a softly folded vertical column, held upright by clasped hands behind his back. A vulnerable posture in my opinion. He made tentative conversation and corny jokes, never once *off-color*. He hung back as the tension became palpable at Scrabble games. Then, he would try a cryptic quip or suggest more coffee. He was a pleaser. He was kind. My mother often commented that her brother had become a eunuch since marrying Dorothy. I never had to look up the word. She clarified without my asking. "He has no balls," she stated. She also liked to joke that the reason they had only one child was because, "Dorothy tried sex once and didn't like it." I loved the neutrality of him. I loved his softness and preferred not to imagine what balls looked like at all. I may have even liked his asexuality. But I understood it was not a quality my mother respected. My mother seemed more at home in a sexually charged arena with men. The playing field was leveled there. She was almost in control. There was tension I wasn't able to grasp.

There were at least ten non-family intermittent males she had unwittingly or irresponsibly exposed me to. These men made it impossible for me not to be aware of the sexually charged nature of their interest and her role and response to it. Mostly, depending on my age, I could ignore what I wasn't sure of. Sometimes I dismissed her flirtatious behavior as her having fun. Other times, I acknowledged my silent disgust at their suggestive remarks or leering expressions. I was skilled at dismissing things as grown up behavior I didn't understand. As puberty and my own sexual awakening began, I understood she was sexually active with at least three of the men. I had successfully buried the details of these men save their names and the nicknames I gave them. Once my own goals took precedence over everything else, I buried those memories more deeply and believed they were irretrievable. They were not. Aunt Dorothy had lit a fire in my memory bank. The ghosts dipped and swirled and danced in my head. It was uncomfortable to honor their presence. I took them on. I had to.

I call the men we shared time with willingly or not so willingly my Baker's Dozen. I feel compelled to categorize them. The three men who were family members have taken their places comfortably in my catalogue under the title of Family. My father, the great mystery in my life. My grandfather the master of stability, and my uncle an example of adaptability to adversity. But there are those other ten in the Baker's Dozen. They have separate titles. There were the Fruit Flies, the Doves, and the Vultures. Collectively, they shaped me as surely as anyone in my family.

36 Fruit Flies, Doves, Vultures

The Fruit Flies were the insignificant but annoying male creatures that gravitated to my mother like flies on an overripe melon. They buzzed about and added nothing but my desire to swat them away. The first Fruit Fly was the husband of our mean landlady. His wife, Sebastiana, was fat, balding, and owned a perpetual scowl. I was sure she hated my mother and her children. She kept the heat turned down in winter, yelled at us to be quiet each and every time we went up or down the stairs, and stood like a sentinel at the bottom landing to insure silence. She had the rickety and warped front porch that led from our apartment to the outside world hacked off one afternoon. It sat above the front door below us and probably added a touch of architectural interest to the ugly house. She hated that my mother liked to sit and read there. Her husband, Lou, was straight out of central casting. He was short and bent and skinny. He lived in an ugly undershirt that exposed small tufts of hair on his shoulders. He had a thin long nose and beady brown eyes. He always had a skinny brown cigarillo cigar dangling from his thin lips. While Sebastiana performed the duties of landlady, he worked in a factory where cheap lace was dyed. Liberty Lace seemed to dye most things red or black from what I could see. They also seemed to specialize in lace panties, thongs, and baby doll nightgowns. At least these were the treasures he smuggled home to bring my mother. He reminded me of a cat proudly bringing home a dead mouse. At any opportunity his wife was out, he would ring our bell and announce himself. "Piney, are you home?" he'd whisper. He either thought the derivation from correct pronunciation was cute, or had vestiges of some foreign language, or was as ignorant as I thought he was. My mother would roll her eyes in mock annoyance but always ended up admitting him to our apartment. He sat bent over a cup of coffee and ogled her legs mostly. "I brought you something, Piney. This is new this week. I think you would look great in it." He smiled slyly and waited.

She'd pick up the item and quickly fold it away. "Oh Lou, these are really not something I wear. But that was so sweet of you. You don't have to bring me things," she'd say as she tucked the offensive item into a drawer. The coffee was quickly consumed in the absence of any other conversation. He'd gotten a closeup look at her long, freckled legs and left before his wife returned. These were the extent of his clandestine visits. He was content to leave and ruminate (or more, I now suspect) over imagined scenes of my mother in a slutty red thong.

She tolerated but didn't invite the intrusions. I think it was her way of getting back at the bitch that delighted in making us miserable. It was her upper hand. There was no other rational reason to explain her not refusing to answer the door. I hated his sneaky visits and leering eyes. I hated how she allowed him into our home, our safe place. One time, he crawled on a ladder to the back of the house. He may have told his wife he was repairing something up there. I can remember him peering in the kitchen window like a hungry squirrel. His adoration and fixation on my mother may have flattered her. Eventually, he died from lung cancer. We attended his funeral. It was strange to see him without a cigar and in a suit. I was relieved to have him tucked away for good.

Another Fruit Fly was Walter the hot dog guy. We called him Walter Post Arrow. That was where he worked and we met him. The hatchet-faced man had a raw but wounded look to him. He was tall and had light-brown straight, sparse hair. He looked like someone who had been in a fire. He was ugly but had a really wonderful smile. His face looked taut and immobile and damaged in some way. I thought smiling may have been painful for him. I always smiled back. He managed the hot dog grill at the nearby fast food and kiddy ride place. He was at least twenty years my mother's senior and had never married. "The poor man has no one in the world. His job is about all he has," my mother would often tell us. The Post Arrow was a place Stephen and I loved. Before their friendship, it was a rare treat to go there. For the next couple of years, we ate as many hot dogs and French fries as we wanted. Walter, wrapped in his soiled white apron, was content to just have my mother stand at the counter and speak to him. He once gave my brother a Yankee baseball signed by the 1956 team. He tried in every way to please her, including through her children. He would always ask her on a date. She would always refuse. Still, the hot dogs and flattery were free. Eventually, he gave up on asking her but continued to feed us and smile longingly at her. I understood, even at ten, that she was plying her wares. He was content with that modest attention from the beautiful young mother. He literally called her "mother" and never by her given name. I found him sad. But are fruit flies as stupid as moths? Attracted to the light where they will perish, but helpless to avoid the attraction. I understood my mother's charade. The hot dogs were served with mustard, pickles, and pity for this helpless man. He was my favorite Fruit Fly.

There was Jack the fabric pimp. Jack was the owner of an impressively large and well-known fabric store. My mother's best friend from my earliest memories was Mary Canava. Mary was the widow of my father's first business partner before my father bowed out and her husband Eugene died of a massive heart attack. The women bonded over being left so unceremoniously and over endless Scrabble games. Mary was cultured and well-traveled. She was a talented seamstress and her clients were the wealthiest matrons of Westchester County. She often made designer dresses for my mother and for Cissy, the Madame Alexander grown-up doll given me by my father. She would order more fabric than the patterns required to assure a well-dressed friend and for Cissy. But the finest of fabrics had high price tags. My mother was masterful at negotiating the best price possible. Jack was shamelessly smitten with her. He loved that my mother was not only beautiful but was Jewish, like him, and spoke Yiddish fluently. "How's my favorite *Shiksa* (Christian girl)?" he'd chuckle when the duo arrived to shop. He was delighted. She would answer in Yiddish, "And how is my favorite *Alte Kaker* (old man)?" My mother would engage him in perfect Yiddish and coy postures while Mary selected the most luxurious woolens and gabardines or silks. When Mary brought her costly selections to Jack, the ante was raised. He would give Mary a price and she would feign shock. My mother would intervene. "Oh Jack, why are you such a *Ganif* (thief)?" He would chuckle and she would sidle closer to him as if to inspect the fabric in question. The close proximity afforded him a brush of her long thigh and slim hips as she crossed in front of him. I knew the routine. I loved the colors and feel of the fine silks. They were like a whisper of breath across my fingers. The tall slouching bolts of fabric were perfect places for me to hide in a folded end or between the caverns of bolts. I studied the predictable ballet and knew the stated price would be drastically reduced with just another pass. Occasionally, his wife would glance over from the register but seemed unaware of the foil. Mary was one of the store's best customers. Another silly Fruit Fly. Maneuvered, stoked, trapped and tricked by a spoonful of honey, a brush of lean leg, and a few foreign words.

My least favorite Fruit Fly was Johnny Chevrolet. His last name was not Chevrolet. My mother first met him on a used car lot after the Studebaker finally died. It hadn't gone in reverse for a few weeks, and it became exhausting to make broken U-turns to accommodate the problem. He was short and blue-eyed. He wore shiny pleated pants and crumpled dress shirts. He had sweat stains on the underarms of those shirts and emitted a sour male sweat smell. He managed the car lot. He gave her a great deal on a used Chevrolet. I can't remember the car. It was one in a series of old cars that died in short order and were traded in his lot. He was married and had two daughters and a son. He spoke reverently of his wife. I know he spoke reverently because he spent so many hours at our kitchen table drinking coffee and staring at my mother. He didn't seem to have a preference for a body part. His leering blue eyes bored, in slow motion from top to bottom every time she got up to refill his cup. Sometimes neither of them spoke. They drank coffee, talked car talk (cylinders, transmissions, engines) and engaged in meaningful looks. The air was charged and heavy with sexual suggestion. In my adult years I had heard the term "eye-fuck." I knew exactly what that meant. I am sure they never dated. But for sure this was cheating on his wife and family. I knew that much. How else to explain long silences over cold coffee and hot looks. In later years he had a stroke and was paralyzed on one side of his body. He continued to work and help select the next car. He was now a more pathetic cheat to me. His left side was useless and braced. But both of his blue eyes continued to bore and leer, moving in perfect alignment. He eventually was forced to retire. The visits ended. An occasional phone call was all that remained. There was nothing left to barter. He flew off. Were the taming and domestication of Fruit Flies for personal gain, a form of barter? Yes. But does it rise to the level of prostitution? My point of view is that it does not qualify. It seems amoral and pathetic. It damaged my budding awareness of men and sexuality. Long buried memories had, nonetheless, made an impression and left their mark. A basic distrust and disdain for too many men is ingrained. I struggle to be fair.

There was a feeble attempt by my mother to date unmarried men. Men she could have dated and had a legitimate, mutually respectful future with. These benign men, the Doves, were creatures without enough fight or ferocity to appeal to her. She dated only two and had no more than three dates with either of them. They may have been too passive. They may have been driven more by love than lust. Her comfort zone was more with creatures of prey. These relationships involved a sexual tension she understood better. Her beauty was as great an asset as a flaw. It attracted predators. She loved the power of her sexuality. But she had flirted casually with the vision of doves.

There was a Dove named Harold Cohen. He was tall and had a fluffy ring of black fringe that was the surviving vestige of what might have once been a full head of hair. The shiny white pate it now framed was high and cone shaped. He was not attractive. He surprisingly came to our apartment to pick her up. He barely greeted me or my brother. I thought he was shy. I think he was an accountant and was introduced to her by one of the Fruit Flies. I'm not sure about that. After the third date, she told us she decided not to see him again. "He's a nice enough guy. Makes a decent living. I don't want to get serious with him." She paused and looked directly at us. "He actually wouldn't mind getting married someday. The thing is, he would like you guys to live in Florida with your father most of the time." Then she waited for our predictable response. At this point I'd seen my father twice, my brother had seen him once. He was a stranger. My brother's hostility persisted. "We don't want to do that," we shouted in unison. Our outraged voices were all she needed to hear to justify her own decision, which may have been driven as much by her lack of physical attraction to him. "Of course you don't, and that will never happen. You guys are my whole world. You are number one. No way any man can come ahead of my children." Her self-sacrifice and unquestionable love were reinforced. The balding Dove was released.

Leo Stormwind was a damaged Dove she met at the one Parents Without Partners meeting she was talked into. He was a grieving widower with a twelve-year-old daughter named, of all things, Barbara. He lived in the Lower East Side of Manhattan with her in Stuyvesant Town. It was a vast postwar complex of apartment houses that has always appealed to young professionals and solid upper middle-class families. My mother traveled there to meet him for just two dates. After the second date, she pronounced any hope of a future as the wife of an accountant or stepmother to another Barbara dead. "What a spoiled brat. He is totally afraid of that overindulged kid of his." An exaggerated exhalation signaled her disgust. "Good God, he asked her what time she would like him home. There was a babysitter and she is twelve. Is he kidding? She is in charge. That man is afraid of his own kid. No balls!" Well, here again was the issue of missing balls. My uncle Walter had the company of other castrated men. Perhaps this wounded Dove had a more seriously injured daughter. They were quickly released by my mother.

The arrival of the Vultures coincided with my own sexual awareness and awakening. My mother couldn't have chosen a more inopportune time to become sexually liberated. I was almost eleven when my mother met a new best friend. Her relationship with Mary had gone sour. There were arguments about religion and race and sexuality. Their views were diametrically opposed on almost everything. Mary was a righteous conservative Catholic. My mother, the daughter of a Socialist, was politically and socially liberal. The rift was inevitable.

She met Elaine by chance over casual conversation one warm July afternoon sitting on a park bench. Both were reading. My mother spoke first. "I see you're reading *Lady Chatterley's Lover*. How did you manage to get a copy of that?" The erotic D.H. Lawrence book had been banned in America for more than three decades. My mother, an avid reader, was impressed. Elaine offered to lend her the book but suggested she might enjoy just reading all her dog-eared pages first. They soon became friends, and she and her biracial, out of wedlock daughter became our extended family for more than a decade. She was one of the most exotic and colorful people in all our lives. A free-love Bohemian, well before Woodstock was a household word, she was the daughter of artists, communists, and well-heeled vagabonds. She wore pounds of turquoise set in hammered sterling silver. They were Navaho treasures. Every finger and available appendage was adorned in shades of skystone. She was a naturalist who awakened our awareness and love of a wide range of flora and fauna.

I am eternally grateful for that. We listened to folk songs by Burl Ives and torch songs by Edith Piaf and sketched and rode bikes. But I have no gratitude for her part in my mother's sexual liberation. It was Elaine who preferred the salt and seediness of 1950s and 1960s Block Island over her own childhood home on Martha's Vineyard. Block Island was home to sports fisherman, sailors, and the lucky few hundred who had lived there for many generations. In summer, it was a bawdy playground for the wealthy boat owners to drink and party. For sure it was not a haven for family outings. Elaine thought it was high time for the two mothers to enjoy a two-week vacation without children. We were shipped off to an overnight camp in upstate New York run by the Jewish Federation. It was nearly free and offered our first exposure to Jewish children and customs. We survived. While we learned unfamiliar Hebrew words and ate challah on Friday nights, our mothers hopped and skipped across the decks of the yacht sized boats of fishermen. This is how she won the trifecta of Vultures who gripped her in their talons for the next several years.

Sal B. owned a sixty-foot sports fishing boat equipped with radar and tuna tower. The huge vessel had sleeping quarters below and ample deck room for parties. It was one of the first boats she was invited to step onto. I thought it was more of a steep downhill slide than a single step. She was impressed with his wealth and loved his jet-black hair and tall muscular build. She loved that he owned two Buick agencies in Babylon, New York. The Chevrolet connection had dissipated. She believed his tale of a miserable marriage to a cold woman. A perfect example of cognitive dissonance. She knew he had children and a sprawling house in Nassau County. Had it ended with the weekend of abandon, I may never have known these details. But it did not end. It continued back home in the Bronx and transformed to a weeknight date every two weeks. The tryst lasted several years. He waited in the latest model of Buick in front of our apartment house. From my vantage point of six flights up, I could see his black hair and broad shoulders. She primped and looked flushed and excited each time the car pulled up. She may have believed his marriage would end, but I knew she didn't care. At twelve and thirteen, than fourteen and fifteen, I recognized someone in the throes of romantic passion. My own libido was budding. Although limited to a few awkward kisses through braced teeth and the smell of Noxzema and Clearasil, I knew there was more after acne and homework had passed as my life's priorities. I knew what sex was. I recognized the symptoms of the illness inherent in us. I knew this was an extramarital affair. She had bagged a prize-winning fish, but this Vulture was feasting on her bones.

Another large Block Island boat owner was Bill Coro. I won't hesitate to use his name. I realized after many years and a little research later on that the man's last name was never Coro. It was his calling card. It was his Boatman's (Cocksman's?) pseudonym. He was a Block Island friend of Sal's. They'd dropped anchor side by side in Old Harbor frequently. I don't know the size of his boat. I imagine there was the equivalent of a pissing contest they'd had. I don't know whose boat or penis was the largest. He lived in Providence, Rhode Island. My mother believed he was the owner or CEO of the Coro Jewelry

Company. Perhaps he was affiliated and the pseudonym bore some truth. The company was founded in 1901 by two men with the last names of Cohn and Rosenberger. Thus, the company was named Coro jewelry. Its offices were based in Providence and New York City. She must have met him during the same vacation. Perhaps Sal had returned to his trusting wife and loving children, leaving other wealthy men to play and prey. They met in the city infrequently. I imagine it was easy to explain away an occasional business meeting in New York to his wife. Their liaison was shorter lived and less passionate. She was as equally impressed with his wealth as she was with Sal's. I imagined Sal and Bill traded off-color and graphic stories about my mother when they met at dockside or country club events. My innocence was sullied by an awareness of my mother's promiscuity. I began my first and, sadly, everlasting disgust for wealthy powerful men and transactional relationships.

The last Vulture was a legacy man. He was as iconic to my mother as the American Bald Eagle. He was the Master of Ceremonies at Old Harbor. His oceanfront restaurant, bar, and beach were the epicenter of all summer debauchery. Ballard's was owned by Paul Felipi. A short, rotund middle-aged Italian who began his career with a small restaurant in Narragansett. He was the most ambitious businessman to have set foot on the island since the turn of the century when grand hotels hosted presidents and socialites. During the declining years of the island's popularity, he invested in a dream. He was a visionary, a millionaire, a charming, phony master of ceremonies and a cheating husband. He had beady brown eyes, a wide crocodile-like grin, and a booming voice. My mother had caught his eye. He was infatuated with the long-legged divorcee just a few years younger than himself. In very little time, my mother was his constant companion and passenger on the back of his easily recognized blue Vespa. He claimed to be in love with her. She claimed he wanted to marry her and move all of us to Block Island forever. I imagine he could have managed a well-hidden family of three somewhere unbeknownst to his wife. He was her inspiration for returning to the island with us in tow for the next several years. Sal was her wintertime lover and Paul her summer promise. I watched as they held hands or rode by on the Vespa. I was sure she was in love with Block Island but not with him. She eventually rejected his offer. She told us it would not have been fair to us. I am sure other women had similar offers. We were there a week or two each summer and stayed in the decaying but affordable and near empty Ocean View Hotel. The lasting love was that of my brother's and mine for the beautiful island. There has never been a year in our own lives we have not returned. The legacy of their time together is our continued love and amusement at how the future unfolded. He eventually divorced the first wife, married a significantly younger woman, and had other children with her. All his children (the older first two and younger three) became the most prominent name (save that of the founder's relatives) on Block Island. Today the island is teaming with tourists and millionaires lucky enough to have bought up the limited amount of real estate. The fishing boats and yachts are at Old and New Harbors. It is a family place and Water Street is thick and noisy with rented Vespas and bicycles. Both Paul and my mother have passed away. Long before she died, we knew the litany by heart. "*If* I wanted, I could have had all this. But I never loved him and was thinking of my children." Was she? I am brought to laughter each time I think of the word "if" in association with my mother. She would chuckle and say of the word in either English or Yiddish "If my grandmother had balls, she'd be my grandfather." There it was—her humor, fixation on balls, and ability to deflect.

Having forced myself to remember these men was painful but not productive. All I had to show for my walk through these hot coals was a renewed blistering anger toward men, not my mother. It was too late for much else. By the time Dorothy had fired the shot that started this race, my mother was in her seventies. Her waist had grown thick and her hair thin. Her jawline had slackened and her step slowed. She was a loving grandmother to my children. Her irreverent humor and sharp mind still there. I loved those most of all. She was always there for me as she had been my entire life. She was there for my children, there through my divorce and even there for my ex-husband. She understood his pain. She loved and helped him through it. It was difficult to reconcile the image of her now with that of a femme fatale or of slut or, even stretching the imagination to its limits, a whore. It was easy enough from the vantage point of my own maturity to understand the complexities of her life. It made sense to me to consider she was a woman scorned. She was abandoned by my father. She was discarded. She was left to fend for herself and denied adequate funds to provide for her abandoned children. It was logical that her self-esteem was damaged. It made sense that other men, wealthier men, could boost her self-esteem. It made sense to see how her greatest asset, her beauty, was an easy ticket to favors. I am not sure if I should applaud her ability to attract Fruit Flies for favors or find shame. Was she resourceful or wicked? Could I resume the greater mystery of who my father was and accept that my mother was simply a survivor? This theory was plausible and more palatable than the alternative. This is the path I took until my mother's death in the fall of 2006.

37 Love And Truth

She was eighty-five. She had become more frail and finally succumbed to death following a year-long struggle with the aftermath of medical mismanagement and the ravages of time. I could not imagine life without her. My children were grown and married. I was happily into the sixth year of a second marriage. It should have been a manageable grieving process. It was as complex as my childhood. As incomplete and confusing as my grasp on their identities. It remained a question of identity, theirs and mine.

I was free-falling. Do all adults feel this return to an infantile need for a mommy? I felt untethered in a bad way. I was adrift and ungrounded. Both my parents were gone and they remained mysterious. In my fifties, what did it matter? I could be unencumbered by their past lives and mistakes if I wanted to be. But I started feeling undefined and unfinished. There would be no opportunity for deathbed confessions or the discovery of exculpatory evidence by a forgotten witness for either of them. They, and my aunt and uncle and all the winged creatures that plagued my memory, were dead and buried by now. I was experiencing the pangs of questionable identity. The five-year-old who asks, "Where did I come from?" came to mind. Where and who did I come from? It wasn't a matter of biology. It was a more substantive doubt. Maybe adoptees experience this as the need for a whole identity as they grow. They might imagine more perfect parents or appealing reasons for their situation. Do they also need to reconcile the real from the imagined as a precursor to loving themselves? Is this why we are all so captivated by ancestry kits? Over twenty-nine million people have spit in a vial to discover lost or unknown relatives. More sophisticated kits offer information on genetic predisposition to disease. I am guilty of submitting saliva. I thought I would find the half brother and sister who had eluded all other avenues of discovery. I found no new relatives. It was, as it had always been, just Stephen and me. I returned to memories. I took to writing and in completing a memoir, I had a revelation as I wrote about my life.

There was a last man I had almost forgotten. He was always in my life. He was unlike any of the others. There was no suggestion of sexuality about him. He was the last of the Baker's Dozen. How could I have forgotten to consider him? What answers would memories of him reveal? He was tall and bald in a professorial, elegant way. He had considerable traces of a German accent. He was a doctor and he was always a part of our lives in a most remote way. My awareness of him may even stretch back to my earliest memories. Maybe as far back as my last memory of my father smoking a pipe in the big sage-green chair. And yet, I don't believe he ever spoke a word to me. He was my mother's person. I'm not sure when he entered her life, but I am sure of the things she told me about him through the years. It never mattered at the time. He was a cold and shadowy man who was no more exciting than faded wallpaper you forget is there. He never intruded in my life. She never embarrassed me with silly comments about his looks. She was never giddy or chatty with him. Their interaction was always solemn. For as long as I can remember, she was going to do some extra work by helping Dr. Leopold in his Upper East Side office. She said she would do typing or filing that spilled over from his busy practice as a psychiatrist. I never questioned it. The work was always an evening now and then. Other times, he brought his briefcase and files to our kitchen. She took out a small portable typewriter we had with a letter E that stuck. She made coffee and they sat quietly in the kitchen. I never heard the rhythmic tapping of striking keys. I avoided bothering them but if I entered the kitchen, he avoided eye contact and conversation. It never occurred to the child I was then that a doctor should be capable of eye contact. But after her death, I thought about his presence. I thought about her stories, and I remembered the love letters from him I had discovered under the lining paper in her lingerie drawer. I was only looking for a pair of stockings. I don't think I was snooping. I was not suspicious. I was about fifteen. There were banded stacks of white envelopes. There were postcards from Zurich. None had a return address but all were signed, "I love you, Harold." I understood then that they were lovers. I forced myself to dismiss those thoughts. It was more weird than salacious.

He was so old. He was a good twenty years older than her. He was so quiet and foreign. He was nothing like the Fruit Flies or Vultures. I thought maybe it was something from a long, long time ago and perhaps they had become friends. I dismissed it. He died many years before her. She told me she had found out by reading his obituary. It was so easy to forget the man and the letters.

It was only five years ago when I started writing in earnest. I revisited so many things. I thought about his life and how she had known him so well and for so long. I felt compelled to remember what she'd told me.

He was much older than her. He fled Germany in 1933 before the Nazis could claim his practice as a respected gynecologist and professor. He fled before they could claim his life. He began a new practice and new life in New York. He married there and had three daughters. His wife was also a professional. I thought she was a doctor but was never sure. My mother first met him when he was a gynecologist. It was always unclear if he was her doctor. A few years later, he switched practices and became a psychiatrist. There was mention of liability and laws he wanted to avoid. She knew so much about his wife and daughters. Sometimes she shared these details. I promptly dismissed them. They, and he, were meaningless people in my life. I thought her own interest was strange. I didn't care. After the letters, I realized she was in love with him as well. Why else to care about his life? After the letters, I also remembered how on his annual trips to Switzerland he brought her small but fine pieces of jewelry. There were eighteen-karat gold bracelets and a watch and a golden apple she wore on a long rope-like gold chain. She fondled it lovingly. That necklace seemed to hold particular meaning to her. I came to terms with their long-lasting love. It was, I thought, the saddest part of her life. He was one more elegant and fine thing she could love but not have. He was different than the Fruit Flies and Vultures. He was a man who valued her brilliant mind as much as he lusted for her body. I began to understand they were in love, but their timing and love were ill-timed and displaced. I thought about how they'd met and I grew more curious. Had my mother met him before she was divorced? I stifled the thought for a few days, but it kept recurring. Had my mother been the one to be unfaithful? Had my father left because of this? That might explain Dorothy's innuendo. That might explain Dorothy's disdain and Nora's hatred. Had she fallen in love with him after my father left? Had he been there to comfort her and fallen in love? Unthinkable to think he may have been her gynecologist. Had he been there cunningly waiting to prey on her vulnerability—another Vulture? Was there a hidden scandal? Why else does a respected gynecologist become a psychiatrist? It was overwhelming. It will always overwhelm and disturb me. How could I reconcile which parent was at fault? Which one had set the table with all the details that would both nourish and starve us? I could speculate endlessly but will never know. Beyond the years of lies and truths, I needed to establish my future, my complete self. That was the challenge.

38 Survivors

The survivors stepped off the ferry. It had been an especially enjoyable hour heading for Block Island. The last half hour, the ferry slowed and plowed through a heavy bank of fog that shrouded the island and made it impossible to distinguish between sky and water. We were Peter and Wendy on Captain Hook's flying ship. We were in the clouds. The rhythmic and sonorous blast of the fog horn lulled as if a lullaby. Without seeing the distant outline of deep green hills and camel-colored cliffs, we knew they were there. We knew the outline by heart. In just a few more minutes, we would be able to see the scattered squares of weathered gray, white trimmed homes that dotted the hills. They had thrived there without growing too tall or wide. They remained humbled by their natural surroundings.

Yes, then there it was. In plain sight. Old Harbor and Water Street. The expansive, mansard roofs and pointed gables of the grand old dowagers. They sat shoulder to shoulder, Victorian hotels welcoming yet resisting the onslaught of visitors. They tolerated the trendy gift shops they sat above as if lifting dainty petticoats and skirts above a muddy street. There had been so many changes in the last century. But they, too, were survivors. Their corbels and spandrels attesting to their dignity like laugh lines and crow's feet on an octogenarian. The ferry drew closer to Old Harbor. It was only then, when the motors reversed to slow and turn the ferry that the human survivors, Barbara and Stephen, drew deep breaths and prepared to assess the changes this year had brought to their beloved island. If they looked to the left and gazed upward, they could easily imagine the Ocean View Hotel as they remembered it from their childhood. Ravaged by a fire more than forty years before, the hill was still a sacred place they'd climb to later. Some wild cornflowers and beach plum bushes would remain. Either of them might search for a precious relic. A piece of brick or stone that proved it had existed. Before then, they would recall the fishing shanties made of rotting clapboard draped in stinking fish nets that had once stood at the left side of Old Harbor. For now, they came to terms with what had become the Grand Central Station of constantly arriving and departing ferries, belching out people. The huge parking lot teemed with rented bicycles and mopeds and small cars. This year, a new intruder was on the scene. A full-sized city bus painted in white advertised group tours and wedding parties. It stood like a vulture waiting to fill up on people who shared as little regard, right, or history of the island as the behemoth of a bus itself.

My husband, Nick, went to the bowels of the ferry to get the car. He had his own sweet memories of our wedding on the island almost twenty years before. Stephen and I waited to be the last people off. We watched as the largest trucks carrying building supplies or fuel exited. Next were the bicycles and surfboards and then cars. Finally fork lifts worked like red ants to lift the pallets of beer and liquor and tee shirts made in China onto the lot where they were promptly picked up and dispersed. We felt our jubilant mood subtly shift. But we were, after all, survivors. We knew how to bend and lean into the wind and how to accept changes when we had to.

Reunited in the lot, Stephen spotted Ballard's and changed the dynamic. "Well, there it is. Bigger and better and more ambitious than ever. It's too early to check in. Let's do lunch and a drink at Ballard's. It wouldn't be Block Island without a stop there." We happily agreed and started walking toward the ever evolving and expanding restaurant. We walked past the lined-up luxury sports fishing boats. It was not quite the fourth of July but in season enough for tightly packed, ready to party boats. Not quite noon, but the drinking and music on board had begun. Bare chested, baseball capped men lounged in canvas deck chairs. Their women, already bronzed and bared enough chatted with each other. The boats sat and bobbled a few feet below the level of people walking by on the concrete path. The boat people stole glances up at the passersby. *Yes,* I thought, *you need our admiration and affirmation. You will not have mine. I have too many memories and repressed thoughts to indulge you.* I thought about my mother's ventures on board similar boats. We continued on and entered the restaurant. The hostess stationed on the porch checked my handbag. This was new. Were they worried about terrorism on Block Island? Drugs? It was early afternoon. The real party and drinking were hours away. I submitted to the search and we were seated outdoors on the newly expanded patio, overlooking the beach and ocean. It was a perfect day. Blue skies above cadet blue umbrellas over white tables and chairs. Matching blue tents covered the bars. A volleyball game was in progress on the beach and small waves capped in heads of foam to match the beer lapped the water's edge. An aerial view could have depicted a five-star resort anywhere in the world.

A handsome young waiter named Juan greeted us. (His name tag claimed he was from Columbia. He admitted he was really from a small town in Florida, escaping their heat.) "Good afternoon," he smiled graciously. "Welcome to Ballard's. Have you been here before?"

Stephen and I looked at each other and smiled. Stephen answered first. "Oh yeah, we are very familiar with Ballard's and Block Island. Let's see, we've been coming almost every year since about 1960."

Wiley and charming, Juan knew just how to answer, "No, no way, you are not that old. That can't be." And with his gratuitous comment, a large tip was assured. We ordered a round of Moscow Mules and Stephen continued the conversation. "Juan, I bet you weren't even born until 1980…"

A loud male voice called out from the next table. "Hey, waiter, come here," it demanded. Juan spun around obediently. He excused himself and pivoted to that table. The loud voice continued. "You forgot the lime in my

Absolut, first of all. The lady's drink only has one ice cube. It's hot out here, buddy. How about a couple of cubes?"

I turned to look at him. Not surprisingly, he was dressed exactly as I would have guessed. His lower half sported Narragansett red cargo shorts. A plain white, short sleeved placket front shirt hung from his square shoulders. His partner wore a cute cornflower blue and lime colored Vineyard Vine floral print shift, their uniforms proclaiming them official members of the inside track. He leaned back and butterflied his arms behind his fat neck linking his fingers. Juan rushed off.

"Pig," I spit out. "Where does he come off calling him buddy? Ugh what a vile pig. I just hate men like that."

"Yep," my brother agreed, "another rich prick who thinks he owns the world."

"Wow," Nick whistled. "You guys mean business. He really pushed your buttons. Lighten up, it's Block Island. You're supposed to be happy." Our drinks arrived just then. Nick took the opportunity of the interruption to raise his hammered copper mug in a toast. "A toast to Ballard's and Block Island." We all took a long slug of the vodka infused mix.

"So," my brother relaxed back in his chair and looked at me. The drink was working its magic. "You hate rich white men as much as I do. That's funny."

"No," I answered, "I think I may hate them more than you do because I'm a woman. Rich old guys with arm candy. Men who think they can buy anything and anyone. That kind of extra crap."

My brother nodded in affirmation but went on. "Well, I'll best you, then. I hate all men in authority positions.

That includes CEOs, principals, other cocksuckers who think they own me." He slammed his hand and drink on the table for emphasis. The metal clanked against the table. It was looking like a game of Knock Rummy, cards being slammed down.

"Okay, I'll up the ante," I said. "I can't stand any man with a very deep voice that considers his voice a sexual tool. I can't stand any man I barely know placing his hand anywhere on my back. It makes me feel like he is commanding me to listen. I feel like a butterfly about to be pinned to a black felt specimen cloth. Shall I continue?'" I smiled in a mock dare. "I hate most any man in a uniform unless he's a fireman or a doctor. Too much unfettered authority. Military uniforms make me especially queasy."

Stephen grinned from ear to ear. "Me too," he said. There was silence. "I think we are officially completely fucked up," he laughed. We ordered a second round.

Narragansett Red and Vineyard Vines stood to leave. I turned to see if they'd left a large tip. No cash on the table. Corporate write off, I thought. Tip and all. They were replaced by a couple of young, bathing-suited women with eyes that scanned the patio. Hunting? Fishing? Flirting? I turned my attention back to our table. I considered how we had never shared this before. We often laughed about our physical similarities and tendency to outrageous and outspoken behavior. But this was different. "Battle scars," I said. "I guess we grew up on the same battlefield."

Nick, still trying to lighten the mood, lifted his second round of copper mug. "To childhood, then."

"Hell yes," my brother added. "Here's to Paul Felipi."

"Actually, it all ended up okay considering," I agreed. Wanting to add on to Nick's attempt at levity. "In the end, we both survived and here we are to testify," I said.

Stephen cocked his head. Not quite ready to relinquish the end of the prickly thread. "So, you think after childhood it was all okay? How do you account for your five years with a gay boyfriend and almost husband before you married at twenty-two? Then, you married a man who most resembled the safe passivity of Uncle Walter? What do you have to say about those thirty-three years you seem to forget? That was a very long detour on your road to happiness."

I was stunned into silence. I was momentarily grateful to be distracted by the activity at the neighboring table. The two young things had successfully lured a couple of perfectly preppy men a decade or more their senior. The men wore silly shorts. One with tiny navy blue whales on beige background, the other wore faded Madras plaid. Above their silly shorts, each wore Oxford cloth pastel shirts with casually rolled up sleeves untucked. Brown boating shoes (Sebago I guessed) with no socks. They could have been Pinterest Pins for "How to Look Preppy after Forty." I thought the men must have considered this a sport much easier than fishing for marlin or tuna.

I'd regained my composure and allowed speech without a plan. "You are almost right," I spoke softly and carefully. "The problem is, it's never that simple. Those thirty-three years were not just a poorly chosen detour. There was nothing absolute about it. There is probably nothing absolute about our childhood or parents, either.

It was good and bad, pleasure and pain, bitter and sweet. I think I'm grateful for all of it."

Nick, now agreeing, spoke about his own parents and his first marriage. He offered up something he often told me. "So, look at me. I married my mother the first time around. I sure did. Anxious, aggressive, explosive and volatile. Then, I married my father." He glanced lovingly at me. "Patient, quiet, thoughtful and kind."

I was always humbled when he said this. His father was beloved by everyone. I was lucky enough to have known him for the first few years of our marriage. I couldn't agree completely but accepted the praise. We understood his intent. It's never just simple. Our parents, and we in turn, are complex and complicated. We continued to drink. The vodka coursed through our blood. It blurred all the sharp edges. There were the dulcet sounds of small waves lapping the edges of the beach, seagulls cried overhead, and we slipped into a comfortable silence. We retreated to private thoughts. It felt like a moment of divine intervention. It was almost perfect. If anything is.

39 Truth

My Ancestry DNA kit had scientifically shown I was seventy-six percent Eastern European Jewish. I knew that to be Russian and Polish. The rest was twenty-one percent English and something else. I had no new-found siblings or famous relatives. The rest of my identity and my narrative is less scientific. It is a complex matrix of second-hand stories and my own lived memories. It is how I want to identify and define myself. I have opted to claim the best of what I gleaned. I love the colorful stories of known and unknown grandparents. It is rich and fits my need for distinctive drama. I decided to believe my father loved me in his limited way. I know my mother loved us completely if not perfectly. I am grateful she instilled my love of books and art. I am grateful for the irreverent humor and attention to detail I seem to emulate, albeit unconsciously. I can't help but try my hand at painting. A genetic gift from my father. I credit my mother for my love of words and irreverent humor and for seeing all the little things in life that are beautiful but often overlooked. Like my mother, I love an underdog and real dogs, too. I am quick to anger but prefer to love. I am grateful to both my parents for their intentional and unintentional gifts. I may come to be grateful for their imperfections someday. There is no room for blame or need for forgiveness. There is a better but still incomplete understanding. I am imperfect also. That seems fair. My parents did not stay a bonded pair in marriage, but they unwittingly managed to bestow bonding upon the siblings who were their children. We belong to each other and to them. I belong to myself. Most importantly I have been able to define myself. It was a difficult journey. The clock was ticking but hadn't run out. At times, it seemed to be an exercise in egocentric futility or a fool's errand. There is no one truth, including my own. There is understanding. I value that most.

Acknowledgements

Truth's Daughter began as a self-indulgent exercise in reconciliation. Writing had always been my catharsis of choice. There was the residual anger I believed was rooted in my parents' dishonesty and misguided choices. After my mother's death, I began to search for facts that might enable me to relinquish the rage that cropped up from time to time. It disturbed my sensibilities, although I learned to embrace it as my "salty side" or bent for brutal honesty. Its triggers were often misogynistic men, transactional relationships, or frivolous dishonesty. I knew the triggers in this minefield.

From the vantage point of *now*, I ventured into a minefield of memories. I ruminated and wrote. I journaled and considered the words reflected back. I relived snippets of time spent with the father I hardly knew. I eagerly wrote down the feelings the memories evoked in order to preserve them. I recalled the mother I treasured and basked in those memories. I breathed life into the bad thoughts and recollections about her as they surfaced like shards of glass against unprotected flesh. I gave myself permission to betray her as well. Writing the thoughts only compounded the guilt. The notepads stacked up and the guilt was offset with the revelation that they both loved me, but only she had sacrificed for me. She evolved as a complex and empathetic woman I could love completely. My father emerged as a victim of his own questionable character or unfortunate choices. The words and pages had served their purpose. There was forgiveness for both.

I shared the pages with the two people who knew me best, my husband and the brother who had shared my life from the beginning. The plan was to take the disordered collection of words and banish them to the recycle bin or to a dusty corner of the attic. They had served their purpose. They insisted the collection was a second memoir with a message for other adults with unresolved issues. I questioned the vanity of a second memoir. Ultimately, I trusted their opinion and it became a manuscript. And so, this book is dedicated to Nick and Stephen and my two wonderful grown sons. It is dedicated to the many men of integrity and commitment. I hesitate to add my father to the list of gratitude. In the spirit of forgiveness and understanding however, I include the father I missed knowing, Charles Payne.

About The Author

Barbara Santarelli RN, B.S- H.C.A, an employed nurse for more than four decades before semi-retirement in 2017, has authored articles on sex education for Tweens as well as on aging gracefully. Her previous memoir, *Everything I Never Wanted* was praised for its relatable, conversational writing style and candor in addressing uncomfortable truths.

A mother and grandmother, she lives with her husband and spoiled ten-pound Dachshund in a one-hundred-and-fifty-year-old home in a Northern Westchester New York suburb.

Note From The Author

Word-of-mouth is crucial for any author to succeed. If you enjoyed *Truth's Daughter*, please leave a review online—anywhere you are able. Even if it's just a sentence or two. It would make all the difference and would be very much appreciated.

Thanks!
Barbara Santarelli

Thank you so much for checking
out one of our **Memoirs.**
If you enjoy this book, please check out our
recommended title for your next great read!

Until Forever by Luisa Cloutier

"An earnest account of a passionate marriage."
-KIRKUS REVIEWS

"... a warm and moving memoir."
-IndieReader

CPSIA information can be obtained
at www.ICGtesting.com
Printed in the USA
FSHW021030130421
80416FS